D0559475

Chinese Entrepreneurs
in the Economic
Development of China

Chinese Entrepreneurs in the Economic Development of China

Rashid Malik

Westport, Connecticut
London

Library of Congress Cataloging-in-Publication Data

Malik, Rashid, 1960–
    Chinese entrepreneurs in the economic development of China /
Rashid Malik.
        p.   cm.
    Includes bibliographical references and index.
    ISBN 0–275–95848–5 (alk. paper)
    1. Tientsin (China)—Economic conditions. 2. Entrepreneurship—
China—Tientsin. 3. Consumption (Economics)—China—Tientsin.
4. China—Economic conditions—1976– I. Title.
HC428.T5M35 1997
338′.04′0951—DC21   97–1918

British Library Cataloguing in Publication Data is available.

Library of Congress Catalog Card Number: 97–1918
ISBN: 0–275–95848–5

First published in 1997

Praeger Publishers, 88 Post Road West, Westport, CT 06881
An imprint of Greenwood Publishing Group, Inc.

Printed in the United States of America

The paper used in this book complies with the
Permanent Paper Standard issued by the National
Information Standards Organization (Z39.48–1984).

10 9 8 7 6 5 4 3 2 1

This book is dedicated to my father, Advocate Abdul Wadood Mallik, and my mother, Professor Momtaz Mallik

Contents

Preface

After the death of Mao Zedong on September 9, 1976 and the fall of the Gang of Four, Deng Xiaoping, who had been purged earlier in the year on Mao's recommendation, reemerged as a political force. Deng's successful struggle to reinstitute economic reform against Hua Guofang's Maoist "two whatever" approach (a position which said that whatever decisions and whatever instructions Mao gave were right) signaled a new epoch of reform commonly termed China's second revolution. Under the new economic reform, the individual economy and the private economy were given the green light to engage in market activities based on risk, uncertainty, and profit. Although from the Western market economy point of view there might not be any difference between individual economy and private economy, in China there are differences. For example, in China an individual business has fewer than eight employees and a private business has eight or more employees. Other differences between individual and private economies will be discussed later in the book.

In this book I examine the role of entrepreneurship in China using the city of Tianjin as a case study. I explore the role of history, culture, and the government in the development or hinderance of entrepreneurship, and the role of entrepreneurs in the development of China's urban economy.

Chapter 1 reviews some of the pertinent literature on entrepreneurship and considers how different scholars have viewed entrepreneurs, and, in the context of China, how the definition of entrepreneurs may differ from other contexts. The chapter also discusses the city of Tianjin, how the research was carried out, and personal experiences in pursuing research in China.

From 1949 to 1976, the Chinese Communist Party (CCP) directly dominated China's economic policy, as well as all other aspects of life. Since 1977,

China's economic and other government policies have been dominated by the newly evolving reform policy. Some understanding of entrepreneurial history is necessary in order to study the development of entrepreneurship in China from 1949 to the present. For this reason, Chapter 2 focuses on the historical development of entrepreneurship in China since 1949. Specifically, this chapter explores the impact of the Three-Anti (*San-fan*) and Five-Anti (*Wu-fan*) campaigns, the socialist transformation of private businesses, and the suffering of private businessmen. The chapter also discusses the reform period from 1977 to June 1989 until the Tiananmen Square incident and the post–Tiananmen Square period.

Chapter 3 relates empirical observations of some of the entrepreneurs I met and interacted with in Tianjin in order to provide a picture of how Tianjin's entrepreneurs behave in their daily life.

In Chapter 4 I discuss the cultural aspects of Chinese life and how the culture affects entrepreneurs and visa-versa. This chapter analyzes the evolving economic culture in the reform era and its differences from the previous culture. It should be kept in mind that the new economic culture that is evolving among the Chinese people is different from region to region, such as northern China versus southern China. This chapter also explores the impact of government policy and behavior on both the culture as a whole and on the behavior of entrepreneurs in particular. The government's behavior should be taken in the broadest sense to include open manifestations of power, as in the crackdown at Tiananmen Square; change of leaders; visibility of top leaders in the mass media; which leader is meeting with whom, where, when, and why, both domestically and internationally; positive and negative news of fallen leaders, and so on. Entrepreneurs' behavior may be described in terms of their actions to curtail or expand their businesses in response to political currents, their level of visibility, and the kinds of interaction they have with society.

Chapter 5 describes the political economy of China and how it affects entrepreneurship and analyzes the relationships between different factions—hardliners and reformers—and what the government is doing to encourage or discourage entrepreneurs to play an active role in the nation's economic development. This chapter also explores how entrepreneurs view, and the extent to which they trust, the policies of the government and whether there is a common understanding and perception of the policies by the officials in Beijing, local officials, and the entrepreneurs themselves. It should be noted that Tianjin is a northern city adjacent to Beijing; entrepreneurs and policymakers there behave in different ways compared to other areas, for example, Guangdong, which is both far from the conservative center in Beijing and close to, and heavily influenced by, the freewheeling economic environment in Hong Kong.

Chapter 6 focuses on the role of entrepreneurs, consumers, and the government in economic development and explores what China is doing, as well as what needs to be done, so that entrepreneurs and consumers are able to play a positive role in China's economic development. Chapter 7 reflects my conclusions and suggestions about the future of entrepreneurship in China, what the government might do to help the development of entrepreneurs and a strong consumer group, who in turn will invigorate the economy and help China to achieve economic development, thus contributing to the good of the people of China and the rest of the world.

Acknowledgments

I thank my undergraduate professors, Stuart Vorkink and Candy Young, at Northeast Missouri State University for challenging me to pursue knowledge with passion. I extend my appreciation to Professor Carl Lande for introducing me to the concept of entrepreneurship. I am greatly indebted to professors Daniel Bays, Clyde Stoltenberg, Keith McMahon, Jaroslaw Piekalkiewicz, and Roy Laird for giving me helpful critical feedback on the manuscript. Special thanks goes to Cynthia Harris, acquisitions editor of Academic Reference Books and Economic Monographs at Greenwood Publishing Group, for her help and support. I also wish to thank Deborah Whitford of Publishing Support Associates for her critical editing of the book.

I would like to thank all my friends and well-wishers. Special thanks to Loyce and Doris Bell. I thank Hamed Ghazali for being a good friend. My recognition and thanks to all my Chinese friends in China. Without their help, I would not have been able to conduct my research in Tianjin, China. The help and friendship they extended toward my wife, Yasmin, and me is unmeasurable. I thank Zongren and his wife, Lu da jie, and their two sons, Wei and Hui, for all their kindness and understanding. I thank my Chinese teacher, Jie, for her help and hospitality. I thank Wang Daifu and Suo Daifu for their kindness. I thank Zengcheng, Tianhui, Yong, Min, Tong, Hao, and Yu Cai. I also thank Xiao Bai, whom I call my little sister.

I thank my parents, Mr. Abdul Wadood Mallik and Mrs. Momtaz Mallik, for bringing me into this world. Heartfelt thanks to my brothers, Mamun, Tariq, Amin, and Mahmood and my only sister, Fahimida Sharmin (Moon), for their support and friendship. I thank my uncle, M. A. H. Mansur Khan, and his wife, Sufia Khan, for their moral support. I thank my mother-in-law,

Hasneara Begum, for helping Yasmin and me to take care of our daughter when we needed it most.

And finally, my deepest appreciation and special gratitude goes to my beloved wife, Yasmin, a great source of inspiration. Without her help, understanding, encouragement, patience, and tolerance, both in China and in the United States, this book would never have been completed. My daughter, Samiyah Ayesha Malik, from soon after her birth, used to wait for me until 1 o'clock in the morning when I returned home from the library. Her tenderness and affection helped me overcome my tiredness and worries. Samiyah provided me with joy and happiness, which I often needed so badly. Again, I thank my wife; without her help and understanding this book would not be possible.

Chapter 1

Introduction

Contemporary Chinese entrepreneurs exhibit great entrepreneurial and management skills. They are contributing more than ever toward the economic development of China. But entrepreneurs in China are very different from entrepreneurs in the West. In China, history and the politics of the 1980s, all influenced by culture, have created an ambiguous and fragile entrepreneurial class. Therefore, entrepreneurs in China often suffer from a lack of confidence and security. This raises the question about the future of Chinese economic development.

The Chinese government plays an important and influential role in entrepreneurs' lives. This chapter discusses the historical and contemporary studies of entrepreneurs in China and defines entrepreneurs in terms of Chinese history, recent politics, and the bias of culture.

To begin, we analyze entrepreneurship in China: how history, politics, and culture play an important role in the lives of entrepreneurs and their efforts to develop a prosperous China by introducing new goods and services for profit, thereby creating jobs, savings, and investment, and promoting the circulation of funds, all of which were lacking during the Maoist rule.

With the rapid economic development of China under the reform policy, the role of entrepreneurs—private economy—will be key to the development of stable and steady economic growth. Due to rapid growth, the economy is overheating (wage and price inflation and overinvestment) but China had to make the choice between stagnation or economic prosperity. With the role of entrepreneurs increasing, the economy will move forward. As the government moves toward efficiency and productivity, many state-employed workers will lose their jobs, which will diminish consumer purchasing. It will be up to the individual and private economies to close this gap. In 1988, 14.53 million urban and rural units of the individual economy employed 23.05 million people. It was reported by the State Administration Bureau for Industry and Commerce in 1988 that there were 235,000 private enterprises, which hired 3.6 million people.[1]

Entrepreneurs not only create jobs and opportunities for people but they also fill in gaps in the economy not provided by the state-run sector. This makes the lives of consumers much easier. As one entrepreneur, an optician, reported, "One day a student came to my shop at 9:00 P.M. He said his glasses were broken and he had to take his final exam. So, I opened the door and helped him. So, I am working for not only money but also self-satisfaction."[2] The government officials of Tianjin's Business Administration Bureau also reported that "the individual business contributes a lot to economic development of Tianjin. It makes citizens' lives convenient. In 1988, each Tianjiner spent 200 renminbi in the free market. Most irrigated vegetables, fruits and foods are provided by individual business people. With the restoration and development of the traditional catering trade, such as *jian bing* and *guo zhi* (pancakes and juice), the problem of people's difficulty in having breakfast was solved."[3]

This creates an interdependent relationship between buyers and sellers that is essential for economic growth. One of the reasons for the Chinese economy's stagnation by 1976, after all, was the state-owned sector's neglect of the desires and needs of consumers and the diversion of most of the nation's talents and resources to keep the drowning state-owned enterprises alive. But "[i]n the economic order based on private ownership in the means of production no special institutions . . . are needed to achieve corresponding success. Free competition does all that is needed. All production must bend to the consumers' will."[4] Therefore, if an entrepreneur fails to meet the needs of consumers, his or her actions become unprofitable. At that point, the entrepreneur must change or exit the economy and make room for others. This was not the case in the pre-1976 era. In fact, by 1976 most of the economy was regulated by the CCP and entrepreneurship of any form ceased to exist aside from some illegal business ventures.

The departure of Mao and the Gang of Four and the advent of Deng brought new life to entrepreneurship. On December 22, 1978, China adopted a new economic policy during the Third Plenary Session of the 11th Central Committee of the Communist Party. The new policy stated that "carrying out the four modernizations requires great growth in the productive forces . . . and requires changes in all methods of management, actions and thinking which stand in the way of such growth."[5] Since then, individual and private economies have become a reality.

Great changes are indeed needed in the Chinese economic system if China wants to achieve economic development. I will elaborate on one of my experiences with the public sector in China to help explain why it is necessary for China to develop private ownership in the means of production for economic development. When I was in China in 1991, I visited different stores, both private and public, sometimes to buy things, but most of the time for observation. Whenever I visited a state-owned store, I often faced a passive clerk whose body language told me, "Please leave me alone and go to some other place to make your purchase." One day I walked into a state-owned store with three clerks, two of them were talking among themselves and the third was reading a newspaper. The door had a bell that rang as the door opened. Because the clerk reading the newspaper was nearest to the door, I approached her. She did not lift her head to great me; the other two clerks kept talking. I then approached the clerk reading the newspaper. I was standing two to three feet away from her on the other side of the counter. I felt that she was ignoring me. After a minute or so, she raised her head and asked me what I needed. After I told her what I needed, she looked at me blankly and said, "[We] don't have [it]," and went back to reading the newspaper. I quietly exited the store and went to a private store and bought what I needed.

This experience suggests that China is indeed in need of entrepreneurs to take the helm. No doubt, foreign joint ventures will continue to have an impact by bringing new technology and management approaches to China, but local entrepreneurs will have to learn these new techniques and implement them in order to set the nation on the path of progress and change China's economic situation, taking each local situation into account, of course. This raises the questions of who these entrepreneurs are and what they are like. To begin, we review the literature on entrepreneurs.

ENTREPRENEURS—HISTORICAL CONCEPTS

Entrepreneurs in different societies behave in different ways. All societies—capitalist, communist, and mixed economies—have entrepreneurs. In communist societies, entrepreneurs appear restricted because of the pressure imposed on them by the government and its agencies. This causes entrepreneurs to be less active in the economic development of the society. On the other hand, entrepreneurs in capitalist societies appear to have more freedom and are able to play an active role in the economic development of society and move freely between buyers' and sellers' markets.

For a long time social scientists could not figure out just who these entrepreneurs were, because they sometimes keep on changing their behavior to adjust to the environment. Adam Smith, author of *An Inquiry into the Nature and Causes of the Wealth of Nations*, did not see the entrepreneur as a capitalist—one who used capital to rent and pay wages for profits. Smith failed to give any credit to the "undertaker" (one who coordinates the factors of production—land, labor, and capital) for his role in inspection and direction, but he acknowledged that something must be given for the profits of the undertaker of the work who hazards his stock in this adventure. . . .

The profits of stock, it may perhaps be thought, are only a different name for the wages of a particular sort of labour, the labour of inspection and direction. They are, however, altogether different, are regulated by quite sufficient principles, and bear no proportion to the quantity, the hardship, or the ingenuity of this supposed labour of inspection and direction. They are regulated altogether by the value of the stock employed, and are greater or smaller in proportion to the extent of this stock.[6]

Although it might be difficult to differentiate between a capitalist and an entrepreneur, the capitalist's survival is based on interest, whereas the survival of the entrepreneur is based on profit. Where there is profit, there is usually the possibility of loss, which means that the profit of the entre-preneur is subject to risk. Therefore his or her labor of inspection and direction is subject to loss. It is often true that a capitalist is also an entrepreneur because a certain amount of capital is needed to venture into something new. But it is also true that a person of talent who works hard may be able to borrow money from a capitalist in exchange for interest. In China and other developing nations, the role of capitalist may be played by relatives and friends, and the concept of interest might have different meanings, such as a personal favor.

In 1874, Leon Walras introduced the entrepreneur as the fourth factor of production, the one who hires the other three factors of production—capi-tal, land, and labor. It is the entrepreneur—the buyer of productive factors and the seller of goods in the market—who links different markets together and moves the market toward equilibrium.[7]

Alfred Marshall, writing in 1890, recognized the entrepreneurs in Adam Smith's "undertaker" as "to a certain extent a class apart."[8]

For Frank Knight, the entrepreneur vastly increases the efficiency of economic production through uncertainty. Knight takes the concept of loss or risk and puts it in perspective. According to Knight, there is more to risk than what it conveys to us. To elaborate the concept of risk, he introduces the concept of uncertainty. In the case of risk, we may be able to calculate it by going back to previous experience, but uncertainty cannot be calculated because it cannot be quantified.[9]

Joseph A. Schumpeter, who acknowledges the idea that uncertainty is always present for entrepreneurs, rejects the notion that entrepreneurs take any risks. For Schumpeter, development is spontaneous and discon-tinuous, disrupts the "circular flow," and moves the economy toward a new equilibrium. A force within the economy causes this disruption because without it there would not be any real development. Schumpeter characterizes this force as the entrepreneur—an innovator who creates new combinations for development. This concept of new combinations appears in five forms: (1) introducing a new good, (2) introducing a new method of production, (3) opening a new market, (4) locating a new source of supply of raw materials, and (5) carrying out the new organization of any industry.[10]

In conclusion, there are different ways of looking at an entrepreneur. Although in the past social scientists could not distinguish between capitalists and entrepreneurs, with the advancement of economics as a science it became necessary to make a distinction. Nevertheless, contemporary observers continue to report on entrepreneurs from different societies in different ways.

CONTEMPORARY STUDIES OF ENTREPRENEURS

Several authors have studied entrepreneurship in different settings. They have chosen to look at entrepreneurs by reference factors such as politics, economics, and social forces.

Gustav F. Papanek, writing on Pakistan's development in the early 1960s, proposed that industrial development would depend on entrepreneurs who are willing to give up their traditional occupations, such as agriculture, trade, and civil service. Papanek's potential entrepreneurs were ruthless and farsighted individuals with abundant energy and a willingness to accept political risk.[11]

Yusif A. Sayigh conducted his research in Lebanon between 1957 and 1959 to determine the role of entrepreneurs in the process of economic development. Sayigh believed that entrepreneurship in developing countries like Lebanon, Pakistan, Columbia, and others, could not be understood as it is understood in Western "stable developed society." According to Sayigh, to understand the concept of entrepreneurship and its function in developing economies, we need to come up with a new definition that takes into consideration the prevailing environment of the entrepreneurs. Entrepreneurs in a developing economy may be engaged in different functions "from primary or creative innovation at the top, down to the point of routine management." The entrepreneur must be innovative and should bring a "new combination" into play.[12]

John Carroll saw Filipino entrepreneurs as decision makers and principal actors who brought together the traditional factors of production—land, labor, and capital—"to form a new enterprise. Whether or not he personally provided capital, technology, or management from his own resources, he saw to it that they were obtained; he coordinated the efforts of others in obtaining them; and he accepted chief responsibility for the outcome."[13]

Wayne Nafziger[14] and Anita M. Weiss[15] analyzed entrepreneurship in India and Pakistan respectively, based on Knight's idea of risk and uncertainty and the entrepreneur. The entrepreneurs in Nafziger's and Weiss's studies were the main contributors of capital and the ultimate decision makers in the enterprise. It was the entrepreneurs who committed the capital and ventured into risk and uncertainty.

Andrew A. Beveridge and Anthony R. Oberschall,[16] in their study of Zambian entrepreneurs, viewed them as innovators. Although in the African countryside an innovation may not be seen as something remarkable, opening a wholesale market, a restaurant, or a bus service is a big achievement. The entrepreneur saw the opportunity and found a way to get the factors of production together. The Zambian captain of industry[17] may not be sailing a big enterprise or industry but should not be excluded from the category of entrepreneur for that reason.

Through his empirical study of Hungarian semiprivate enterprises and their managers, Kalman Rupp came up with an empirical definition of entrepreneurs. Entrepreneurs were those "plant leaders who had no previous affiliation with the given cooperative and who have initiated, established, and run a given industrial plant with little assistance from the co-op central management." To Rupp, innovation or success was not necessary to be an entrepreneur, an entrepreneur was someone who demonstrated a certain degree of success as manifested by empirical observation.[18]

Anthony Jones and William Moskoff, in their study of contemporary entrepreneurs in the former Soviet Union, found that present-day entrepreneurs already had some entrepreneurial spirit. The communist system was not able to destroy entrepreneurial skills completely. The central planning system in some ways cultivated different kinds of talents in the managers of government-run enterprises. How so? The managers were forced to be creative, due to supply shortages, and find ways to obtain raw materials and meet the output targets demanded by the central authority. Also, because of chronic shortages of consumer goods, an underground economy evolved in the Soviet Union before the advent of a legal private sector.

When the legal private sector appeared mostly middle-aged men became involved with the cooperatives as emerging entrepreneurs, but not for profit only. A lot of entrepreneurs mentioned that "the primary reason was the possibility of realizing their creative potential, entrepreneurship, and talents," and to avoid an "administrative-bureaucratic yoke."[19]

ENTREPRENEURS OF CHINA

This discussion demonstrates that scholars have tried to define the concept of entrepreneurship in the context of the environment in which they carried out their research. It was reported in a 1915 case study of rice markets in Hangkou that Chinese entrepreneurs were diligent, honest individuals who made their living through hard work.[20] During the precommunist era, entrepreneurs were not involved in politics because of the uncertainty created by warlordism. During the Guomindang (GMD) era, it was reported that many entrepreneurs were unscrupulous and used foul play to make economic gains. The GMD used terror to keep the entrepreneurs under its control and extract money in an unfair fashion, yet somehow the entrepreneurs were able to survive. But the rise to power of the CCP in 1949 signaled the end of entrepreneurship in China until 1978.

The definition of an entrepreneur used in this study is based on empirical observation and interviews with entrepreneurs in China who are gravely influenced by history, recent politics, and culture. I have chosen to define Chinese entrepreneurs as those individuals who are engaged in business, or were engaged in business, after 1978 for the sake of profit and are willing, under the conditions of life uncertainty, to take the risk of loss and find new ways to fill gaps in the economy which are, or were, left by the state-run economy. In addition to the usual factors of uncertainty, entrepreneurs in China, who willingly venture into businesses with their own resources and find new combinations or adapt new techniques for profit, must constantly confront the fear that they will someday lose not only their businesses but perhaps their very lives. The government of China might decide to alter its presently permissive policies toward entrepreneurship and entrepreneurs may once again face the wrath of mass campaigns. Under this "life-uncertainty" factor, an entrepreneur fears the possiblity of being thrown into jail and possibly paying the price for engaging in business with his or her life through execution or suicide.

The power of life uncertainty may become clear if we look into the contemporary history of China. In June 30, 1949, Mao Zedong in his report titled "On the People's Democratic Dictatorship," in commemoration of the twenty-eighth anniversary of the CCP, said that private businesses were important for Chinese economic development and they would not be destroyed.[21] This kind of assurance somehow caused the entrepreneurs to become involved in corruption involving party members that eventually led to the *San-fan* and *Wu-fan* campaigns.[22]

In 1952, the CCP launched the *Wu-fan* or Five-Anti campaign against private entrepreneurs. By using the standard of the "five poisons," the government could charge virtually any business or entrepreneur of "tax evasion, bribery of government workers, theft of State property, cheating on government contracts, and stealing economic information from the government for private speculation."[23] Massive taxes or large fines were imposed on those who were found guilty. The harassment and pressure were so great that one businessman after another gave up his or her business and surrendered to the government. Mao was very pleased with the Five-Anti campaign and later told his party colleagues that nationalizing private businesses was like getting a cat to eat chili. How so? "Rub the Chili into the cat's ass, and when it begins to burn, the cat will lick it off, and be glad of it."[24] As in other campaigns, Mao also set a quota of criminals to be found guilty from different types of suspects. For the Five-Anti campaign, the quota required 90 percent of businessmen or entrepreneurs to be found guilty of a given crime. In this tiger hunt, thousands of businessmen experienced the humiliation of public trials. Millions of workers and employees denounced their employers in mass meetings. "The flood of secret denunciations, accusations, and condemnations, compounded by the psychological threat of professional ruin, drove many to suicide."[25] According to official reports, out of 450,000 private businesses in nine major cities, 340,000 (76%) were found guilty of various illegal transactions. An official survey in 1953 in Tianjin found that "the amount of working capital private factories and firms had possessed (taking 1949 as 100) was 232 in 1950 and 319 in 1951. In 1952, as a result of the Five-Anti campaign, the working capital dropped to only 182, a 43 percent decline."[26]

The fearful memories of these campaigns did not fade from the minds of China's entrepreneurs, and the recent Tiananmen Square incident brought them back. As a result, in 1989 there was a decline in the private sector economy. The political cannot be separated from the economic in China and political issues, in particular, affect the outcome of economic reforms. In Soviet Union–type economies, official information about private businessmen gives a politically biased picture by stressing the private businesses' exploitation of the masses. In China, according to one interviewee, "some propaganda from the state gives the message to the people that individual businessmen always cheat people but I do not think so."[27]

Private entrepreneurs in China are always cautious about their businesses because they are unsure of the future. In the past, any kind of mass campaign had a tendency to spill over into the economy. This association is not going to be forgotten by present-day entrepreneurs regardless of the level of profit made from private enterprise in a rapidly expanding market economy.

One of the entrepreneurs I interviewed, one of the first three individual entrepreneurs in Nankai District, Tianjin, did not hold a high opinion of other entrepreneurs:

> They [entrepreneurs] earn a lot of money. However, they are from the lowest class of social culture and morality. Business people are becoming worse and worse because of competition. Before liberation National Party Government restricted the number of business people, but now there is no such restriction. Many business people lack education and social responsibility and do not have business morality, social values. They are not human.

When I asked him why some businessmen do not want to expand their businesses after some success, he replied, "They are very wise because individual business is sure to be canceled in China in the future. China is a socialist country, and it will extirpate capitalism."[28] Another interviewee, when she was asked the same question, replied,

[W]hen they [private businesses] reach a certain level, the government will come to confine them. Most of them are not, and dare not be, in the limelight and are afraid of the slogan, "Cut off the Capitalist Tail." For example, a private restaurant XYZ [name intentionally omitted] previously expanded its business and, as a result, is now a collective restaurant. It enjoys preferential treatment from the government.[29]

At this point it should be noted that it is not only the bureaucracy, the government, or CCP members that hinders the development of the private sector; opposition also comes from the local people who feel excluded from the benefits brought about by the present reform. Accordingly, it would not be surprising to see local people working together to take over a successful private business by manipulating the relevant government agency to get a share of the pie, that is, economic benefits by any means. In Chengdu, the capital of Sichuan Province, Zhang Wu is a successful entrepreneur and the owner of a construction firm, an appliance store, a beauty shop, and a nightclub. However, Wu feels ostracized. "People look down on me because I was in jail for political reasons," he says, perhaps ignoring the fact that some may suffer from what the Chinese call red-eye disease, or jealousy.[30]

A report in *China Daily* said that almost all directors and managers in China are worried about their future because of the possibility that they might be misunderstood, wrong, or criticized, or they might even go to jail for some minor mistake or for no reason at all. The report stated that a retired factory director of a state enterprise by the name of Xiong ZhiCai in Anqing, a port city on the Yangtze River in East China's Anhui Province, related that during a meeting he and his friends found that they had all, without exception, been investigated, criticized, or attacked in some way. Xiong said, "Luckily we were finally proven innocent, otherwise I wouldn't be here talking to you."[31] Similarly, the official newspaper, *Renmin Ribao*, lamented that reformers in some cases might be criticized in a humiliating manner or pestered to death by anti-reformers instead of correctly handling errors to protect the initiative of reformers.[32]

This suggests that it is not only entrepreneurs in the private sector economy who are suffering from uncertainty. The same phenomenon is experienced by public sector entrepreneurs who are willing to innovate and take risks to improve the functioning of the units they are working for—a government-run store, factory, or research center. We can easily understand what kind of risk and uncertainty the private entrepreneurs live with if even the entrepreneurs in the public sector are not safe.

When I asked entrepreneurs in China about the future of private entrepreneurs, some of their answers were quite alarming. One entrepreneur
said, "I cannot speak easily about the future of individual businesses in
China. It is hard to say anything because I do not know if the policies will
change or not. Maybe the government will go back to the 1960s when they
[private businesses] were collected together."[33] Another interviewee said,
"I do not know about government policy. We somehow know that the future
is not stable, so we are very afraid to expand and risk what we have."[34] Two
other interviewees expressed their concerns about a change of policy in the
future and were afraid to express their opinions.

Uncertainty that has nothing to do with economic activities involving
profit and loss gives rise to a lot of frustration. One interviewee, a recent
college graduate of Nankai University, expressed his frustration by lowering his head and shaking it sideways while answering. He said, "I do not
know [about the future]. I do not want to think about it, it is of no use. The
situation is changing in the world and China, I do not know what the
government wants."[35]

This uncertainty is no doubt shared by all entrepreneurs in both the
private and public sectors, but one group of entrepreneurs bears the
greater risk—private businessmen. China makes a distinction between
the individual economy (*geti jingji*) and the private economy (*siren jingji*).
As noted earlier, individual businesses have fewer than eight paid employees. From my observations in Tianjin, most of the employees are
family members. Private businesses have more than eight employees and
use hired labor. This distinction is necessary because ideological reservations about private ownership apply more to private businesses than to
individual businesses. As Robert Hsu has written, to a Chinese economist
"private ownership is acceptable only to the extent that it remains an
appendage of public ownership, supplementing it but never threatening
to dominate or overwhelm it."[36]

It is not only the economists or party members who have ideological
reservations about the private sector economy. The recent Nankai graduate
quoted above, when asked what he thought about private companies,
replied,

> I am not clear [about private companies]. I think I do not like private
> companies. But sometimes they think that private companies are good
> for the national economy. Private companies can do those things
> which government companies cannot do. Private companies are flex-
> ible. Their effect [work] is fast. Private companies information systems
> are fast, so they work fast.[37]

It might seem that many Chinese are unable to separate themselves from
the past. Although the government is advocating a market economy, many
people may still want to revert to the state-run economy where they feel

secure with their "iron rice-bowl," that is, their jobs and livelihoods are protected by the government. One day some individual entrepreneurs might turn against the owners of private companies and make them scapegoats in order to save themselves from mass campaigns and persecution. The fear felt by entrepreneurs is logical because China remains a communist country with anticapitalist sentiment.

One approach entrepreneurs have taken to avoid the type of uncertainty they confront in China is to keep a low profile by concealing their recently obtained wealth. Most of the entrepreneurs I met, with few exceptions, lead a simple life in public. However, through close observation of the food they eat, the soft drinks they drink, the brand of foreign cigarettes they smoke among other things, it becomes clear that many private entrepreneurs are very wealthy. Another approach some private and individual entrepreneurs take to avoid uncertainty is to run a business under collective operation or to keep the business under the name of their retired parents, while working their iron-rice-bowl jobs at the same time. The latter was true for some of the entrepreneurs I met in Tianjin. About the former, Willy Kraus reports: "It can also be assumed that considerable numbers of firms fall under the heading of collective business which could be regarded as being individual. This is especially true for collective-individual joint enterprises, for which, however, no definite figures are available."[38] Another approach taken by some entrepreneurs doing business mostly in small jeweleries, clothing, fruits, vegetables, and so on, is to conduct business without a license and move from place to place to avoid detection by the authorities.

PURPOSE OF THE STUDY

My research in Tianjin revealed that along with history and culture, the government plays a very important role in the life of the Chinese people, from allocating jobs to the allotment of food stamps. Since 1949, government policies, and Mao's thoughts in particular, have not only affected the life of its citizens but also played an important role in formulating a sociopolitical life-style for the people in China. The impact of Mao can still be felt in China, and an increasingly significant group of Mao supporters can be detected. For this reason, my analysis includes not only history and culture, but also government policy and how it affects China's entrepreneurs in their effort to develop China's economy.

After its victory, the CCP took over the economy and converted it to a socialist planned economy. The CCP, which destroyed the private sector economy from the early 1950s to 1976, is now helping to build the private sector economy since Mao's death in 1976. In effect, the CCP wrote the history of entrepreneurship in China with its own ink, and it is still writing, but with a different color of ink. The government also affected the culture of the people by trying to create the Communist Man; now it is trying to convert the Communist Man into a capitalist man with Chinese characteristics.

This book examines the role of the government vis-à-vis entrepreneurship in China. Historically, what role did the government play in making and breaking entrepreneurs in China since 1949? How did the government affect the culture of the people in relation to the private sector economy? What role can government play in developing entrepreneurship in China? What can entrepreneurs do to contribute to China's economic development? My quest to answer these questions took me to Tianjin in February, 1991.

SETTING

China has a population of 1.1 billion people. It is the largest country in Asia, with a total area of 9,562,904 square kilometers (3,692,244 square miles). China has common borders with fifteen countries: Outer Mongolia, North Korea, Russia, Buthan, Sikkim, Nepal, India, Burma, Laos, Vietnam, Afghanistan, Pakistan, Kazakhstan, Kyrgyzstan, and Tajikistan.

China is rich in minerals and other natural resources necessary for industrialization. All known economic mineral resources—more than 150—are found in China; 136 were proven to be reserves.

China has twenty-three provinces and five autonomous regions (*Zizhiqu*) that represent national minorities—Inner Mongolia, Guangxi, Ningxia, Tibet, and Xinjiang—and the administration of the three largest and most important cities—Beijing, Shanghai, and Tianjin—reports directly to the central government.

Research for this study was conducted in the city of Tianjin. Tianjin has a population of over 8.3 million with an urban population of 5.5 million. Tianjin was developed as a coastal port for goods coming from the sea to Beijing. Tianjin means "the ford of heaven." It was an important city but gained its popularity when it was occupied by British and French troops in 1858 and 1860. At that time, Tianjin became a treaty port and was used as a base for trade between the West and China. There is architecture reminiscent of early twentieth-century Western style, similar to some parts of Washington, D.C. There are Western style houses surrounded by high walls and iron gates. The old city walls were razed by the Western powers in 1900 as retaliation against the antiforeign Boxer rebellion, but parts of the old city walls remain.

Tianjin serves as the port for Beijing and is the corridor for transportation of goods for virtually all of North China. The city was raised to municipality status in 1967. Even before 1949, Tianjin was known for food processing, wool textiles, carpet manufacturing, and a large cotton industry. At present, Tianjin stands as China's second largest producer of soda ash and bicycles, and is the third largest producer of cameras and sewing machines.

In spite of all the promise observed in Tianjin there is some pessimism conveyed by the city's entrepreneurs. When asked how they would develop the economy of Tianjin there were many different responses; two answers are provided below. One entrepreneur said:

[It is] hard to [develop Tianjin's economy] because Tianjin is the door of Beijing. Leaders in Tianjin follow Beijing very closely. What Beijing does, Tianjin also follows. Tianjin is too poor. They [leaders] do not dare to take bigger strides as Guangdong province has done. However, the [central government's] policy is changeable.[39]

A similar sentiment was expressed by another entrepreneur:

It is a tough job to run Tianjin well. Tianjin is the door to Beijing. It is too near to Beijing. And geographically it is less favorable than other coastal cities, either up to the north or down the south. Tianjin's policy is quite conservative. Besides, Tianjin is an old industrial base of north China. A big job needs to be done to promote reform when compared to other developed cities.[40]

Regardless of the disadvantaged position of Tianjin portrayed by some entrepreneurs, when I went to Tianjin in February, 1991, I found a lively city with lots of activities. I saw billboards advertising different products. I went to import-export fairs and other shopping centers. I found these places to be full of buyers and sellers. The entrepreneurs were very energetic and were trying to catch the attention of the buyers by enthusiastically advertising their products. They seemed very confident and friendly. I bargained with them, even if there was no need to bargain. It was very seldom that I came across an entrepreneur who became tired or angry because of my bargaining, though it could be that they treated me nicely because I was a foreigner.

From 1986 to 1991 individual businesses developed steadily in Tianjin. Some 100,000 to 110,000 individual businesses were established during that time. There are seven categories of individual businesses: industry, transportation, real estate, general business, food, repairing, and services. Individual information advisory services and technological services also developed. The total retail business in 1990 among individual businesses was 146 million renminbi (RMB), which was 2.9 percent of the total state and private sectors combined together in Tianjin.

As for private entrepreneurs, in 1991 there were about 360 private enterprises in Tianjin, including 30 limited companies. The largest number of employees in any one firm was 194 in the Jinnan assembly factory. In 1987, the trade revenue of private enterprises in Tianjin was 3 million RMB, putting it far behind the southern areas of China, the main reasons being the lack of investment in and the location of Tianjin.[41] It was also stated by the government officials in Tianjin that before 1988, due to hazy policies about individual and private entrepreneurs, Tianjin was able to keep up with the speed of development experienced by other cities. In the murky waters of these policies everybody had an equal chance to take advantage of policy loopholes. But after 1988, when the official policy was established, Tianjin, because of its closeness to and influence by conservative Beijing, failed to keep pace with the south. Cities such as Guangzhou and Shanghai pursued more favorable local policies for individual and private entrepreneurs and experienced faster growth. Tianjin needed more reforms in order to catch up with other fast moving cities.

I went to Tianjin planning to conduct interviews with the managers of state-owned enterprises, collective enterprises, and the private sector. I quickly determined that it would be nearly impossible to conduct interviews with the state-owned and collective enterprises without the backing of government officials. Having been advised by my Chinese friends not to deal with the state and collective enterprises, I gave up that idea. However, upon the suggestion of a Chinese student in a class I taught at Nankai University, I talked with the officials of the university's foreign affairs office and was given a letter of introduction to the officials of Tianjin's Business Administration Bureau. The student believed that being introduced to the officials by the university would be the best way to proceed. If I was caught interviewing private sector entrepreneurs in the future, the letter would provide evidence of the officials' prior knowledge of my activities.

RESEARCH METHODOLOGY

From my knowledge of China and of research methodology, I developed my own research method that was quite different from the conventional methods of conducting research. I knew that I would not be able to interview a random sample of the population for my research in Tianjin, China. Also, because of the June 4, 1989, Tiananmen Square massacre in Beijing, which brought back memories of the Cultural Revolution, it would be very difficult to obtain information from entrepreneurs.

Before leaving for China, I planned how to conduct interviews in Tianjin. Knowing the importance of name cards in Chinese culture, I had two kinds of name cards made. On one card I mentioned that I was a visiting research scholar, and on the second card I introduced myself as a businessman from the United States. I used the visiting scholar card with government officials and the business card with all others.

In February 1991, my wife Yasmin and I went to Tianjin to collect data on entrepreneurs. According to our plan, Yasmin and I started making friends from the very beginning. We took distinctly American gifts to help build friendships in the customary Chinese way. Yasmin played a very important role in developing friendships with females, and because of her it was possible to invite female friends to our room without the risk of offending them. Yasmin and I also developed friendships with families among both Nankai University employees and other residents of Tianjin. I found that as part of a family it was easy for me to become friends with other Chinese families; they also helped me in other ways with my research.

Making many friends had practical advantages. I was familiar with the importance of the *guanxi* (connection) factor in China. I taught a class in the political science department at Nankai University entitled Economic Development and Government Policy, to undergraduate and postgraduate students. Also, I privately tutored eight Chinese students in English. I did not take any fees to teach them English; instead we exchanged favors—I taught them English and they helped me establish contact with local entrepreneurs. Two students from my political science class played a very important part in my research. Their knowledge of economics and social sciences helped me to understand the economic and social behavior of entrepreneurs in Tianjin.

Other friends were willing to help me in a limited fashion. As we became closer, they felt obliged to help me arrange meetings with entrepreneurs in order to save the friendship and to save face (honor). But after arranging one meeting, successfully or not, I found that many people did not show enthusiasm for arranging a second interview. I think that some of my friends felt that they had fulfilled their responsibility to me by arranging one such meeting. In fact, one of my friends told me frankly after attempting two meetings, that he was not going to try any more. Knowing the social and political situation in China, I never tried to persuade them to try a second time. I was careful not to put a strain on the friendship.

I was able to interview nineteen entrepreneurs from the private sector. I arranged six interviews on my own. As mentioned before, I spent the first two months in Tianjin establishing connections with the local people. I would venture into the marketplace to find entrepreneurs who were friendly and willing to talk and exchange ideas. I found six entrepreneurs who were open to me, and I started meeting with them often. Three of them had general stores where they sold cigarettes, food items, or stationery. Of the remaining three, one was a photographer, one was an optician, and one was a barber. From the photographer, I used to buy and develop my film. The barber cut my hair (though he charged one extra yuan). I bought a new pair of glasses from the optician, but often we would just talk.

Of the remaining thirteen entrepreneurs, twelve interviews were arranged by my friends and one was arranged by government officials. The venue of the interview differed from interview to interview. Some of them were conducted at our mutual friend's place, some in the back of the entrepreneur's store, and some were carried out in my room.

We were given one room with an attached bath in Nankai University's international housing. Whenever any interviews were carried out in my room, Yasmin and I extended our hospitality to the interviewees and our friends. We offered them hot tea, cookies, sweet peanuts, and sometimes coffee, which we bought from the Friendship Store. Some of the interviewees wanted to leave in a hurry and some wanted to sit and chat before and after the interview. I tried to accommodate each situation.

As previously mentioned, upon the suggestion of my student I obtained a letter of introduction from the university's foreign affairs office, which introduced me to Tianjin's Business Administration Bureau officials, who arranged one meeting with a private entrepreneur. I found out that an interview carried on in the presence of government officials lends a superficial touch to the research. Though I was able to observe the setting of the environment where the entrepreneur worked, during the interview the entrepreneur was very cautious and chose his words carefully. His answers to my questions seemed designed not only to give me information but also to please the government officials. He also arranged to videotape the interview. I believed he wanted to keep a record of the interview so he could not be blamed for saying anything against government policy. The interviewee was very pleasant and extended his hospitality with a six- or seven-course dinner and foreign cigarettes. But it should be kept in mind that not all hospitality extended by private entrepreneurs in the presence of government officials is sincere. Private entrepreneurs often must act to please the government officials, save the officials' face in front of a foreigner, and save himself or herself too. As a result, it is important to critically analyze the environment and the data obtained from interviews in the presence of government officials. After the interview was over, I expressed my appreciation for their help and support and pretended that I was pleased with the interview and did not need more information to file my report. I was also able to interview the government officials.

During the first two months, while I was developing friendships with the local people, I found that tea and cigarettes played a very important role in China. Foreign cigarettes were valued by entrepreneurs in Tianjin, particularly Kent cigarettes from the United States. Often, when I visited entrepreneurs, they offered me cigarettes, sweets, peanuts, and watermelon. I always accepted their hospitality. I also carried my Kent cigarette packet, or some other expensive brand, and offered cigarettes in return. I also brought sweets, peanuts, and other things with me when I visited them.

Altogether I arranged thirty-three interviews with private sector entrepreneurs. Of these scheduled interviews, I was able to interview only nineteen entrepreneurs. Often the entrepreneur did not show up at the designated place or was not present in the store. Sometimes when the entrepreneurs were present in the store, they were reluctant to talk. Therefore, even when approached by my friends, an entrepreneur might agree to an interview, but later change his or her mind. On such occasions, I became very disheartened. Yasmin encouraged me to have patience and try to understand the position of the Chinese people. Patience paid off with nineteen interviews.

During some of the interviews I was able to take notes; during others I was told bluntly not to take any notes. In such cases, I relied on my memory and the memories of friends to write up the interviews. In the beginning my interviewing technique was inefficient, but as time went by, it improved. I wrote down a set of questions (see Appendix A) to ask and I tried to memorize them in order. Most of the time, I took an open-ended approach. I would start by asking the entrepreneur to tell me something about him or herself and about the business. Some entrepreneurs would respond by asking me what, in particular, I wanted to know. I would reply, "anything you feel comfortable to talk about." Often some entrepreneurs would not answer a question clearly. Through experience I learned that most of the time they wanted only to give a certain amount of information. It was wise not to press for information which they were not willing to give. However, from my experience with the six entrepreneurs whom I knew personally, I learned that information they were unwilling to share initially might be gladly shared later on. Patience paid off. Also, in the course of an interview it often proved possible to phrase a question differently to get an answer. An example of this concerned questions about income. Many entrepreneurs felt uncomfortable talking about income and savings; answers often appeared to state less than the actual amount. I began to ask for information on their initial investment in the business and followed up with a question on the present investment. This gave me a better idea about income and the status of the business.

The Chinese people have been suppressed for so many centuries they have become very cautious. The CCP's rule from 1949 to the present, the anti-movements, the Cultural Revolution, and the Tiananmen Square massacre have made the Chinese even more careful. Manchu Princess, Aixinjuelo Xuanqi, the youngest of the thirty-eight children of the Qing reformist Prince Shu, said this about the Chinese people: "Chinese have been so long oppressed, they've been obliged to become selfish and more analytical. They seem submissive, but they're just waiting for their chance."[42] I agree with the princess. My observation of the Chinese people told me that to conduct research and understand China, it's important to have a good knowledge of politics and culture as well as an understanding of the history of China and its people. Without knowing the history, it is impossible to understand present-day China.

Chapter 2

The Historical Development of Entrepreneurship in China from 1949 to the Present

This chapter discusses the role of entrepreneurs at the end of the Qing dynasty and their position during the time of Sun Yat-sen (leader of the 1911 revolution) and Yuan Shi-kai (president of the Chinese Republic). It also summarizes how entrepreneurs were befriended by the Guomindang (GMD) and CCP only to be later betrayed.

After the CCP victory in 1949 over the GMD, the CCP, under the leadership of Mao Zedong, destroyed private entrepreneurship by means of the *San-fan* and *Wu-fan* campaigns, among others. This gave rise to the life-uncertainty factor. The lingering effect can still be felt among entrepreneurs in China today. The position of entrepreneurs in Chinese society is very delicate, vague, and conspicuous. In addition, the Confucian culture and communist ideology of looking down on private entrepreneurship and profit-making, along with Confucian authoritarianism and CCP dictatorship in the lives of entrepreneurs, has made them overly dependent on the government for protection and direction. This has hindered entrepreneurs in their efforts to contribute toward China's economic development. Entrepreneurs must maintain a low profile and a slow approach toward business expansion until a better system or environment evolves in China that allows them to contribute freely to China's economic development. Due to this fragile position, many entrepreneurs are unwilling to expand their businesses and are afraid of any policy changes.

After Mao's death, Deng Xiaoping and his reform-minded followers, against the wishes of the hardliners led by Chen Yun, helped open up the economy to move toward a market economy. This presented an opportunity for the *getihu* (individual) and private entrepreneurs to flourish again in China after the terror of the Cultural Revolution.

Historical events, such as the *San-fan* and *Wu-fan* campaigns, the Cultural Revolution, and the recent Tiananmen Square massacre in June 1989, still influence the contemporary Chinese people's views of business life, and life in general.

ENTREPRENEURS IN THE POST–QING DYNASTY

At the end of the Qing dynasty, China had a growing population of merchants in the coastal areas involved in commercial capitalism, who dealt in trade rather than industry.[1] The commercial system of the late Qing period functioned in two different ways: one was managed by foreigners dealing with overseas markets and the Chinese ports; the other was managed by the local Chinese between treaty ports and the interior. "Although it may seem paradoxical to conclude that at the end of the Qing dynasty the merchants served Chinese trade much more than they controlled it, it is clear that to a large extent the Chinese did use them for their own ends."[2] The increasing power of the merchants as a bourgeois class and the contemporaneous decline in the Qing dynasty's power contributed to the 1911 revolution led by Sun Yat-sen. The bourgeois class supported Sun in the hopes of creating a strong China. However, these hopes would not materialize.

The rise of Yuan Shi-kai to power in March 1912, and his rule of China for four and a half years (until his death in June 1916) delivered a serious blow to the bourgeois class in their pursuit of political power. Although Yuan Shi-kai wanted to move China toward economic development by promulgating commercial legislation, stabilizing the fiscal and monetary system, and supporting private enterprise, his willingness to encourage business contrasted sharply with his refusal to grant any power to the bourgeoisie.[3]

Chinese entrepreneurs, after the 1911 revolution, did not present themselves as an organized group to share political power. However, they enjoyed some prosperity after the death of Yuan Shi-kai because of the international situation created by World War I, the Nationalist Revolution of the 1920s, and the ascension to power of Chiang Kai-shek, who brought the merchants under the umbrella of state capitalism. A 1923 *Peking and Tientsin Times* editorial described the Chinese merchant class as passive and submissive to authority.[4]

The era of warlordism started during the presidency of Yuan Shi-kai and gained momentum after his death in 1916.[5] In the absence of a strong bourgeois or proletariat class, the militarism of the warlords increased tremendously.[6] The era of warlordism caused great damage to the economic development of China. Agriculture was constantly threatened in many ways, including the conscription of peasants as soldiers or carriers, confiscation of farm animals and vehicles, raids by robbers, and the exploitation of the villagers. The effect of warlordism on agriculture was so serious that by 1929 famine conditions existed in about nine provinces in northern and central China.

Trade was also affected by the warlords when they began to impose arbitrary taxes. In 1912, there were 735 customs barriers to tax goods in transit. If the substations were included, the total number of tax points were in the thousands.[7] In spite of the negative impact of warlordism on the economy as a whole, China saw a rise in entrepreneurial activities in many areas, such as during World War I. Western businesses, unable to compete with the Chinese and Japanese, had to curtail their production of civilian goods and decrease their shipping capacity. Both the Chinese and Japanese seized opportunities. One such area of opportunity was the textile industry (see Table 2.1), the fastest growing business in pre–World War II China.[8]

Entrepreneurs were not only active in the domestic market; they also picked up momentum in exporting cotton yarn (see Table 2.2). Shanghai's cotton textile industry grew rapidly. Because England was unable to supply the finer quality of yarn during World War I, the Japanese seized the opportunity to move in as the major manufacturers of finer grade yarn. This opened the market for coarser grades of yarn, and Chinese entrepreneurs moved in to fill this gap. In Shanghai the number of spindles quadrupled and the number of looms increased more than sevenfold. Imports of raw cotton for the Chinese textile industries doubled from 1914 to 1919, and from 1919 to 1925 it increased ten times. By this time, local entrepreneurs controlled the market. In 1913 Chinese-owned mills controlled only 38 percent of the domestic market, but by 1920 this figure had risen to 70 percent.

World War I also assisted the development of China's second most important light industry—flour milling. Before the war, China had fifty-three flour mills, ten of which were in Shanghai, but from 1914 to 1921, twelve new mills came into existence in Shanghai and about forty-eight mills were built throughout the country. However, "after the war, the return of foreign competition, the changing value of foreign exchange, crop failures, and finally the loss of Manchuria (in 1931) put the industry into a decline from which it never recovered."[9]

Though the warlords disrupted trade in both the agricultural and commercial sectors, both peasants and merchants found common ground to interact economically in common markets. Buyers and sellers bargained hard with each other, leading a Western observer to comment that "in no other country are the free play of competition and the law of supply and demand still so completely relied upon for the regulation of prices."[10]

There were some powerful merchant guilds that might have used some restraint of trade in some markets, but most of the merchants let the brokers do the selling and buying to avoid risk and uncertainty. At the same time, there were so many merchants in China that no one was able to establish total monopoly of the market. Rice marketing in Hangkou in 1913–1914 provides an example of honest trade in the market.[11]

Table 2.1
Distribution of Cotton Spindles in China by Ownership, 1913–1936

Ownership	Number of Spindles	Percent
1913		
Chinese	484,192	58.8
Japanese	111,936	13.6
Other Nationals	227,024	27.6
Total	832,152	100.0
1925		
Chinese	1,907,504	55.4
Japanese	1,326,920	38.5
Other Nationals	205,320	6.1
Total	3,439,744	100.0
1931		
Chinese	2,566,642	54.7
Japanese	1,946,840	41.5
Other Nationals	170,610	3.8
Total	4,684,092	100.0
1936		
Chinese	2,919,708	51.8
Japanese	2,485,352	44.1
Other Nationals	230,006	4.1
Total	5,635,066	100.0

Source: Yen Chung-p'ing, Chung-Kuo mien-fang-chi Shih-kao (Draft history of China's cotton
textile industry, Peking, 1963), 354–355. Reproduced from Kang Chao, "The Growth
of a Modern Cotton Textile Industry and the Competition with Handicrafts," in
China's Modern Economy in Historical Perspective, ed. Dwight H. Perkins (Stanford:
Stanford University Press, 1975), 170.

This discussion suggests that in spite of the disruption created by warlordism, entrepreneurs were able to carry on activities in both agriculture and
industry, especially in coastal areas such as Shanghai, Qingdao, and Tianjin.
However, Gail Hershatter offers a different picture concerning Tianjin. According to Hershatter, the officials and warlords in Tianjin used their power
to develop industry, but most of the merchants were less enthusiastic about

Table 2.2
Export and Import of Cotton Yarn, 1922–1932 (thousand bales)

Year	Export	Import
1922	13	406
1923	30	254
1924	49	188
1925	22	216
1926	64	153
1927	113	98
1928	117	95
1929	115	78
1930	110	53
1931	206	16
1932	116	32

Source: Shanghai Cotton Textile Mills Association, Chung-Kuo mien-fang-chi tung-chi shih-liao (Statistical records of China's cotton textile industry, Shanghai, 1950), 123. Reproduced from Kang Chao, "The Growth of a Modern Cotton Textile Industry and the Competition with Handicrafts," in China's Modern Economy in Historical Perspective, ed. Dwight H. Perkins (Stanford: Stanford University Press, 1975), 172.

investing in industry. They preferred to invest in less risky projects such as banks, pawn shops, private gold and silver stores, cloth shops, medicine shops, and breweries. The merchants in Tianjin rarely invested in factory production. When they did invest, they typically invested modestly in ventures such as flour mills.[12]

During the era of the warlords, the merchants in Guangzhou acted differently. The rapprochement between Sun Yat-sen and the communists, as well as subsequent actions taken by Sun against the merchants' wishes by threatening to seize the Guangzhou customs receipts by force, were viewed as hostile actions against the merchants' interest. As a result, conflict broke out between Sun and the merchants in the summer of 1924. On October 15, 1924, the merchant militia was defeated decisively, and the Xiguan business district on the west side of Guangzhou was looted and burned to the ground.

However, the death of Sun and the ascension to power of Chiang Kai-shek, who had close links with the bourgeoisie, brought the merchants back into the limelight. Nonetheless, Chiang did not let them organize into a political force.[13] This policy of containing the merchants within the realm of economic activity was vigorously pursued by Chiang after his victory in the Northern

Expedition. The Northern Expedition was headed by Chiang himself on July 9, 1926 to eliminate the warlords. Chiang also broke with the communists in 1927, almost eliminated them, and chased them to Shaanxi in 1934.

NANJING PERIOD

Chiang and his followers, in the name of economic development, advocated bureaucratic capitalism and harassed entrepreneurs, thus preventing them from contributing their resources toward the economic and political development of China. However, the Guomindang (GMD) also neglected their responsibilities toward the economic development of China as a whole by ignoring the needs of the common people, which contributed to purchasing power and disrupted the normal circulation of funds and money. The GMD also consciously deprived potential entrepreneurs from borrowing money from the banks for investment and the creation of jobs.

After the establishment of the Nanjing government in 1928, the GMD, under the leadership of Chiang, tried to develop the economy. In 1928, the government established the National Reconstruction Commission with the intention of developing utilities and the coal industry. In 1931, the National Economic Council was set up to work on road building, water works, cotton and silk culture, and to establish an elaborate program of technical cooperation with the League of Nations. In 1934 the National Defense Council was set up to focus on heavy industry. In spite of all these councils, there was no strong leadership from the central government to carry out its projects, and the resources allocated to the projects were insignificant when compared to the total resources of the national government.

There were, however, some developments in other areas. Between 1927 and 1937, about 50,000 miles of roads were built. Railway construction saw an average of 700 miles added each year from 1931 to 1937. China-owned steamships more than doubled their tonnage, and a national airline network was put in place. Electric power output more than doubled and coal production nearly doubled. Cotton cloth production also increased almost fourfold during the decade. "Industry, mining, and utilities as a whole (excluding Manchuria, seized by Japan in 1931) increased by 6.4 percent per year between 1926 and 1936. Evidently, China's economy in the modern sector was not stagnating."[14]

However, a close observation at the micro level reveals that the GMD failed to support private entrepreneurship, which was important for the creation of jobs and the circulation of money for economic development. For a long period of time, Western observers thought that the cooperation between the GMD and the bourgeoisie during the Northern Expedition lasted until the downfall of the GMD regime in 1949, but this was not the case. After the success of the Northern Expedition, the Nanjing government started laying down its strategy to bring the merchant organizations under

its control. The GMD used different strategies, including "setting up paral-
lel structures, reorganizing or eliminating old institutions and progres-
sively reducing the field of the bourgeoisie's political and social activity."[15]

A look at Shanghai's merchants during the time of the Nanjing regime
will reveal how adamant Chiang was about establishing his hegemony over
political and economic organs of the country. The cooperation between the
merchants and GMD came to an end because of the high pressure exerted
by the GMD on the merchants to contribute money to the party. When the
merchants refused to pay, Chiang resorted to force and terror, initially under
the guise of eradicating communists and their supporters. The Nanjing
authorities wanted a businessman named Fu Cong Yao—managing director of the China Merchants Steam Navigation Company, general manager
of the Commercial Bank of China, Chairman of the Shanghai General
Chamber of Commerce, and one of the wealthiest merchants in Shanghai—
to help in absorbing a loan of 10 million yuan by raising the money through
his enterprises, personal funds, and connections in the Chamber of Commerce. When Fu refused his arrest was ordered. Fu escaped to the International Settlement and then fled to Dairen, but he later made a large
contribution to GMD coffers to clear his name.

In Fu's absence, Nanjing assumed control of Shanghai's General Chamber of Commerce and the China Merchants Steam Navigation Company,
both of which were handed over to the bureaucracy. Chiang also used his
personal connections with underworld gang members to harass and kill
rich merchants who refused to pay money to the GMD.[16] If the terror and
force led to merchant resentment, it also convinced them to submit to the
government, thus ending any political role for the bourgeoisie as an independent group.[17]

The terror created by Chiang and the gang members was not limited to
trade and commerce; it affected industry too. Economist H. D. Fong observed that in Shanghai and Tianjin management was "polluted by igno-
rance, favoritism, and squeeze," thus resulting in great economic loss.[18]

The near anarchy that resulted from the lack of a sound GMD economic
policy was not limited to the bourgeoisie class or industry, but also
affected other areas of the economy. Unlike in Hangkou in 1913–1914,
when the rice merchants did not use foul play to manipulate the market
for extraordinary profit or cheat the rice suppliers, in Wuxi (located
between Shanghai and Nanjing) in 1934–1935, we find an extraordinary
case of market manipulation by the merchants. In January 1935, Qian
Zhaoxiong wrote that in the cocoon market, strong cocoon firms used
their advantageous position to cheat the peasants who came to the
modern market to sell cocoons.[19]

These cases demonstrate the GMD regime's failure to put forth any
long-term plan for economic development or to create an economic environment where entrepreneurship might flourish. Instead, they tried to
suppress the very entrepreneurs who were willing and able to modernize

China. Even a faction of the GMD named *gexin* or renovationist, which originated in early 1944, complained about this bureaucratic capitalism. This corruption, inefficiency, and bureaucratism of the system under the GMD not only dampened entrepreneurial endeavors, it failed to provide the leadership needed to move the new economy forward.[20]

CCP IN SHAANXI

While all this corruption and promotion of self-interest against the interests of entrepreneurship was going on in the areas controlled by the GMD government, a new government of the CCP was evolving in Shaanxi with its own economic institutions. In the areas controlled by the CCP based on Marxist ideology, a combination of private capitalism, state capitalism, and cooperatives existed at the same time. In fact, private enterprise and industry were permitted and encouraged because the CCP needed rich peasants and entrepreneurs to raise production to meet local needs. In addition, the GMD placed a blockade against the whole region, which meant that the CCP had no choice but to cooperate with the private entrepreneurs. Private transactions in land and its products were allowed, but with some restrictions. The state did not establish a total monopoly on all commodities, such as cattle, hides, salt, wool, and cotton; it allowed private competition to exist. In the case of cooperatives, the government and private entrepreneurs cooperated with each other as partners and competed with private capitalism as well as with state capitalism.

Though these economic interactions may seem contradictory, in Shaanxi they complemented each other. Just as Chiang in Guangzhou had established the ground work to subdue the merchants and bring them under state capitalism in the future, the CCP also had its own plan. In the 1935 *Outline for Cooperative Development*, the CCP defined the cooperative as "an instrument to resist private capitalism and develop a new economic system," and expressly included as one of the five cooperative system objectives: "to combat the exploitation of the masses by merchants."[21]

In addition to trade and commerce, the Communists were able to set up an industrial base. They operated the richest tungsten mines in China, with an annual output of over 1 million pounds of ore, which they exported to Guangdong. They also opened weaving plants, textile mills, and machine shops. The Communists claimed that they had a "foreign export trade" of over $12,000,000 in 1933.[22]

The government of China, whether republican or communist, cooperated with private businessmen to gain support in times of crisis. When Yuan Shi-kai thought that he did not have any need for the merchants, he turned against them; the same story was repeated by Chiang. In the case of the Communists, we find that before 1949 the CCP encouraged private entrepreneurs to become strong and develop their economic base. But in the post–1949 period, the government turned against the private businessmen when it no longer needed their assistance to pursue political goals.

The merchants and private businessmen were used as pawns by the ruling groups to further their interests; the latter did not share the apparatus of policymaking with the private sector to improve the economy of China. This inability of the Chinese government to create an environment in which the entrepreneurs could function economically and also have input in the decision-making process for the betterment of the economy was lamented by Thomas R. Jernigan, ex-consul general of the United States in Shanghai. In 1903, Jernigan wrote that the Chinese entrepreneurs were superior to other Asiatic merchants and able to survive in a hostile environment created by the Chinese government. However, "under a better system of government their merit would be more favorably known and no agency could be so potent in developing and making China wealthy and respected as her mercantile class."[23]

CHINESE ENTREPRENEURS IN THE POST–1949 ERA

Before coming to power in 1949, the CCP, under the leadership of Mao Zedong, viewed private entrepreneurs in a different light. In an interview with Helen Foster Snow in the 1930s, Mao stated that Chinese society at that time was made up of three segments: individual capitalists, the national government, and the imperialists. These three segments together formed the capitalist structure of the Chinese economy. However, because of imperialist capitalism, the other two forms of capitalism, national government capitalism and individual capitalism, could not flourish. On top of this, the existence of a feudal economy hindered the development of Chinese capitalism.[24]

From the Shaanxi period onward, the CCP did not want to isolate private businessmen in their struggle for victory over the colonial powers and the GMD. At a meeting on December 25–28, 1947, in northern Shaanxi, the CCP Central Committee adopted a report by Mao Zedong entitled, "The Present Situation and Our Task." In section VI of the report, Mao stated that the CCP had three major economic policies: (1) to confiscate the land of the feudal class and distribute it to the peasants; (2) to confiscate the properties of the four big families—Chiang, Soong, Kung, and Chen—and turn them over to the communist state; and (3) to protect the industry and commerce of the national bourgeoisie. Mao also emphasized that wherever the power of the CCP reached, it should protect the interests of the national bourgeoisie (those who did not have ties with foreign powers or the GMD). He went on to elaborate that the CCP should distinguish between political attack and economic annihilation. Under such a philosophy, only the landlord class and the bureaucrat–capitalist class would be wiped out, and the upper petty bourgeoisie and middle bourgeoisie (small businesses oppressed by the landlords and the GMD) would be allowed to function.[25]

The main objective of the CCP, aside from land distribution, was to confiscate the property of bureaucrat–capitalists. When Harbin, the capital of Heilongjiang province, was taken over by the CCP in 1946, it started to confiscate the property of bureaucrat–capitalists. In 1948 and early 1949, after the successful campaigns of Liaoxi-Shenyang, Beijing-Tianjin, and Huai-Hai, the CCP confiscated all property belonging to bureaucrat–capitalists north of the Yangtze River. After the final victory at the end of 1949, the CCP took over all property of the remaining bureaucrat–capitalists.[26]

It has been reported that before the CCP came to power, "bureaucrat–comprador capital accounted for 66 percent of the country's industrial capital and 80 percent of its industrial, mining, communications and transportation fixed assets."[27] In spite of the confiscation of property by the communist government, when the CCP came to power in 1949 and founded the People's Republic of China, there were 7.2 million individual industrialists and businessmen in China's cities and towns. In the entire country, the number of people involved in private business was estimated to be 30 to 40 million.[28]

The CCP had not expressed any intention to destroy the private sector completely. As a matter of fact, those businesses that were not confiscated did very well, and in some cases established new enterprises. The government gave them protection in the form of stable prices, labor peace, and clean government. The state also provided raw materials, working capital, and utilities. The business environment presented by the CCP government was good at the time, leading a former capitalist to comment, "the communists provided the best business climate we had ever known!"[29]

But like Yuan Shi-kai's regime and the GMD regime, the Communist regime also disappointed the energetic entrepreneurs of China and did not hesitate to destroy them. It was governments in China that gave hope to the private entrepreneurs, and it was government that took it away. As Willy Kraus wrote, "At any rate, China lost its private economy in 1956 and with it a lot of its most indispensable, dynamic entrepreneurs, risk-taking businessmen and innovative decision-makers."[30]

The following account will demonstrate how the CCP, from 1952 to 1976, successfully planted the seeds of fear in the minds of Chinese entrepreneurs. Beginning in the early 1950s, Chinese private entrepreneurs had been suffering from a life-uncertainty factor that differed greatly from the Western model of capitalism. The situation created by the CCP gave rise to terror and uncertainty, which bore no relationship to the idea of economic uncertainty described by Frank Knight. At the same time, the entrepreneur as defined by Joseph A. Schumpeter ceased to exist because the CCP did not leave any room for innovation in either the private or public sectors. The public sector was supposed to take the leading role in innovation, but failed miserably. As one of Nankai University's graduate-turned-entrepreneurs said:

In China, in the government company, I cannot work hard because the people give me trouble and criticize me for working hard. They ask me, "Why do you work hard?" If I work hard, they will have to work hard, so they criticize me. If I do not work hard and take rest, they criticize me. So if I work hard, they criticize me and if I do not, they criticize me. They just want me to look busy but I really end up doing nothing. I met some friends and they had the same problem and we decided to open our own company and work for ourselves. Money is not important, but success is more important. I want to be a challenger, just to have good achievements.[31]

Before the new entrepreneurs of China became active contributors in the late 1970s to the economic development of China, their predecessors had to survive the wrath of the CCP from 1952 to 1976. This began with the Three-Anti (*San-fan*) campaign, initiated by the CCP on August 31, 1951, to cleanse the government of the three evils of corruption, waste, and bureaucracy. This campaign eventually rolled over in January, 1952, to incorporate private businessmen under the slogan of the Five-Anti (*Wu-fan*) campaign.

The memories of these campaigns are still vivid in contemporary China. Entrepreneurs are reluctant to talk openly to anyone. In particular, older entrepreneurs who survived Maoist rule and the Cultural Revolution are very careful about their delicate and uncertain position in the society. On at least two occasions when their parents walked in unexpectedly in the middle of interviews, the interviewees and I became the victims of scorn. The fear displayed by the parents was very clear. The terror of Maoist rule was relived by the parents, at least for that moment. These two incidents left a lasting impression in my mind. The parents looked filled with shame, fear, and anxiety. They were exasperated with their children for their foolishness. As for myself, I learned to view the terror of Maoist anti-campaigns in a different perspective. The fragile position of the entrepreneurs due to historical and recent political events has become even more clear to me.

PRELUDE TO THE FIVE-ANTI CAMPAIGN

To understand the Five-Anti campaign, we need to understand the origin of the Three-Anti campaign and even go further back to the late 1940s to explore the position taken by the CCP toward private entrepreneurs. This in turn, may shed some light on the business activities of the industrialists and merchants in the early 1950s.

On January 18, 1948, Mao Zedong presented a report to the CCP Central Committee entitled, "On Some Important Problems of the Party's Present Policy." In section II, Mao stated that the party should avoid taking drastic measures with respect to middle and small industrialists and merchants and that the industrial and commercial holdings of landlords and rich peasants should be protected. The holdings of bureaucrat–capitalists and counter-revolutionaries, however, could be confiscated. On June 30, 1949, Mao presented a report entitled, "On the People's Democratic Dictator-ship," in commemoration of the twenty-eighth anniversary of the Communist Party of China. In the report, Mao stated that the national bourgeoisie at the time were of great importance to the CCP and China and that "[o]ur present policy is to regulate capitalism, not to destroy it."[32]

The foregoing discussion includes two main points. First, Mao purposefully led private business to believe that the CCP was only interested in political power and macromanagement of the economy, so that private businessmen need not worry about future security and would be allowed to carry on business as they did before the CCP came to power. Second, the industrialists and the merchants who chose to stay or could not flee the country in the face of CCP threat to private entrepreneurship, with their fresh memories of the Yuan Shi-kai and GMD regimes, hoped that, though deprived of their political roles, their economic roles as a whole would not be challenged. Moreover, during the rule of Yuan and the GMD, the bourgeoisie, willingly or not, accepted their role as observers of political affairs in return for freedom to pursue microlevel economic activities. This was a quid pro quo for the middle and lower bourgeoisie groups and they accepted their status. In this context, the statements of the CCP during the late 1940s were interpreted as encouraging the bourgeoisie to carry on with their business activities. As one commentator noted, the CCP's statements,

> appear to have caused many capitalists' to assume that they would not be subjected, at least for the foreseeable future, to strict controls; consequently, they persisted in a variety of corrupt business practices which frequently involved the connivance of Party and government cadres who succumbed willingly to the "sugar-coated bullets" of the bourgeoisie.[33]

After the victory in 1949, the CCP had taken over the economy as master caretaker. In urban areas, government regulation of industry, commerce, and finance led the capitalists to depend on the party and government cadres, which gave them greater control over the economic survival of any industry. A government contract could make a firm very rich. On the other hand, any disapproval by the government would mean an economic threat to the firm, or even bankruptcy. In similar fashion, the cadres also controlled labor activities. If the cadres wanted it, there was labor peace, otherwise there would be workers' protests over wages and working conditions. The cadres also controlled the banks. It was up to the cadres to decide who would get loans for new investments. These factors led to deep corruption and bribery.[34]

Many party members were happy with their achievements and took an attitude of "eat well, sleep well, the job is finished."[35] Not only did some new party members exploit their official position for personal gain, many veterans embraced corruption to make themselves rich by taking bribes, using public properties and funds for private gain, and even selling public property to private individuals.[36]

It is reported that a group of Shanghai metal merchants formed an organized network for the purpose of bribing government officials to get information on the government's future orders for metals. On obtaining the information, merchants would raise the prices of metals. Another case involved drug merchants in Shanghai. Because of the labor insurance provided by the government, the demand for medical supplies increased. According to one report,

> Wang Kang-nien, a private drug merchant in Shanghai, took advantage of this to bribe functionaries who made bulk purchases and induced them to accept faked medicines. . . . In the food industry, the Ma Ling canning factory in Shanghai, which had received ¥30,000 million [$1,347,000; ¥30,000 million in terms of old currency. The amount would be ¥3 million in terms of the currency in use since March 1955] worth of government orders, substituted inferior meats for those specified and gave short weight.[37]

These corrupt activities led to the *San-fan* campaign. It began on August 31, 1951, by Gao Gang, a party leader in Manchuria, to cleanse the government there of the three evils of corruption, waste, and bureaucracy. By December 1951, the campaign spread to the rest of China. On New Year's Eve, 1951, Mao Zedong called a meeting of high-level party members of ministerial rank, chiefs of administrative districts, and mayors of municipalities directly under the control of the central people's government to notify them that the party was going to launch the Three-Anti campaign. Mao told them to direct the campaign carefully, "Among us, there are some who are guilty of corruption, extravagance and bureaucratism, perhaps rather seriously guilty. I hope that they will change their ways and what they have done will not be prosecuted." This statement made the higher officials feel safe; they understood that they could attack others with impunity.[38]

The free hand given to the party officials to cleanse the government was not limited to waste, corruption, or bureaucratism; they attacked anybody who did not meet their political standards, sometimes even because of activities of their forefathers. According to Chow Ching-Wen, many cadres committed suicide. Among his friends, Si Fu-liang, deputy minister of the Ministry of Labor, was accused of harboring anti-CCP thoughts. Si was given such a hard time during a "struggle meeting" that he became ill with high blood pressure. Chang Nai-Chi, vice-chairman of the China Democratic

National Construction Association, was interrogated for eight days and eight nights, not because he was corrupt, but because of his bourgeois thoughts. In similar ways other top officials were interrogated and physically abused.[39]

Most of the time, party members were physically abused or punished; however, some were sentenced to death. In Tianjin, two longstanding party members were found guilty of large-scale misappropriation of public funds and sentenced to death.[40] One month after the Three-Anti campaign was launched in Beijing, it was reported that in twenty-seven central government bodies, 1,670 cases of corruption were unveiled. A month later it was officially reported that several thousand cases were exposed in Beijing. This pattern of findings was common all over the country. In Guangzhou alone, party officials declared that they had exposed seventy to eighty "tigers" (big corruption cases) and hoped to find 400 to 500 more big cases and 4,000 to 5,000 medium and small cases. The purpose of the campaign "was not only to reduce corruption, waste, and bureaucratism, but also to cleanse the Party and the entire bureaucracy of 'rightist' deviations and 'bourgeois' thought."[41]

If party leaders and members were not safe from the tiger hunt of the Three-Anti campaign, it is easy to understand what happened to the capitalists. The Three-Anti campaign began mainly to purge the government of dishonest officials whose corruption derived from the presence of private businesses under a communist regime. If the main source of corruption were the capitalists, it was not surprising that the CCP proceeded to attack them so they were powerless to create any future problems for the party. The result was the Five-Anti campaign of 1952. The campaign was the beginning of the end of private capitalism in the PRC until the late 1970s. The consequence of the movement was almost total annihilation of private entrepreneurship in China.[42]

ENTREPRENEURS AND THE FIVE-ANTI CAMPAIGN

The Five-Anti campaign was formally aimed against alleged capitalists on grounds of tax evasion, bribery of government officials, theft of state property, cheating on government contracts, and stealing government economic secrets for private speculation. In January 1952, Zhou En-lai started a direct attack on the bourgeoisie based on the Three-Anti campaign. During the campaign momentum built up and by March 1952 it became official.

The CCP organized the employees of big industry and other business firms to vigorously criticize the owners and managers. During struggle meetings, the owners and managers were often tied up or forced to kneel down or bend over for an extended period of time. They were interrogated for many days and nights, deprived of sleep, and threatened with death if they did not confess. After a confession, they were allowed to wait for trial.

In Shanghai, a manager of a big company was locked in his office for seventeen days and forced to confess real and imagined evil acts. The weather of Shanghai was cold and wet when another businessman, wearing only his underwear, was questioned for three days and nights. These kinds of mental and physical punishments, handed out to thousands of Chinese businessmen, were intended to humiliate and horrify them, and to destroy private entrepreneurs as a force in Chinese society. Entrepreneurs were made to confess their "illegal earnings" and were forced to pay back the state. "It was all-out psychological warfare."[43] To escape, some entrepreneurs resorted to suicide.[44]

The campaign left an everlasting impression Chinese businessmen. Even today, entrepreneurs in China suffer from the life-uncertainty factor. They still do not trust government policy, and they try to hide information from others. In the West, where economic uncertainty rules, entrepreneurs are generally free with information related to their businesses and even their families. However, in Tianjin, when I asked the owner of an electric appliances store to tell me about his business and family life, he told me about his business in general but refused to talk about his family.

Entrepreneurs in China are extremely careful about their affairs and are distrustful of other Chinese. They are aware that neighbors, friends, and even relatives acted against the capitalists in the past and accused them, with or without valid reasons. In some cases when I interviewed entrepreneurs in their workplaces, the interviewee would come to a dead stop in the middle of the conversation when another customer or even a friend walked into the store. The fear of some unknown consequence or danger was clear. Though entrepreneurs might want to be helpful, they often feel a sense of helplessness (*Wu ke nai he*). This distrust and fear limits the smooth and natural flow of information from one entrepreneur to another prospective entrepreneur. Perhaps the roots of this present distrust can be traced back to the anti-campaigns carried out by the CCP.

In addition to the wave of suicides that swept Shanghai (involving as many as several thousand during that time)[45] and the dispatch of about 300,000 people to "reform through labor,"[46] there was another impact on Chinese society. The concept of *guanxi*—the personal relationship based on kinship, friendship, common village, school, or workplace, and the paternal relationship between an employee and employer—was challenged and, to some extent destroyed. It is reported that the Shanghai capitalists had close relationships with their employees. In light of the concept of extended family in China, it was common to find relatives of the employer working under him. In a metal shop in the Laocha district, for example, many employees were relatives of the owner and others maintained a good relationship with the owner. This close relationship between employee and employer prevented the campaign from growing. In the Chung Nan Rubber Company some of the employees were relatives of the owner and some were from the same village (*tong xiang*). Although it is not possible to determine the full scope of *guanxi*, reports of difficulties faced by the CCP in persuading workers to turn against the capitalists in the initial stage of the campaign testify to the phenomenon's existence and strength.[47]

The impact of *guanxi* eventually was diluted not only because kin and employees denounced the owners, but because very close relatives denounced each other. Wu Wen-fu, son of the owner of the Wu Fu Medical Instrument Enterprise in Xincheng district, told his father to admit his mistake in public. Another case involved the owner of the Ta Hua Copper Company. The owner confessed at a mutual help and criticism meeting that he had gained 50,000,000 yuan through corruption. When he returned to his shop, his employees again called on him to confess, and when he went back home, his mother-in-law and daughter admonished him. He became so worried and ill that he developed a sense of helplessness and confessed to obtaining 2,300,000,000 yuan illegally. Along with these pressures, his own "capitalist class, become meritorious small teams," also persuaded him to confess.[48]

Because of all these broken promises and trust, the *guanxi* factor became highly volatile. The *Wu-fan* campaign weakened the business class and left it without capital, unity, or the morale to advance its cause. The *Wu-fan* campaign laid the groundwork for the final takeover of private business. As Zhou En-lai said seven years later, the campaign "pushed private industry and commerce a great step forward towards state capitalism." As the Chinese were guided through stages by the state to fulfill the government's requirements for processing, manufacturing, and purchasing, they easily accepted their socialist transformation in 1956.[49]

PRIVATE BUSINESSES AND SOCIALIST TRANSFORMATION

The hangmen in ancient times put a man to death by hanging him several times—hanging him until he lost consciousness, reviving him, and hanging him again. Mao Tse-tung must have learned from these hangmen because this is what he is doing to the Chinese people [and businessmen].[50]

After the Five-Anti campaign came to an end, the private sector of China began to revive, but only for a short period of time. In 1953, there were more than two million people involved in private industry, excluding individual handicraftsmen. More than 45,000 private industrial enterprises, each employing more than ten workers and staff, were functioning in 1953. They employed altogether over 1,500,000 workers and staff. In the field of commerce about 200,000 individuals were involved in wholesale trade, about 2,000,000 were engaged in retail business, and several million small traders and peddlers were involved in the private economy.[51]

Nonetheless, the official report about the decline of the gross value of industrial output and distribution of retail sales makes it clear that the health of the private sector was declining quite rapidly. In 1949, the gross value of private industrial output was 55.8 percent of total output, in 1952 it was 17.1 percent, and by 1953 it had declined to 14.0 percent (see Table 2.3). In the area of retail trade the story was similar. In 1950 distribution through retail sales was 85 percent; in 1952 it was 57.2 percent and by 1953, it was down to 49.9 percent (see Table 2.4).

The actual process of socialist transformation of the private sector started in 1953, the same year the CCP initiated the first five-year plan. The state started the process of joint ownership and then began buying off private shares with dividends payable over ten years.[52] In the process of joint ownership, the state gradually took over the large and medium private firms. The handicraftsmen, food stalls, and small peddlers were eventually organized into collectives.

The transformation of private industry and commerce was carried out in two steps by the Chinese government. The first step was to transform

Table 2.3
Socialist Transformation of Private Industry in China, 1949–1956* (percent)

Year	Socialist Industry	State–Capitalist Industry			
		Total	*% Joint State–Private Enterprise*	*Private Enterprises Executing Orders and Processing Goods for the State*	*Private Industry***
1949	34.7	9.5	2.0	7.5	55.8
1950	45.3	17.8	2.9	14.9	36.9
1951	45.9	25.4	4.0	21.4	28.7
1952	56.0	26.9	5.0	21.9	17.1
1953	57.5	28.5	5.7	22.8	14.0
1954	62.8	31.9	12.3	19.6	5.3
1955	67.7	29.3	16.1	13.2	3.0
1956	67.5	32.5	32.5	—	—

* Percentage distribution of gross output value of industry, excluding handicrafts. **This indicates those produced and marketed privately.

Source: P.R.C. State Statistical Bureau, *Ten Great Years* (Beijing: Foreign Languages Press, 1960), 38.

Table 2.4
Socialist Transformation of Private Commerce in China, 1950–1957* (percent)

Year	Socialist Commerce	State–Capitalist and Cooperative Commerce	Private Commerce
1950	14.9	0.1	85.0
1951	24.4	0.1	75.5
1952	42.6	0.2	57.2
1953	49.7	0.4	49.9
1954	69.0	5.4	25.6
1955	67.6	14.6	17.8
1956	68.3	27.5	4.2
1957	65.7	31.6	2.7

* Percentage distribution of retail sales.

Source: P.R.C. State Statistical Bureau, *Ten Great Years* (Beijing: Foreign Languages Press, 1960), 40.

capitalism into state capitalism. The second step was to transform state–capitalism into socialism. State capitalism was the transitional stage from which the state eventually moved to socialist transformation of private industry and commerce.[53] Article 10 of the 1954 Constitution stated the reason for the socialist transformation of the private sector and the end result:

> The policy of the state towards capitalist industry and commerce is to utilize, restrict, and transform them. The state makes use of the positive sides of capitalist industry and commerce which are beneficial to national welfare and the people's livelihood; restricts their negative sides which are not beneficial to national welfare and the people's livelihood; encourages and guides their transformation into various forms of state-capitalist economy. It gradually replaces capitalist ownership with ownership by the whole people, and this it does by means of control exercised by administrative organs of the state, the leadership given by the state sector of the economy, and supervision by the workers.[54]

This account of the transformation of the private sector into socialism tells us something about the situation of the private entrepreneurs but leaves some questions unanswered: Why did the CCP choose to take a gradual approach toward this transformation? Why did entrepreneurs not challenge the government policy? If on the surface entrepreneurs seemed not to challenge the government policy, did they challenge it in some other ways? How did entrepreneurs suffer and what happened to them?

The reason the CCP chose to take a gradual approach toward transforming the private sector to socialism is very simple—they did not have the necessary management expertise to move more quickly. The rural origins of much of the party's leadership meant their knowledge of the economy was very basic, and they were starting a new economic system that was very different from the traditional system. The CCP knew that it would take a long time to develop the expertise needed to run the economy well. What the CCP failed to recognize was that human nature forces people to function well because of the rewards they expect from hard work and innovation. While individuals are willing to venture into uncertainty and risk to create something new, the communist regime took away the incentives from China's dynamic entrepreneurs.

The CCP replaced hard work and innovation with fear and terror through Mao's anti-campaigns, thus giving birth to the life-uncertainty factor. That terror still haunts present-day entrepreneurs in China. During most of the interviews, and from casual interaction with entrepreneurs in Tianjin, Beijing, and other places, I was left with the impression that entrepreneurs fear some unknown due to the country's history and uncertain government policy. This is further accented by the Chinese and Communist culture in which the entrepreneurial talents and spirits are dampened, thus frustrating the effective use of resources to create jobs and opportunities.

When China's entrepreneurs were challenged by the CCP after the Five-Anti movement, they were not in a position to fight back. One commentator said that after the Five-Anti campaign, Shanghai was like a malaria patient who had just gone through a severe fever; the patient was recovering and returning to normal temperature but was still very weak and wondering when the next attack would come.

The next attack did indeed come, but in a gradual way. Chinese entrepreneurs found they could no longer figure out the government's policy on entrepreneurs or their position in the economy. They were like tadpoles swimming in communist water, going through a slow metamorphosis and finally turning into frogs, without knowing what really happened. But when the process became clear to the Chinese businessmen, they were not happy. They reacted in a strange way. It was reported that, in Shanghai, businessmen spent their money lavishly on eating, drinking, and other things while they could.[55]

With the gradual disappearance of a capitalist market and entrepreneurship where profit could be made through the acceptance of risk and uncertainty, and the introduction of the life-uncertainty factor by the CCP, private businessmen lost their interest in business. Many decreased production and were unwilling to improve management or expand their business. This resulted in great waste, poor quality products, the unnecessary accumulation of raw materials, and unnecessary inventories. Also, because private businessmen's profits were calculated in terms of processing charges, they were not pleased about reducing their costs, and sometimes even raised costs by purposefully wasting raw materials and paying excessive wages. This led the government to adopt the policy of state–private joint enterprise in an effort to exert more control over enterprise management.[56]

The policy adopted by the government, and other ways of manipulating power, directly affected the private entrepreneurs who sought to minimize their risks and transfer loss and risk to the government one way or another. This caused the whole economy to suffer by reducing saving and investment by entrepreneurs.

When entrepreneurs were caught in the policy trap of the government, they became passive and economic liabilities. Clearly, party policy and entrepreneurs' responses, beginning in the early 1950s, combined to undercut the aims of policymakers and the business class. For an economy to develop a marriage of policy and entrepreneurial activities must occur. This would not happen in China again until 1978. Even after 1978, private entrepreneurs do not have faith in the government and still suffer from the life-uncertainty factor which makes them very cautious and indecisive about the future. Most entrepreneurs are not willing to invest and expand their businesses. Many of the entrepreneurs I talked with like to enjoy life while they have money and keep a low profile. It will take time for a better system or environment to evolve in China where entrepreneurs feel comfortable enough to be innovative and expand their businesses in the face of risk and uncertainty. This directly reflects the legacy of history and the past actions of the government, as two recent entrepreneurs noted. One of them said: "If I get bigger, I will have more trouble. All kind of person will take money from me. The tax collector, the traffic administration and health administration. . . . If I do not have these problems, I will surely expand but I am not sure of the [government] policy."[57] And the other entrepreneur said:

> I do not know about the [government's] policy. I do not know about the future of the individual business. The policies are so unstable. I do not want to go into risk by expanding and investing money. There are a lot of problems of opening a business. The bureaucracy gives you troubles, you need a lot of connections [guanxi], like the police and the heads of departments. I am making money to enjoy life. I am not thinking about the future. The future you do not know.[58]

These observations by two Chinese entrepreneurs reflect not only their distrust of government policy, but the powerful presence in their minds of the country's history. They want to enjoy life while they can. In the following chapters, we will find that Confucian authoritarianism and the CCP's dictatorship, accentuated by culture, makes entrepreneurs excessively dependent on the government for their survival and continuity. This makes entrepreneurs sensitive to any change of policy, thus creating fear and life uncertainty. This no doubt hinders their contribution toward economic development of China.

Present-day entrepreneurs are indeed aware of their country's communist history along with the recent Tiananmen Square massacre. For this reason entrepreneurs are very sensitive about the policy of the government and profess to not trust it. To understand entrepreneurs in China, we must look at history and analyze what happened to the Chinese businessmen during the socialist transformation.

THE SOCIALIST TRANSFORMATION AND THE SUFFERING OF BUSINESSMEN

Beginning in 1949 the state gradually started to control the economy and increased its ownership of the means of production. By the end of 1952, about 70 to 80 percent of heavy industry and 40 percent of light industry were owned by the state. Sixty percent of large-scale industrial output was produced by state-owned enterprises, 6 percent was from joint state–private enterprises, 3 percent was produced by state-controlled cooperatives, and only 31 percent was produced by private industries. In other words, less than one-third of China's large-scale industry was run by the private sector. (See Table 2.3.)

The same story prevailed in the field of commerce (see Table 2.4). By the end of 1952, there were more than 30,000 state stores in China, or 4.7 times the number in 1950. The state sector and cooperative sectors coordinated their functions in supply and marketing cooperatives in the countryside and consumer's cooperatives in the cities. During 1952, the state and cooperative sectors together controlled more than 50 percent of the total business turnover in China's domestic market. The state controlled about 30 percent of retail businesses in the major cities. Total retail sales controlled by the state in 1952 increased by 306 percent over 1950 and, in the case of cooperatives, increased even more. In wholesale trade, the state controlled almost 100 percent of certain commodities. In 1950, the state's share of wholesale commerce was 23.9 percent, but by 1952 it had risen to 63.8 percent. In 1950, the share of state and cooperative commerce in total retail sales was 14.9 percent, by 1952 it had risen to 42.6 percent. The state sector also managed approximately 93 percent of all foreign trade in 1952. All this was a precursor to eventual socialist transformation.[59]

In accordance with its socialist goals, the state moved rapidly to gain control over economic life beginning in 1952 with the wholesale business. The state bought staple farm products, awarded contracts for manufacturing and processing goods, and purchased important industrial products in large volumes. From the second half of 1953, the state planned, purchased, and supplied grain, oil-bearing seeds, cotton, and cloth, and excluded private wholesale dealers from the bulk purchase of industrial products.[60] The state trading agencies consisted of thirteen specialized companies with branches all over China and employed 400,000 workers. By the end of the third quarter of 1953, these specialized companies controlled 65 percent of all wholesale trade in the country and purchased most of the output of private industry. In Tianjin, three-quarters of private industries' output was purchased by the state. In Guangzhou, 64 percent of output in the last quarter of 1953 was produced based on government contract. In Beijing, state agencies bought over half of private industries' output during the first two quarters.[61]

Although state capitalism left some room for retailers to function in commerce, the CCP held tenaciously to the doctrine that all private dealers were exploiters and should be strictly controlled by the CCP. In 1954, the phrase, "strike at the private merchants' speculations" rose to the status of a catch phrase.[62] In the lowest form of state capitalism in commerce, private retailers bought goods from state-owned factories for cash. The retailers, in turn, sold the goods to consumers at a price fixed by the government, making a profit of 5 to 10 percent depending on the trade and locality. In the secondary form, private retailers acted as sub-agents for the government, distributing goods for state factories. The private retailers paid a deposit of 50 to 80 percent for the goods obtained from the state factories; after selling the products at a fixed price they were given a commission of 5 to 9 percent. Sample figures for August 1955 showed that about a quarter of China's private retailers were then functioning under one or another of these classifications. In the highest form of state capitalism in commerce, the whole trade was taken over by the government in major industrial and agricultural areas. For example, the entire cotton piece-goods business in Beijing was converted into a single state–private business.[63]

The highest form of state capitalism—state–private joint enterprise—developed in Shanghai where more than sixty large factories were transformed into state–private joint enterprises by 1953.[64] By the second half of 1954, this transformation moved on to whole trades. In Shanghai, eight branches of production—cotton, wool, linen textiles, paper, cigarettes, enamelware, flour milling, and rice hulling—were transformed into state-private joint enterprises. By 1956, all private industry had been converted to joint ownership in Beijing. Tianjin, Xian, Shanghai, and other cities followed shortly. As one private businessman described this phenomenon, "We used to cross one by one in row boats. Now so many want to go over, we have to charter whole steam ships."[65] In Shanghai alone a majority of the city's 200,000 private industrialists and merchants surrendered to the government, which gladly accepted the private entrepreneurs' mass application.[66]

It is easy to understand the suffering of private entrepreneurs who had been demoralized by the Five-Anti movement. Those who could not stand the suffering committed suicide while the rest waited for the next attack and simply surrendered to the will of the government. The government decided how the private entrepreneurs would be paid and what position they would have in the very industry they themselves had built. It was painful to see the takeover of one's own company and still work as a government employee in return for a small fixed interest:

> Annual payments between 1956 and 1965 were set at 120 million yuan a year, or an equivalent of $50 million. The recipients numbered 1,140,000, each receiving an average of $44 per year. Many capitalists elected to forfeit their payments, because they thought it did not pay to be labeled a capitalist in return for a few dollars.[67]

The process of taking over private businesses and the treatment given to the private entrepreneurs by the government after the Five-Anti movement amounted to nothing but pain for the private entrepreneurs. To overcome the suffering, they developed the ability to look at the humor of the situation and laughed "at the government sent agents' maladroit attempts at improving their factories."[68]

Along with this kind of passive role displayed by private businessmen, some tried to regain their monetary and social losses in other ways. In some cases, when private factory owners received orders from the government for certain products they "[lowered] the quality of their products, [raised] expenses, [used] for their own purposes the raw material provided by the government, [did] not deliver the goods on the fixed date; thus causing great loss to the people."[69]

For example, at the end of 1954 in Shanghai there were 27,772 industrial factories and workshops with 478,000 workers. Two hundred forty-five public–private factories with 110,000 employees produced 19.7 percent of industrial output. More than 9,000 factories were working on state processing orders. The quantity of goods produced since 1952 for the state had more than doubled, making Shanghai's total production by private factories 78 percent. The services offered by private businesses were minimal but very costly. It was reported that because of low quality in rubber manufacturing, the government suffered a loss of 4,600 million yuan (about $200,000) during the first eight months of 1954. Similar losses occurred in paper, thermos flask, and other industries. In Wuhan, 60 percent of automobile accessories were said to have been rejected because of low quality. Even strict punishment did not "deter private owners from sabotaging State orders."[70]

It can be argued that present-day entrepreneurs, like their predecessors, are not contributing fully to the economy. This is due to the CCP's past and present uncertain policies and brutal oppression of any move by the citizens away from traditional submission to authority, further accentuated by the position of entrepreneurs in Chinese culture. However, in the following chapter it is shown that the status of entrepreneurs is changing slowly in a positive direction, and they are feeling more secure about their future.

In spite of indirect or passive resistance by private businesses, the CCP was slowly able to take over the private sector and convert them to public–private joint ownership under dictated conditions of compensation.

PAYMENTS TO THE PRIVATE SECTOR

After the transformation to public–private joint ownership, the government assigned jobs to the private businessmen and their associates. In Shanghai, 563 private businessmen and their associates were involved in the transformation of the eight trades—cotton, wool and linen textiles, paper manufacturing, cigarettes, enamelware, flour milling, and rice hulling. Of these 563 businessmen, 22 were given jobs as managers or deputy managers, 190 were assigned to factories as directors or deputy directors, 28 were assigned as engineers or technicians, 267 were given jobs as department heads or assistant department heads, 26 were given positions on boards of directors, and 13 were retired due to old age. Of all 563 individuals involved, 11 were not given any jobs on the pretext that they had been law breakers or counterrevolutionaries.[71]

In Tianjin, the second largest industrial city in China, 55 factories were converted to public–private joint ownership in 1954 alone. In the first three months of 1955, 43 were transformed, and on April 22, 1955 it was decided that 74 more would be converted. By the end of 1954, 19 percent of private factory clerks and workers worked for the public–private factories.[72]

Along with assignments of jobs and responsibilities after the transformation of private enterprises, the government also shared the profits with the private sector until the end of 1955. Article 17 of the provisional regulations on public–private jointly operated industrial enterprises (September 2, 1954) stipulated that

> [t]he balance of yearly profits after payment of income tax should be distributed by the jointly-operated enterprises among reserve funds, bonuses and dividends according to the following principles. Dividends for shareholders and remunerations to board directors, managers and factory directors may absorb around 25 per cent of the yearly profits.
>
> An appropriate amount may be taken out as bonuses, taking into consideration the relevant provisions of state enterprises and the welfare facilities formerly provided by the enterprise.
>
> The balance left after payment of dividends and bonuses shall be set aside as reserve funds.[73]

But the profit sharing came to an end in 1956. With the virtual elimination of private enterprises in the urban areas, the interest system was imposed on businessmen. They were given fixed interest at five percent of their shares and the owners became the staff of the state enterprises. "As a social class the national bourgeoisie had vanished."[74]

Another report said that by the end of 1956 the number of industries and businesses dropped to 160,000, there was a decrease of 32.1 percent in commercial undertakings, and the number of catering businesses had dropped by 44.8 percent compared to the previous year.[75]

SOCIALIST TRANSFORMATION AND SMALL BUSINESSES

The socialist transformation not only affected big business, it touched small businesses too. In the process of socialist transformation in 1956, small traders, handicraftsmen, peddlers, and individual laborers (*getihu*) were organized under industrial and commercial cooperatives, and some were assigned to state enterprises.[76] Before the socialist transformation, the big cities in China had been full of tailor shops, food stores, small traders, different kinds of peddlers, repairmen, and pedicabs, and many offered convenient services until midnight. But with the socialist transformation, service hours were reduced and employees were given fixed wages instead of earnings based on labor. Small business experienced the same process as the industrial sector. Business volume grew but the variety of goods presented to consumers decreased. Handicrafts accounted for approximately 17.4 percent of China's gross output in 1954, and nearly 20 million individuals were involved in this field. Of these 20 million, 9 million were full-time and 11 million were part-time peasants who worked during their free time.

A look at Shanghai gives an idea of the situation characterizing the individual economy in China's cities. During the early 1950s in Shanghai, individual businessmen were involved in 150 kinds of trades in three major categories: 24 percent were in handicraft, 40 percent in repair and services trades, and 36 percent in commerce. Before the socialist transformation in 1956, Shanghai boasted more than 200,000 individual producers and operators, but by 1960 there were only 14,000. Though there was a slight increase in this number during the early 1960s due to economic difficulties brought about in China by the Great Leap Forward, a clean-up movement in 1964 brought the number to 34,000. The Cultural Revolution brought the number down to 8,000, and the rest were either absorbed by the collective economy or moved to rural areas.[77] In Beijing by 1978 about 259 individual businesses were in operation.[78]

Regardless of the Cultural Revolution, private entrepreneurs were doomed as long as Mao Zedong was in power. As Mao said in his speech "On the Correct Handling of Contradictions Among the People" in 1957,

Some people contend that the Chinese bourgeoisie no longer has two sides to its character, but only one side. Is this true? No. Even when they stop receiving their fixed interest payments and the bourgeois' label is removed, they will still need ideological remoulding for quite sometime.[79]

For Mao, class struggle and revolution were a perpetual state of affairs. The Cultural Revolution was a tool used by him to subdue his opponents in the CCP leadership so he could carry on his revolution and remain in power. The message that was given to the private sector during the Cultural Revolution was that they were already dead and should stay in the grave. The Cultural Revolution left an everlasting impression on private entrepreneurs that caused them to believe that they would not be able to escape the life-uncertainty factor as long as the CCP was in power. Entrepreneurs in China are still suffering from the shock of Mao's rule, and the uncertain policy of the 1980s continues to feed that fear.

PRIVATE BUSINESS AFTER THE CULTURAL REVOLUTION

After the completion of socialist transformation of private industry and commerce in 1956, there was a severe drop in the number of private businesses. In 1957, due to policy adjustments, the number of individual industrial and commercial operators rose to 1.04 million. This figure remained basically the same until 1965. With the advent of the Cultural Revolution in 1966 any hope for survival of the private sector came to an end. In 1967, fixed interest payments to private industrialists were stopped and the joint state–private ventures came completely under the socialist economy. As a social class, the capitalists were eliminated. During the ten years of the Cultural Revolution, the individual economy was mostly eliminated as a tail of capitalism. By 1978, only 140,000 small retailers and repairers run by individual operators survived the wrath of the Cultural Revolution. Other reports say that the number was reduced to 180,000 or 150,000.[80]

Whatever the actual number, the Cultural Revolution can be said to have temporarily ended the several thousand years of history of private economy in mainland China. It was not until 1977 that the private economy was able to start breathing again.

The chaos of the Cultural Revolution left the CCP and the Chinese system as a whole paralyzed to manage the economy. It was time to let the people take their economic destiny into their own hands. There was a huge number of unemployed—recent graduates, urban-educated youth who were sent to the countryside, people released from prison and reform-through-labor and education programs, and retirees. Many retirees were below the formal retirement age (sixty for men and fifty-five for women). About 10 to 25 million, or 8.5 to 18 percent of the nonagricultural workforce were unemployed.[81] Faced with this situation the CCP, under the leadership of Deng Xiaoping, let entrepreneurship flourish in China along with economic reform and opened China up to the outside world vis-à-vis trade, information, tourism, travel, and so on.

On March 5, 1978, the Fifth National People's Congress adopted at its first session a constitutional amendment that mentioned the legal status of private individual businessmen. Article 5 of section one stipulates:

> There are mainly two kinds of ownership of the means of production . . . at the present stage: Socialist ownership . . . and socialist collective ownership. . . .
> The state allows non-agricultural individual labourers to engage in individual labour . . . within the limits permitted by law . . . [state] guides these individual labourers step by step on to the road of socialist collectivization.[82]

Since the adoption of Article 5 of the constitution, private businesses have been growing at a rapid pace. Although there has been some disruption in the process of development of the private sector, it is dynamic and growing. Although certain segments of the government might at times try to slow down the process, the mainstream of the government continues to advocate development of the private sector. During 1981 to 1982, there was a popular saying in China: "The two ends are hot but the middle is cold," which meant that the top level and bottom level wanted the reform to continue but the middle-level bureaucrats did not want change.[83]

Whatever form opposition to development of the private sector took, it did not deter the government from carrying on reform. The third plenary session of the 11th Central Committee of the CCP in the fall of 1978 put its authoritative stamp on continued development of the private sector when it unequivocally declared that for modernization to be successful, China needed a great growth of the productive forces.[84]

The Dengist party's open support for private entrepreneurs is needed in China. The party plays a very important role in the life of the Chinese people and greatly influences the decision-making process of the private entrepreneurs. Chinese entrepreneurs look to the government for new directions and a sense of security, without which they are afraid to move into unknown areas of private economic interaction. On the other hand, reform-minded government officials are careful not to take bigger strides toward opening up the private sector because any failure in that sector would play right into the hands of the anti-reform group. In light of this, the 1978 constitution's characterization of the private sector as leading toward socialist collectivization manifested a struggle within the government and served as a subtle effort to appease the anti-reform group.

However, with the continuing success of the private sector, the National People's Congress, in its new constitution adopted on April 22, 1982, did not mention the collectivization of the private sector. This was a real boost to the confidence of private entrepreneurs. Entrepreneurs in China are always looking for signs from the government. Article 11 of the 1982 constitution stipulates:

> The individual economy of the urban and rural working people . . . is a complement to the socialist sector of the economy. . . . The state protects the lawful rights and interests of the individual economy.
> The state guides, . . . the individual economy . . . through the economic links of the state and collective economy with the individual economy.[85]

This wait-and-see policy adopted by reform-minded officials in China is not typical of the Chinese communist system. In the former Soviet Union similar behavior was observed in the early 1980s. Officials would take a small step and, with success, became bolder. The first experiment involving the private economy took place in Estonia in 1983 and with success entrepreneurs were allowed to "engage in any activities which were not forbidden."[86]

What we see in communist systems, as demonstrated by China and the former Soviet Union, is that the policy of private ownership is an experiment with something new. The result is not a product of a well thought out plan vis-à-vis private ownership. When I asked one private owner, "How do the government policies help you?" he replied,

> I do not know [how the government's policy helps me]. Maybe they make some laws to help the individual economy. I did not read the government policies. In China, the policy is used by the leaders according to their understanding; level of thinking is different, sometimes good ideas and sometimes wrong decisions. So it is not easy to say about policy, which one is good or which one is wrong. Policy changes fast but people's [officials] understanding is very different.[87]

In a communist system like China, there will always be a group of people who will try to hinder the development of private ownership because of their loss of interest and power. In many developing economies, it is not money that begets power, rather it is the political power in the office that begets money and comfort. As a result, any loss of power due to decentralization will be opposed vehemently. In the case of China, where entrepreneurs look to the government for guidance and assurance of safety (not only for economic well-being and freedom) it is necessary for top-level government officials to come forward with words of assurance and actions that comfort private owners.

A look at other communist systems and China reveal the connection between power and money and why some Communist cadres are so unwilling to go along with the economic reform movement. Nicolae Ceausescu, Romania's Communist ruler for twenty-five years, spent money lavishly. Erich Honecker of East Germany spent thousands on sport cars. Bulgaria's dictator, Todor Zhivkov, who never made it past eighth grade, thought that he owned Bulgaria. Czechoslovakia and Poland's communist dictators were no exception. This kind of abuse of power for economic gains led Boris Yeltsin to say, "The higher you climb, the more comforts surround you."[88]

China's cadres (*ganbu*) are no exception to abuse of power for economic privileges. In Beijing, the children of cadres went to high-quality kindergartens whereas the children of common citizens were deprived of the same luxury. High officials were supplied with luxurious cars and special train compartments for personal use.[89] In China, CCP officials are immune from criminal punishment unless they participate in a political blunder, like the Gang of Four, and are dismissed.

In August 1983, after a long tug of war between the anti-reform group and the reform-minded group, Hu Yaobang, late general secretary of the Central Committee of the CCP, came forward and assured private businesses of their continued survival and government protection. Hu expressed this support by saying that the party supported the individual economy. Hu criticized the prevailing notion that working in state-owned enterprises was more respectable than working as private businessmen and termed the notion outdated. He further said, "Every job which benefits the country and the people is to be respected."[90]

This kind of open assurance from time to time to private entrepreneurs by the government gave them renewed hope and confidence in the policymakers, which is one of the key preconditions for positive entrepreneurial behavior in China. Confidence in the government's policy helped to reduce the life-uncertainty factor and entrepreneurs were able to produce results that, in turn, helped reform-minded policymakers take innovative actions. In 1982, a farmer named Wu Jilong of Hebei Province successfully turned around the failing silicon workshop of a big copper works in Shanxi Province. "From a four-year loss of 1.9 million yuan, the workshop made a profit of 4.2 million yuan in the following three years."[91] These kinds of success stories were not kept secret from the reform-minded government officials. In his report to the National People's Congress on May 15, 1984, Zhao Ziyang, then Premier of the State Council, declared that "[s]mall state-owned enterprises may be run by the collective or by individuals under contract or lease."[92]

The reform-minded officials led by Deng Xiaoping knew very well that this kind of timely support of private entrepreneurs was needed in order to reduce the life-uncertainty factor and move China toward economic development. Support for private entrepreneurs was evident again in October 1984. Each time, reform-minded officials first lay the groundwork for supporting the reform movement. In October 1984, the government, led by Deng, started talking about urban reform. Deng declared that the wisdom manifested during the Third Plenary Session of the 11th Party Central Committee in 1978 helped in adopting the reform policy for the rural areas. The rural reform policy proved to be successful; 80 percent of the Chinese population lived in rural areas and enjoyed a good life. But to sustain these achievements urban reform was needed.[93]

By laying the groundwork and silencing anti-reform-minded officials, the CCP opened the door for urban entrepreneurs. The Third Plenary Session of the 12th Central Committee of the CCP in October 1984, stated that rural reform was a success and urban reform was needed to liberate the forces of production so they can complement the consumers' demand in the rural areas, where 800 million people live. At the same time, government discouraged the prevailing idea of "eating from the same big pot."[94]

This declaration helped reduce the life-uncertainty factor and created a new trust in the continuity of government policy. China saw a rapid development of private ownership in 1984 (see Table 2.5). In 1983 there were 5,980,000 individual businesses in China, in 1984, the number jumped to 10,000,000. For example, in Chengdu, capital of Sichuan Province, before 1983 there were 7,200 individual business with 9,000 operators. By 1985 there were over 100,000 individual businesses with 120,000 operators. In just two years in Chengdu, the number of restaurants

Table 2.5
Progress of Individual Business

	Number of Units		
Year	Urban Areas	Rural Areas	Total
1978	140,000 (46.7)	160,000 (53.3)	300,000 (100)
1979	250,000 (44.6)	310,000 (55.4)	560,000 (100)
1980	400,000 (44.6)	497,000 (55.4)	897,000 (100)
1981	867,000 (47.5)	961,100 (52.5)	1,828,900 (100)
1982	1,358,000 (50.3)	1,340,000 (49.7)	2,698,000 (100)
1983	1,821,000 (30.5)	4,159,000 (69.5)	5,980,000 (100)
1984	2,911,000 (29.1)	7,089,000 (70.9)	10,000,000 (100)
1985	2,764,000 (23.7)	8,916,000 (76.3)	11,680,000 (100)
1986	2,910,000 (24.0)	9,200,000 (76.0)	12,110,000 (100)
1987	3,383,000 (24.6)	10,342,300 (75.4)	13,725,000 (100)
1988	3,823,000 (26.3)	10,704,000 (73.7)	14,527,000 (100)
1989	3,694,548 (29.6)	8,774,386 (70.4)	12,471,934 (100)

Table 2.5 (continued)

	Individuals Employed		
Year	Urban Areas	Rural Areas	Total
1978	150,000 (44.9)	184,000 (55.1)	334,000 (100)
1979	320,000 (47.3)	356,000 (52.7)	676,000 (100)
1980	810,000 (48.9)	848,000 (51.1)	1,658,000 (100)
1981	1,056,000 (46.4)	1,218,000 (53.6)	2,274,000 (100)
1982	1,470,000 (45.9)	1,730,000 (54.1)	3,200,000 (100)
1983	2,086,100 (27.9)	5,378,300 (72.1)	7,464,400 (100)
1984	3,390,000 (25.1)	10,120,000 (74.9)	13,510,000 (100)
1985	4,500,000 (24.6)	13,823,000 (75.4)	18,323,000 (100)
1986	4,831,000 (25.1)	14,383,000 (74.9)	19,214,000 (100)
1987	5,690,000 (26.5)	15,793,000 (73.5)	21,483,000 (100)
1988	6,590,000 (28.5)	16,460,000 (71.5)	23,050,000 (100)
1989	5,604,545 (28.8)	13,809,860 (71.3)	19,414,405 (100)
	Turnover in Billion Yuan (in current prices)		
1978	—	—	—
1979	—	—	—
1980	—	—	—
1981	1.13 (53.6)	0.98 (46.4)	2.11 (100)
1982	5.07 (50.3)	5.00 (49.7)	10.07 (100)
1983	7.24 (34.3)	13.86 (65.7)	21.10 (100)
1984	12.27 (26.8)	33.49 (73.2)	45.76 (100)
1985	21.41 (28.5)	53.65 (71.5)	75.06 (100)
1986	27.44 (30.0)	63.98 (70.0)	91.42 (100)
1987	33.60 (32.4)	70.23 (67.6)	103.83 (100)
1988	44.23 (37.15)	74.84 (62.85)	119.07 (100)
1989	54.22 (40.4)	79.70 (59.6)	133.92 (100)

Percentage distribution between urban and rural areas in parentheses.

Sources: Statistical Yearbook of China 1981-1990; Liang Chuan-yun, "The New Development of Individual Industry and Commerce in Cities and Countryside," *Almanac of China's Economy 1985-86* (Beijing 1986), 332; Xinhua News Agency, News Bulletin; *China, Statistical Abstract 1989* (Beijing 1989), 17; Statistical compilation by State Administration for Industry and Commerce. All sources cited from Kraus, 1991, p. 64.

increased by 40 times, tailor's shops by 25 times, and repair shops by 7 times.[95] This rapid increase reflects a few phenomena. Private entrepreneurs in China were ready for entrepreneurial activities but were waiting for some kind of positive signal from the government—the signal was that rural entrepreneurs and urban entrepreneurs are the same and they serve the same purpose. There was no distinction made between a peasant entrepreneur and a city entrepreneur. This signal was enough to reduce the life-uncertainty factor, allowing the entrepreneurs to venture into new activities. In the rural areas where the experimentation started vis-à-vis private ownership, the number jumped to almost double. This shows that rural entrepreneurs are also very sensitive to the government's actions and many potential entrepreneurs were waiting for the right moment to see the government policy applied to the whole country rather than just rural areas.

This trend continued with a slow development in the number of individual businesses (see Table 2.5), but the Tiananmen Square incident caused the number of individual businesses to plummet again. The entrepreneurs felt threatened, and the events of the 1950s and the Cultural Revolution came back to haunt them, causing them to reduce their business activities. Consumers also lost confidence in the government. To understand the role of government and entrepreneurs in the economic development of China, one cannot ignore the role of the consumers. (This triangular relationship of government, entrepreneurs, and consumers is discussed in detail in Chapter 3.)

After the Tiananmen Square massacre, consumers bought goods selectively and in 1989 businessmen started panic selling to move inventory quickly:

> An analysis of the consumers' attitude towards consumption reveals that since the latter half of 1989, the increase rates of commodity prices have [slowed], interest rates have decreased, and the value-guaranteed deposit has lost its appeal to people. Some people have chosen to purchase commodities to guarantee value instead of depositing their money.[96]

Before the Tiananmen Square massacre shocked Chinese entrepreneurs and consumers, a few important steps were taken in the late 1980s that, in my view, ensured the rapid comeback of private ownership in the early 1990s. By the end of October 1987, the individual economy flourished, increasing to 13 million businesses and employing 20.37 million people; total capital was 21.6 billion yuan. From January to October 1987, the individual economy's business turnover was 76.1 billion yuan, which included 49.9 billion yuan from retail services, accounting for 13 percent of China's total retail sales.[97]

He Jianzhang and colleagues discovered through a 1981 study that private businesses (businesses that consist of more than eight employees) already existed in China. In Guangdong Province, in the Miancheng town of Chaoyang county, twenty unemployed youths collected 5,000 yuan to open up an electrical repair shop. In Jiamusi City in Heilongjiang Province, sixty youths pooled almost 20,000 yuan to open their own company.[98] The government chose to take a wait-and-see approach toward these private businesses. The government neither prevented the private businesses from developing nor promoted them. With the success of individual entrepreneurship, private entrepreneurship started to grow by soliciting idle funds to create businesses, which then facilitated growth of productive forces. "The social and economic benefits arising from private enterprises have led to a more unified understanding of their role."[99]

With the unofficial growth of private businesses, it was time for reform-minded officials to move in and declare the next step toward the development of private ownership. At the 13th National Congress of the CCP on October 25, 1987, Zhao Ziyang announced the official stand on private businesses. He said, "Co-operative, individual and private sectors of the economy in both urban and rural areas should all be encouraged to expand. . . . [And] we must formulate policies and enact laws governing the private sector as soon as possible, in order to protect its legitimate interest."[100]

In April 1988, the National People's Congress formally passed a constitutional amendment to accept Zhao's proposal. On June 28 1988, the highest administrative body in China, the State Council, published China's first regulations on private enterprises. The regulations defined a private enterprise as a private company that can hire eight or more employees. At that time, China had about 225,000 private enterprises with an employment of 3.6 million employees and an average of 16 employees per business.[101]

This number of private enterprises does not truly reflect the number of private enterprises and their activities. Due to the life-uncertainty factor of private entrepreneurs and *getihu* in China, many entrepreneurs chose to evade the possible wrath of the conservative anti-reform group by disguising themselves. Some small individual businesses simply did not register with the authorities. As one interviewee said, "All the individual businesses are not good. Most of the individual businesses do not have a license, so there is an unfair competition. . . . The businessmen without licenses are better off because they do not have to pay taxes."[102]

Some larger private businesses arrange their disguises in different ways. Some borrow their names from other administrative units; others take the names of collective enterprises. A survey by Baoding city officials in 1988 found that in the Baoding area alone, there were 9,797 private enterprises, whereas the Hebei Provincial Statistical Bureau reported in 1988 that in the whole province the number of private enterprises was no more than

20,000.[103] It was reported in 1990 that private enterprises borrowed the names of collective enterprises to evade tax and detection by the authorities. The collective enterprises acted as a protective umbrella over private business.[104] It was reported in January 1993 that approximately 33 percent of the collective enterprises were, in fact, private business.[105]

It was no surprise that Deng Xiaoping had to take personal steps to help private entrepreneurs overcome their fear of persecution by government officials and the masses. For this reason, Deng took the southern train trip in the beginning of 1992 to show support for reform and to give new hope to private entrepreneurs.

ENTREPRENEURS IN THE POST–TIANANMEN PERIOD

The train tour of the south by Deng Xiaoping and his open support of reform to cultivate productive forces should not come as a surprise. Chinese entrepreneurs had two choices. One was to stay put and wait for positive change; the second was to give up on business altogether. Either choice would have moved China toward an economic disaster. It was up to Deng to come out in favor of the reforms, reduce the life-uncertainty factor, and try to erase some of the fearful memories of 1950s and the Cultural Revolution and the Tiananmen Square massacre that haunted entrepreneurs.

Deng's trip can be viewed in two ways. One was the message sent to government officials, private entrepreneurs, and foreign investors that the reform toward private ownership was to continue even after the Tiananmen Square massacre, and the incident should have no bearing on the economic activities of the private sector. But the question still remains, why did Deng have to make a long trip to the south to spread the message of freedom to the private sector? He could have made the announcement while lying in his bed. The second view states that in the context of China, the physical presence of Deng was necessary to convince the private sector that the reform toward private ownership was genuine and enduring. It was wise on Deng's part to visit the power base of private ownership and economic development to prove his committment to the reforms to the anti-reform officials and private entrepreneurs.

It was reported that the coastal leaders made an appeal to Deng to make the trip to help them remove the fear of life uncertainty from private entrepreneurs and potential investors, and to combat the threat of the hardliners.[106] Deng said during his southern train tour, "Don't hinder the development pace. . . . Be good at grasping opportunities, and right now there are good opportunities.[107]

However, during the train tour, hardliners in Beijing's propaganda department chose not to publish Deng's comments and his call for bolder reform.[108] The victory of the hardliners was very short-lived. Upon Deng's return to Beijing, he fired them. Among the hardliners who lost their central committee posts were Gao Di, publisher of *The People's Daily*; Wang Renzhi, director of the propaganda department; and He Jingzhi, the acting culture minister.[109] The train tour and subsequent actions against the hardliners were well received by the reformers and private entrepreneurs.

Since the train tour, private entrepreneurial activities have been increasing in number. Chinese entrepreneurs are active in the Chinese market; they are venturing outside the country to bring in capital; and they are investing in other countries. Except in a few areas, they are also competing with the state sector, surprisingly with CCP approval.[110] Gone are the days when ideology dictated economic outcome. Now in China, anything economically good is considered good capitalism with a good socialism coating.

Jiang Zemin, in his report to the 14th National Congress of the CCP on October 12, 1992, said that China should not get bogged down in an argument over socialism versus capitalism; rather, the nation should work hard to encourage economic forces, including private enterprises, to promote economic development. He continued, sounding more like Ludwig Von Mises than a communist *ganbu*, "Practice in China has proved that where market forces have been given full play, there the economy has been vigorous and has developed in a sound way."[111]

Positive signals to private entrepreneurs helped them overcome their fear and insecurity and venture into new projects and entrepreneurial activities, thus contributing toward the economic development of China. In 1992, from January to October, private businessmen sold 267 billion yuan (about $46 billion) worth of goods in the free market. During the same time frame, the volume of business in private trade in aquatic products, vegetables, industrial products, poultry, meat, and eggs increased 25 percent over the same period in 1991. It was reported in December 1992 that retail sales in free markets accounted for 24 percent of total retail sales. In edible oil, vegetables, aquatic products, and eggs free market sales accounted for 21 percent, 20 percent, 27.8 percent, and 14 percent respectively.[112]

With the success of the private sector, the number of individual entrepreneurs is increasing. At the end of 1992, China had 15.34 million individual industrial and commercial businesses, which employed 24.68 million workers.[113] The case of private enterprises is very different and deserves explanation. As mentioned before, in June 1988, there were 225,000 private enterprises employing 3.6 million employees, but the 1992 and 1993 reports show the number to be decreasing.[114] One explanation for this drastic drop in numbers is that businessmen decided to pull out of their businesses. I question this explanation. Another explanation is that they have chosen to evade the authorities by taking the names of collective enterprises, not only to receive special benefits, but also to escape the life-uncertainty factor, the legacy of the past, and cultural lashing. As mentioned previously, 33 percent of collective enterprises were actually private enterprises. On the other hand, it was reported that private businesses were excluded from investing in the special economic zones, forcing them to assume the disguise of collective or overseas firms. Similarly, in Shanghai's Pudong New Area private enterprises were excluded from investing on an equal level with state- or foreign-funded firms. That "prompted many private firms to take the guise of a collective or overseas-invested enterprise in a desperate bid to operate on an equal footing with their rivals."[115]

The amount of private ownership in China will definitely rise, but it will continue to be important for the government to maintain support for the private sector. At this point, I would like to mention an indicator that is a good sign of the development of private ownership in China. In Beijing, the first pawnshop in forty years, Jinbao Pawnshop, opened. During the communist regime, pawnshops were shut down because they preyed mostly on the poor. However, at present, most customers are well off and the properties pawned are jewelry, antiques, fur coats, and so forth. Interestingly, 90 percent of the loans taken from pawnshops are by private entrepreneurs, who still find it difficult to borrow money from the banks.[116]

In conclusion, it has been shown that CCP history has deeply affected entrepreneurs and is continuing to do so. In Tianjin, entrepreneurs are the product of China's history, recent politics, and traditional culture. The next chapter contains personal accounts of entrepreneurs from Tianjin. They exhibit collectively different kinds of traits—the fear of repeating history, the fear of uncertain government policy, and respect or disdain for the Chinese culture that looks down on individuals who venture into entrepreneurial activities for profit, but respects intellectual pursuits and education.

Chapter 3

Entrepreneurs of Tianjin

A s previously mentioned, I had the opportunity to interview nineteen entrepreneurs. During and after each interview, I understood more about business in China, as well as facets of the entrepreneurs' lives. Though the interview setting and experience of each entrepreneur was different, each entrepreneur conveyed messages that were common to most other entrepreneurs in China. Entrepreneurs still suffer from the life-uncertainty factor and are heavily influenced by government policy; but in spite of the unusual fear of China's past and current government policies, which are influenced by traditional and communist culture, Chinese entreprepeurs are working hard to improve their lives and contribute to the economic development of China.

In some cases entrepreneurs lamented about the government officials, different governmental departments, and tax collectors—specifically how taxes were collected arbitrarily. Due to uncertain government policy, entrepreneurs usually chose to maintain a low profile by keeping businesses small. Also, to avoid harassments by government officials, most entrepreneurs gave money or "in kinds" to officials. Some entrepreneurs expressed reservations about conducting business in light of Confucian values about education in which educated people are held in higher esteem than business people.

Banks usually do not give loans to the *getihu* (individual entrepreneurs). So most entrepreneurs borrow money from family members and friends. In most cases, entrepreneurs worked as a family, demonstrating family unity and cooperation. The entrepreneurs I met in Tianjin worked exceptionally hard, devoted long hours (10–12 hours per day on average), and manifested a high level of determination and sharp, quality management style, in spite of a lack of college education and the burden of the *San-fan* and *Wu-fan* campaigns, and the Cultural Revolution. In short, the communist rule was too short to eliminate the entrepreneurial skills of these dynamic Chinese entrepreneurs.

In the following discussion I give my own account of some of the entrepreneurs I saw and interacted with while I was in Tianjin. The names and particulars of the entrepreneurs have been changed to protect their identity; some of their business information has been withheld for the same reason. The structure of the interview was informal. All interviews followed a natural course, though I had a set of questions I asked during each of the interviews.

MR. XU

It was a cloudy day when my Chinese friend and I went to meet Xu. Xu ran a fruit business. I had not met Xu before and did not know what to expect from him. In the past, this kind of rendezvous had both positive and negative results—most of the time the interviewee did not show up or was not present in his or her store. Sometimes when the subject was present, he or she did not want to talk if, for example, there were too many people present, or the entrepreneur was too busy. I had mixed feelings about this interview.

Xu was waiting for us in front of his fruit shop. He was a tall man, about 5′10″ with wide shoulders and a big beer belly. He welcomed us with a wide smile, which I was very glad to see. My mixed feelings were replaced with hope. It was a wonderful feeling, as thought I had conquered something impossible. In front of the store there was a big pile of watermelons. As we got off our bicycles, Xu greeted us with handshakes. My friend looked worried and his greeting in return was brief. We quickly went behind the store. My friend's nervousness reminded me of the effect of China's brutal past and the recent Tiananmen Square massacre. My friend, who was a college student, may have felt a little embarrassed because of his association with a business person. In Chinese culture, entrepreneurs are culturally looked down on.

Xu's junior partner was a childhood classmate of my friend and a relative of Xu. My friend approached his classmate about the interview and the classmate arranged it. From previous experience, I knew that it was very difficult to arrange an interview between a foreigner and a Chinese national. My friend and his classmate were close friends as children and in spite of their separation after high school they kept in touch. My friend went to university after high school, but his classmate did not have high enough grades to continue his education. My friend told me that his former classmate was more than glad to assist me because of their friendship.

I came to realize the importance of friendship, or *guanxi,* in China. During my stay, I discovered that establishing *guanxi* is very important, and that the Chinese are often willing to take a risk to help friends.

It seemed my friend did not want to cause any problems for his old classmate, or for himself, with the authorities. Xu pulled up three chairs and we sat down. Xu offered me a cigarette, but before he could stretch his arm toward me with the cigarette packet, I had my own Kent cigarette packet, a U.S. brand, stretched toward him. He accepted the Kent cigarette graciously.

Xu was wearing the usual dress of cotton pants and a t-shirt. When he started talking, I noticed his wide, strong jaws, which gave the impression that he was a person with strong determination. Indeed, in China's historicopolitical and cultural context, an individual with strong determination and courage is needed to salvage China's decaying economy. Without entrepreneurs like Xu, true risk takers, China would be doomed. It is because of these courageous self-made individuals that China's economy has within a short period of time, become the third largest economy in the world. As we were talking in the open, Xu was looking around with cautious eyes. He talked slowly and carefully and seemed knowledgeable about government and policy. Xu's partner was running the store while we were talking. He did not seem worried about his business.

None of the entrepreneurs I talked to seemed worried about the financial health of their business. They expressed more worry about government policy, which is historically unreliable and changes at the whim of powerful individuals in the ruling group, about outsiders getting the impression that they have a lot of money, and about society's traditional negative views of profit-maiking ventures. It has been reported that private businesses make high profits. One of the largest businesses in Chengdu, which "[admitted] to assets of 800,000 yuan in 1988, started out in 1983 as a clothes stall worth a few hundred yuan."[1] From my interactions with entrepreneurs, I am certain that they do not deposit much money in their bank accounts. Most savings are kept at home. Official reports stated that bank deposits in 1992 totaled 1,000 billion yuan, about 1,000 yuan ($181) for every man, woman, and child. "Since sensible Chinese do not want the world to know their wealth, there could be a further 300 billion yuan hidden under the nation's mattress."[2]

Xu chose to venture into business to make more money than he was making in a government company. Xu started a restaurant in 1983 with 3,000 yuan as investment money. He and three other friends joined together to rent restaurants for eight months. Altogether Xu rented three restaurants. In the beginning, the business was successful and profitable because there were a limited number of individual businessmen in the restaurant business and the tax rate was low. Xu's income from the restaurant was about 1,000 yuan per month. He paid 100 yuan in taxes every month, which was comparably low. In 1991, the restaurant tax rate was 400 to 800 yuan per month. Restaurants were taxed according to their size and documents of expenditure and income provided by entrepreneurs. The tax fluctuated from 400 to 800 yuan due to the profitability of the seasons. Goods were cheap and Xu and his partners made a 40 percent profit. When the cost of running a restaurant business began to rise, Xu switched to the fruit business in 1986, with an investment of 1,000 yuan. By 1991 his investment in the fruit business was 10,000 yuan.

In the fruit business, according to Xu, the tax was a fixed 127 yuan. In addition, Xu had to pay 40 yuan for administrative fees and 3.75 percent sales tax to government-run fruit suppliers in Tianjin. If profit exceeded 4,000 yuan, the tax was 127 yuan; if it was less, the tax collector would reduce the tax after negotiations. Xu was satisfied with the tax policy but he had one complaint: he did not like the idea that many individual businesses did not have licenses, which produced unfair competition. To Xu, real businessmen like him were protected by the laws of the government. The businessmen without licenses did not pay taxes. The illegal businessmen discouraged Xu from maintaining a legal operation that forced him to pay taxes.

However, it can be argued here that the individuals without licenses were just protecting themselves by hiding their businesses from the government because of their fear of the past, uncertain policy, and cultural disdain for entrepreneurs. But one thing is certain, the illegal economy is not contributing fully to the economic development of the country or to the common wealth of the nation, thus depriving China of much needed tax revenue that could be used for public goods and services—infrastructure, parks and recreation, public protection, research and development, and so on. Thus, the removal of the life-uncertainty factor and the erosion of traditional attitudes about profit-making ventures is essential if China wants to achieve maximum economic benefit from its given resources. However, cultural values are changing in a favorable direction for the entrepreneurs. China is moving toward a better system, where entrepreneurs, the government, and consumers are building a marriage based on social contract. These changes are very slow and close observation is needed to understand the process.

Xu and his relative worked long hours in the fruit business, one of the key characteristics of privately run businesses. As one entrepreneur said, "[To build up my business] . . . was tiring, but I never complained. The harder I worked, the more I earned. . . . Holidays only mean more work for me. I work seven days a week. I get up at six every morning and close my store at six in the evening. I hit the sack after dinner and have no time for any entertainment."[3] Xu and his partner kept their business open from 8:00 A.M. to 11:00 P.M. Xu was 46 years old in 1991, and he had one 28-year-old son; his wife had died in a car accident. Xu planned to remarry after his son married. Xu, I think, did not want to hurt his son's feelings by marrying for the second time. Chinese families are very close, they care deeply about each others feelings and support each other in times of need and crises. Xu was motivated to work hard because he could not get social welfare benefits and he did not have life insurance. He said, "If I do not work hard, then what will happen—no work, no food. Government will not help me or give me benefits, government will say you are a strong looking person. The government will not help me, so I must do business."

According to Xu, since it is very difficult for individual businessmen to borrow money from the government's banks, he borrowed money from his relatives. But there was no concept of profit sharing based on borrowing money. Xu gave his relatives some of the profit as he saw fit, but he stressed it was not profit sharing. His relatives simply wanted to help him out, and Xu felt that this family aid was a part of the Chinese culture. The Industrial and Commercial Bank of China had given some loans to *getihu* (individual businesses), but most of them relied on their own savings or money from relatives and friends to start a business. Although China's standard of living is very low, many people were able to save money, primarily because the cost of commodities were low. In addtion, besides basic provisions, there was not much to purchase. Few houses were built between 1959 and 1979, which meant that in urban areas three or more generations lived together in one flat. This also contributed to family savings, close family ties, and trust. "Like a Panyan tree, a Chinese family spreads its cool shade over all its members."[4]

For Xu's fruit business the government signed the contract and chose the location of the business. At first, the businessmen were sent to the free market for a particular kind of business to sell their goods and services. Xu did not like the free market because the profit was less. But according to the season, the government would allow an entrepreneur to set up shop at a convenient place, and at that time the profit was higher. When I interviewed Xu, his shop was located conveniently on an intersection, between the main town and a residential area. After the season was over, Xu planned to move to another place. Xu felt that the government did a lot of good things for individual businesses. For example, during the watermelon season the government would cancel the 3.75 percent tax because watermelons did not sell well and profit was low.

In spite of positive feelings about the government's assistance with his business, Xu was unsure about the future of individual businesses in China, because policies could change. He was afraid the government might revert to the policies of the 1960s, when individual businesses were collectivized. This fear (which arose from the concept of life uncertainty) prevented Xu from expanding his business. Xu felt that the business was doing fine; if it expanded, he might have more trouble. Different people would take money from him—the tax collector, traffic administration, and health administration. At another point, I asked Xu why some businessmen did not want to expand after they reached a certain level of success. Xu replied, "First thing, maybe the person does not want to expand or the management is not good and he [entrepreneur] may be smart." But when I asked him how the society would view him if he expanded his business, Xu replied that the society would look highly on him. He said that if he did not have the above-mentioned problems, he would surely expand, but he remained unsure of the government policies. Xu also said that he would not have any problems opening another business, any business. Xu said, "I would not have to give any bribe; one cigarette would be okay." This phenomenon of easily obtaining a business license was reported elsewhere in China, thus indicating that the performance of the industry and the commerce bureau's work is considered to be improving.[5]

Xu said individual businessmen were looked down upon by the people during the Cultural Revolution because they had less education. Now the people had high regard for individual businessmen because they made a lot of money. But Xu started his business regardless of how people looked at him. During the 1980s, when people still did not have high regard for individual businessmen, business was good. Presently, the psychology of the people has changed, and there are more businessmen, but business has slowed and there is more competition. But Xu says with determination, "I will go on doing my business, success or failure." Xu's comments regarding public opinion of businessmen in Chinese society is not new. It was observed by an official and famous prose writer, Yun Ching (1757–1817), that considering commerce a shameful occupation was good for the merchants because they could make more profit, but in later dynasties when it was considered to be less shameful, more people engaged in commerce and profit was less.[6]

Xu was not only determined, he was quite knowledgeable about his position in history. He also understood the role of demand and supply in economic interaction and how individual entrepreneurs played an important role in the economic development of China. Xu's father was a businessman. After 1949 there were many individual businesses. After 1956, businessmen were joined together to sell goods at a fixed place and at a fixed price set by the government. They were not allowed to engage in individual business. The fixed price was the same as that charged by the government-owned businesses, which ceased all competition.

However, Xu observed that after 1979 things started to change. The open door policy made way for the reform policy, allowing farmers to sell their surplus produce in the market. Individual businesses shortly emerged, improving the quality of life for both buyers and sellers. Unlike the 1950s, buyers and sellers did not depend on the state-run economy.

Xu also believed that individual businesses were helping the economic development of China by paying taxes. In 1990, according to Xu, individual businesses paid a huge amount in taxes. Xu conveyed the message that individual entrepreneurs were dynamic and sensitive to the market's behavior. Individual entrepreneurs could freely engage in business, including lowering prices to sell products quickly and make a profit, unlike government-run businesses, which could not change their prices based on the market's demand and supply, because the managers of the businesses would not let it happen and for other reasons that went unexplained.

My understanding is that the managers of publicly-owned enterprises also suffer from life uncertainty and do not want to be innovative. For instance, after the June 4, 1989, Tiananmen Square massacre, entrepreneurs in China became sensitive about government policies and their place in society. It was reported in June 1990, that entrepreneurs in the state-owned enterprises had become "over cautious," and some quietly changed their desk mottos of "eager to open up and create" to "inaction is better than action!" Some factory managers became very careful not to say anything controversial, pay one cent less in wages, or offend anyone.[7]

If entrepreneurial managers did not try to bring about change, there would be no success or failure and no accountability. No accountability, coupled with no life uncertainty, meant stagnation. In state enterprises wages and salaries were basically fixed, with weak linkage to economic performance. In these situations, enterprises acted like bureaucratic organs obeying orders and lacking independent initiative in order to avoid criticism. This stagnation meant, said Xu , that government-owned businesses could not meet the needs of customers, thereby improving the role of private entrepreneurs. Entrepreneurs, even in the face of life uncertainty are willing to venture into an unpredictable marketplace to create opportunities and jobs by utilizing given resources, thus invigorating the economy. As previously mentioned, for an economy to develop a triangular relationship among buyers, sellers, and the government has to evolve. This was not able to happen with the government-run businesses.

Xu also understood the difficulties of private entrepreneurs. When I asked him, "If you met Jiang Zemin and he asked you about the economic development of China, what answer would you give?" he replied:

> I want Jiang Zemin to sell goods at my counter to experience what it is like dealing with the tax collectors and others. I tried to contact the last mayor [of Tianjin] about problems but I have failed to contact him. My opinion will not be regarded. So Jiang should experience it himself.

This last statement by Xu during our interview is thought provoking and echoes the statement of the Manchu princess (see final note in Chapter 1). Xu told me positive things about the government's tax collection policy— how low it was, how the government could waive the 3.75 percent tax during the bad season, how easy it was for him to open a new business, and so on. But Xu also expressed concern about the future of individual entrepreneurs and government policy.

Most entrepreneurs I interviewed in Tianjin chose to give a vague answer. They did not want to be blamed for saying something against the government. It should be noted here that Chinese entrepreneurs, regardless of whether they were interviewed under government auspices or during a guerilla interview, will always be vague and analytical, and in the presence of government officials, they will be extra careful and attempt to please the government officials.

Xu's last statement, however, told me that Chinese entrepreneurs are still suffering from an unknown threat. They are constantly harassed by government officials, such as the tax collectors. A close look at the suffering of peasants, specifically an entrepreneur named Luo Qingguo, in present-day China as reported in the *New York Times* will shed some light on this aspect of suffering by the Chinese people and entrepreneurs.

For Luo Qingguo, his nightmare became reality when tax collectors showed up at his door on shiny new motorcycles and confiscated his rice and money and left Luo and his four children to starve. Luo said that there would have been money and food to eat if the tax collectors had not taken away 110 pounds of Lou's rice and corn. The officials also took money in the form of different kinds of taxes, such as an irrigation tax, the subsidy payment to local officials, land rents, a contribution to support the elderly, housing insurance, and electricity fees. It was reported that the tax collectors were using illegal means to collect taxes beyond the 5 percent limit set by the government. The extra money went for personal aggrandizement of the government officials.

A case study of Guizhou, mentioned in the same *New York Times* article, makes this point even more clear. A thirty-five-year-old woman complained bitterly about fees that she and her family were forced to pay. She had to pay 17.5 percent of the family's gross annual income in addition to more than one-third of the grain her family harvested in 1992.

To collect these illegal fees, officials formed different work teams—fee collection work teams and branch brigades or attack teams. These teams collected grain and money from peasants. The "excessive tax burdens have led peasants to commit suicide."[8] Urban entrepreneurs are also subject to the harassments of the tax collectors. In Chengdu, Sichuan, entrepreneurs are also at the mercy of tax collectors.[9] This kind of abuse of power for self-gain contributes toward the entrepreneurs' fears and a distrust for government policies and those who implement them. This breeds the life-uncertainty factor and no doubt inhibits economic development.

This practice of abusing taxpayers has its roots in the history of China. During the Qing dynasty, tax collectors were sometimes known as *jianmin* (mean people). If anyone failed to pay taxes, he or she was threatened, beaten, or jailed. All county Yamens hired runners to collect taxes. The runners were illiterate, unskilled males who made their living by forcing *lougui* (illicit fees) from the taxpayers, who did not receive any legal protection. The runners were social outcasts whose activities transgressed all canons of a "kingly government."[10]

The entrepreneurs of China would like to express themselves to others but feel they cannot, so they provide small amounts of information about their misery. The final analysis of Xu's interview tells me that he is a determined and creative individual who wants to contribute toward the economic development of China. Given the proper opportunities, sound policy, and removal of the legacy of the past, the erosion of cultural attitudes about profit-making ventures, and removal of traditional arbitary uses of official power, entrepreneurs like Xu will be able to positively contribute to China's economic development.

After the interview was over, Xu asked us to stay for a while and have a cup of tea, but since a storm was brewing, we declined. We thanked him; he politely said that he was glad to be of any help and wished me luck. My friend talked with his classmate for a moment, and then we left.

MR. YU AND HIS WIFE

I visited Yu and his wife quite often. They were a very nice couple, and the wife treated me like a son. Whenever I visited them, they were always glad to see me. The wife would offer me something to eat, along with a cigarette (foreign brand) and a cup of jasmine tea. Both the husband and wife smoked, so they enjoyed the company of another smoker. Drinking tea together is a very important part of Chinese friendship. I found during my research that eating a snack, drinking tea, and smoking cigarettes are important aspects of friendship among contemporary entrepreneurs in China. In general, traditional Chinese tea customs are very important to Chinese culture. It conveys the idea of honesty, harmony, and mutual respect.[11]

Both the husband and wife were from the south, Guangdong Province, and very proud of that. They were both in their early sixties, looked and behaved like ordinary Chinese, and were very friendly. They wanted to lead a quiet, peaceful life and were without grand expectations. They had a daughter who lived in Beijing. The couple would take turns visiting her there every week. When one of them was gone, the other one was even more glad when I paid a visit.

The couple ran an eyeglass shop. Both of them had studied optometry but did not elaborate on it. Yu checked the eyes of customers with the help of an English alphabet chart, which hung eight feet opposite a mirror. He would ask his customers to sit for a while with special glasses on, or to walk around for a few minutes to determine if a prescription needed to be altered. I was one of his customers before leaving Tianjin.

The store was 8' by 10' with a wooden door and a window with bars. The walls inside were rough, the white paint was faded, and the plaster was chipped off in different places. On the walls were eyeglass posters with Chinese characters, but the models were from Western countries. The floor was made of red brick laid side-by-side without cement or mortar. There was an L-shaped glass counter with different kinds of glasses on display, a small black-and-white television, a radio, two wooden chairs, a small furnace for winter, a revolving table fan, and a folding metal bed. Most of the time, the television was on when I visited them.

The couple lived in their shop. The wife would cook outside the store, but most of the time they ate in a nearby cafeteria. Business was good, and Yu and his wife were not worried about business profits. When I visited them, we talked lightly about politics, economics, society, and compared the cultures of China, the United States, and Bangladesh. It was a pleasant experience.

Yu worked for a state-owned eyeglass factory before he ventured into business in 1982. He had to receive permission to go into private business. There were two forms of businesses. The first involved a group of employees who formed a collective enterprise (though not a pure collective) that was connected with the mother company in terms of security and investment. The group had to pay 3 percent of their profits to the mother company. The second option was purely private and separate from the mother company. Yu chose the second option. Being an entrepreneur, he saw opportunity in northern China. In southern China, according to Yu, there was more competition and shop space was in short supply. He chose to come to Tianjin and open his business.

He was proud of being a Guangdong citizen and claimed that southerners were good at business. He said that many individuals from his hometown went to other provinces to engage in business. In Beijing, there were several thousand shops, which, Yu proudly said, "are established by us." Yu claimed that people admired the southern businessman. Every corner of China had southern businessmen, even in places like Qi Qi Har (a city in Heilongjiang). Some university graduates from the south quit public jobs to pursue private business.

Yu started his business with an original investment of 10,000 yuan in 1982. Previously, he rented a stall for 3,200 yuan a year. By the end of 1988 he was able to open his own shop. Yu and his wife worked long hours—they kept their store open from 8:00 A.M. to 8:00 P.M., seven days a week. They earned 300 yuan per month, compared to the 100 yuan per month Yu made when he worked for the state-run factory. It is my impression that Yu made more than 300 yuan per month due to the foreign cigarettes he and his wife smoked and shared with me, the foreign soft drinks he would sometimes generously buy for me in private, and the frequent trips they took to visit their daughter in Beijing.

Entrepreneurs often hid their actual income and true identities. Yu and his wife certainly remembered the brutal persecutions of the 1950s and 1960s, when neighbors and friends turned against entrepreneurs to escape the wrath of the CCP or to vent their jealousy or disdain. With their fearful memories intact and refreshed by recent political events like the Tiananmen Square massacre and uncertain government policies, rational entrepreneurs like Yu and his wife do not spend money openly or make public their actual income. Thus, entrepreneurs often keep their money at home, which needless to say, adversely affects capital accumulation and the circulation of funds.

Yu was in business for money, but also for self-satisfaction. For example, once a customer came to his shop at 9:00 P.M. and knocked on the door. The customer said that he needed to replace his broken glasses. Despite being closed for the day Yu opened the door and helped him. Yu was determined to make his business a success. When asked what made him continue in the face of failure, he replied, "Failure is the mother of success. If I failed this year, I will work harder to make a profit next year." This kind of strong determination expressed by Yu was also demonstrated by most of the entrepreneurs I met in China. In a hostile environment like China, there is a need for strong, self-made types of entrepreneurs who are willing to be a class apart from the mainstream and be the pioneers of entrepreneurial development. The Chinese entrepreneurs of the 1970s and 1980s are the individuals described by Alfred Marshall who are willing to trade their "iron rice-bowl" for the freedom to make their own decisions. These types of individuals are willing to take risks, not only in the face of economic uncertainty but also in the face of life uncertainty, which undoubtedly makes them a distinct group of people, a class apart.

In spite of the strong determination expressed by Yu, he was unwilling to expand his business. Though Yu claimed that it was relatively easy to open a business, operating it well was difficult. Yu cited a lack of funds as the reason, (it was very difficult for small businesses like his to borrow money from banks). Then Yu elaborated on the process an entrepreneur had to go through to borrow money:

> [First] it is very difficult [to borrow money from the bank]. The security bureau must check your real estate. You must have large amount of real estate. In that way you can borrow money. And the pay back period is very short. Half a year later you must pay back.
>
> [To get a loan, one] must deposit money at first. The deposit rate is—if you deposit 1,000 yuan, you can get 9 yuan. The loan rate is—if you borrow 1,000 yuan you must pay 16 yuan. For example, this month, if you deposit 4,000 yuan, you will get 4 x 9 = 36 yuan interest. Then next month you can get 10,000 yuan as loan. Actually the loan you will get is 10,000 - 4,000 = 6,000 yuan and you will have to pay 16 x 6 = 96 yuan as interest.

The fear of borrowing money from the bank is another reason why Yu did not want to borrow money. The security bureau must check his family's property, and if he was unable to pay it back the family property would be confiscated and the business would be closed down. The stress would then be on the entire family.

When I asked Yu how government policies helped him, he replied that he paid a fixed tax of 150 yuan per month and industrial and commercial administrative fees. On top of those, he paid the electricity bill and other charges, such as for land use. Because of all these fees, Yu felt that he did not get any help from the government. But Yu also knew that individual businesses were beneficial to both the country and to the owners, so individual businesses had a great future. Individual businessmen worked much harder compared to the collective enterprises. In collective enterprises, Yu said, the worker's initiative could not be aroused, and they accomplished little during the eight-hour work period. The workers in collective enterprises came to work late and left early. By contrast, in an individual enterprise, an entrepreneur could work twenty-four hours a day, and the attitude toward service was much better.

Yu did not experience corruption directly, because in his small business there was not enough room for corruption. Yu believed that there was corruption in large companies but did not want to talk about this factor. I did not press the issue. His fear of government officials and the fear of a change in policy was clear. Yu is, after all, a product of Chinese history and traditional attitudes, which compels him to submit to authority, whether the ruler is benevolent or merciless.

After the interview was over, I visited Yu and his wife many times. Our friendship grew closer after the interview. There was more laughter, more tea and cigarettes, a reduced charge to replace my eyeglasses, and a very strong desire to visit them again.

MR. CHANG

This was the only interview arranged and carried out in the presence of government officials. Chinese officials always like to show the best of China to outsiders, so I was sure to see a success story of private entrepreneurship. I was told by the official to meet in his office at 9:00 A.M. I arrivedd at the arranged time and after half an hour, two officials escorted two other government officials and me to a blue sedan car. The car looked new; later I learned that the car belonged to the owner of the factory, whom I interviewed.

When we reached the site, we were welcomed by the owner of the factory and his assistants. They had a video camera ready and started filming when we got out of the car. The owner acted as the host and took us to his office. There were trophies in the office given to the owner as a symbol of recognition by the government and other organizations. He then took us on a tour of his factory, which made machines for making bags to hold dry cement mix.

The factory was next door to Chang's office. As we reached the entrance of the factory, I saw a yellow banner with big red Chinese characters saying, "Welcome our Bangladeshi friend." I felt like a VIP. Inside the factory we saw people working hard. Sections of the factory were divided according to the manufacture of different machine parts. Chang showed us a complete machine that makes the bags and told us how advanced it was. The factory had few lights (it seemed dark even during the daytime) and was about 100' long by 25' wide. I remember thinking, "I wish there were more lights inside." The owner then took us to the design room and showed us different designs and a model of a new machine, for which he held the patent. He seemed to be very proud of his success.

After seeing the factory, we returned to a different room, similar to a living room. There was a big bowl of fruit on the table. We all sat down and started talking. The video camera continued to film us throughout the interview. The owner appeared to be in his mid-forties. His face told me that he was not only rich and lived well, but that he was also happy.

During the interview I concluded that he was very smart and knew how to use the system in his favor. His interactions with the officials indicated that he knew them well, but the exchange of greetings and body language told me that their friendship was professional. There was a different level of connection between them, perhaps it was a money *guanxi* relationship. The owner had great ambition and will certainly be very successful.

After the interview was over, Chang escorted us to the dining room. We sat down at a round table for a six- or seven-course lunch. We talked about business, import–export, the U.S. market, and so on. The employees' meals were prepared in the same kitchen, but I am sure they did not eat the same dishes. My friend told me that the dishes served to us were the most expensive dishes of Tianjin. After lunch, we said goodbye and drove back in the same car to Tianjin's Business Administration Bureau. Later, I tried to contact the owner of the factory to get a copy of the videotape. I could never reach him. Perhaps he did not want to have anything to do with a person associated with the government officials.

Chang followed his father's footsteps in the packaging machinery business in 1977, after resigning from his government job. Chang's father used to make packaging machinery by hand and Chang learned the trade from him. The factory, which was run by Chang at the time of the interview, was completed on August 22, 1988, and officially opened in 1989. Though Chang claimed that he built the factory with his own money, I soon learned that his financial support came from a relative living in Hong Kong.

At the age of thirty-nine, Chang was very successful and proud of his achievements. His initial investment was 100,000 yuan, and in 1991 it was increased tenfold to 1,000,000 yuan. The rate of tax for a private company like Chang's with sixty employees was 35 percent; state-owned firms and collectives paid a rate of 51 percent.

In spite of employing sixty workers, Chang believed he needed one hundred employees because the demand for his product was high. Chang clearly understood the market, and demand and supply. Chang said that in 1991 China produced 200 million tons of cement, the most in the world, but lacked paper bags to package the mix. The cement industry needed packaging power for 800,000 tons of cement and all the state-owned and collective enterprises together could provide bags for only 300,000 tons. Being an entrepreneur, Chang seized the chance and went into the cement packaging business to fill the gap.

Besides understanding the market's demand and supply, Chang was aware of the quality of the factory's machines and the necessities of upgrading the technology. He believed that his company had successfully integrated the mode of production and scientific research. By 1991, his company had already applied for two national patents for new packaging machines, beating the patents deadlines by two to five years. Chang claimed that his machines were sold in all the provinces of China, except Tibet. His packaging machine had a variety of functions: It could be used to produce two-sided, three-colored packages for cement or chemical fertilizer, and, compared to other packaging machines, Chang's machine saved 50 percent on paper. Chang also expressed the desire to expand his business. He had already applied to establish a limited company and was researching new products and looking for international partners to make his enterprise a transnational corporation.

Chang understood the importance of management. This was demonstrated twice during the interview. Chang acknowledged that he had the right to hire or dismiss any employee, while in a state-owned enterprise in China, a director did not have that right. Chang claimed that his relationship with his employees was good; his company not only provided all the welfare of state-owned and collective enterprises to the employees, but also provided other benefits. Chang's company provided 10 yuan to each employee as a contract fee, and every year after that the contract fee was increased by 10 percent. Moreover, there was a policy of income distribution according to work. At the end of each year, each employee was given one Red Package (a symbol of happiness and good fortune) with a large allowance. Chang said that he paid a lot of attention to the investment in feelings. He helped the employees to solve many problems, whether marriage or funerals.

Entrepreneurs like Chang are badly needed in China. Thousands of state employees are being laid off and will continue to be laid off, because the state-owned enterprises must compete with private enterprises and the international market. To compete with privately owned enterprises and joint ventures, the state-owned enterprises must be efficient and learn to calculate their transactions in terms of profit, not in terms of cost. The government is no longer willing to carry the burden of state-owned enterprises. The rise of the private sector and the maturity of the tax collection process by the government will force the government to shy away further from the state-owned enterprises. This, in turn, will force state-owned enterprises to look closely at the concept of efficiency. Those who will suffer most are the workers. It was reported that China had laid off 100,000 coal workers and will lay off hundreds of thousands more in the coming years.

The same source also mentioned that China planned to close thirty inefficient mines in 1993 alone and lay off 30,000 miners and 70,000 workers in related jobs.[12]

Such layoffs do not go smoothly. It was reported that in several cities workers have attacked factory directors, and some directors and managers were killed by laid-off workers. The workers have also been involved in strikes and acts of sabotage. In Liaoning Province, an outstanding woman entrepreneur named Wang Suqin was murdered by a laid-off worker named Li Dan. Later, Li was sentenced to death.[13] In another case, a bank director named Huang Chuanying, hailed as a daring reformer, laid off so-called inefficient bank employees. One laid-off worker, named Cao Weihua, reacted by fire bombing Huang's house, seriously injuring Huang, his wife, and their two children. Cao was sentenced to death. "The incident seemed to reflect a broad concern among many Chinese that while a market economy may be more prosperous and efficient than a communist one, it may also be less cozy."[14]

To lessen the negative effects of being laid off, China needs entrepreneurs like Chang who understand the needs of workers, and who are historically used to the protections provided by the state, such as job security and medical benefits. With proper guidance and tax incentives from the government to entrepreneurs like Chang, China might be able to eliminate some of the major problems created by layoffs. Chang understood the psychology of Chinese workers who were used to working for state-run businesses. When I asked him about the working hours and wages of the employees, he answered, "Like at state-owned enterprises, we work eight hours, from 8:00 A.M. to 12:00 A.M. and from 1:00 P.M. to 5:00 P.M., six days a week. We pay wages each day according to work. I do not agree with a 24-hour work system. It is beyond human endurance."[15]

Chang was a creative entrepreneur who carefully balanced prevailing social and political variables with good business practices to run his enterprise. When I asked him a hypothetical question about advising a friend who was about to start a new business, his answer again reflected his understanding of the importance of good management. Chang replied: "He must have three conditions. First, he must have his own products; second, he must have enough funds; third, he must reach a certain level of management." Chang went on to say that "Chinese [entrepreneurs] are very smart. Unlike Japanese, we Chinese pay attention to mutual benefits. We would like to do some business that benefits both sides. We are frank to each other, and honor is the most important thing to us."

At the end of the interview Chang again expressed his interest in building a transnational corporation and, after retirement, writing a memoir about his experiences. He echoed Confucius by saying, "I have an 11-year-old son, and I hope he studies hard and contributes a lot to the society."

MR. WANG

Wang and I became very good friends. His wife was a quiet person, so I did not come to know her very well, and most of the time I saw her spending time with her grandchildren. I called my friend *lau pengyou* (old friend). Wang was in his mid-sixties and a very energetic and cheerful person. In my opinion, he was in business because he wanted something to do, but he mentioned to me that long ago, after his retirement, he needed the money.

Wang and his wife ran a small general store. They had different kinds of commodities, mostly intended for students, such as stationery, t-shirts, postcards, among other things. Their store was about 7' by 11' and was used mostly for storing goods. Inside the store there was a small bed, a kerosene stove, and two stools. Red bricks were laid side by side on the floor and covered with earth. The walls were painted white, but the paint was very old. There was only a dim light inside the store, which they did not turn on during the day. There was only one wide window and a single door. Family members took turns sleeping in the store for security reasons.

Wang did all his business from the sidewalk. Each morning he set up a table outside the store and brought out the goods he wanted to sell. He hung the mostly Western t-shirts on a long string overhead. Every time I passed by his store on my bicycle, I yelled to him *"Ni hau Lao Pengyou?"* (How are you old friend?) and *"Mai yige, song yige"* (Buy one, get one free). The entrepreneurs in Tianjin were not aware of this concept and were surprised whenever I mentioned it. They asked me if one could buy one and get one free in the United States. When I replied in the affirmative, they did not want to believe me. If Wang was not busy, he would tell me to stop by and chat with him.

One day he asked me to sell him a U.S. dollar. When I asked him why he wanted to buy a dollar, he replied that some international students wanted to sell U.S. dollars to him on the black market, but he did not know anything about the dollar. He also asked me to explain about rates and how the dollar worked. I sold him a dollar and explained everything I knew about exchange rates.

I thought that Wang must have trusted me to ask me something as sensitive as this, because the store next to him did business on the black market, but he did not ask them. The Chinese are shy to ask other Chinese about sensitive things, but they are often willing to open up to close friends who are foreigners. The roots of this distrust of fellow Chinese can be traced back to the anti-campaigns and uncertain government policies. This distrust definitely hampers the smooth flow of business information from one entrepreneur to another.

It was about 1:30 P.M. when I went to interview Wang. We went inside the store while his wife stayed outside with one of their grandchildren to take care of the shop. Wang retired from his government job in 1979. At that time, all of his children were in school. Wang's eldest son tried to support the family with his income, but it was not enough.

Before starting the present shop, Wang tried his hand at other businesses, demonstrating his self-determination and dignity. Several years ago, Wang tried to sell soft drinks. When he bought his commodities from wholesalers, he observed that, unlike entrepreneurs, state-owned enterprises were able to buy as much as they wanted. In addition, traditional Chinese attitudes caused the individual entrepreneurs to be looked down upon. He chose not to beg for more goods and stopped selling soft drinks. In another attempt, Wang met with failure. When he faced failure, he felt regret at first and then made up his mind to stand up for himself. Wang had bought several thousand *jin* (one *jin* is equal to a half kilogram) of fruit but was only able to sell several hundred *jin*. The rest of the fruit rotted, and he lost a lot of money. Though saddened, he did not give up. Wang made up his mind to earn more money to overcome his loss.

In 1984 Wang opened his own store. He registered his business under his wife's name with the Industrial and Commercial Bureau and obtained a license. Wang had an initial investment of 300 yuan. He sold only small items like toothpaste. At that time he was only allowed to buy retail products, but beginning in 1991 he was able to buy wholesale products. Working long hours (from 9:30 A.M. to 8:00 P.M.) Wang and his wife were able to increase their investment to about 5,000 yuan in 1991. On Sundays, the couple received some help in the store from their children.

Wang's monthly income was unstable. He earned about 500 to 600 yuan but about half went toward paying taxes and other charges. The tax rate for Wang was not fixed and government officials always collected taxes, taking money from entrepreneurs in any way they could. Wang said the government officials always found reasons to collect money. In addition, when Wang bought wholesale goods, he paid 3.39 percent in taxes. Because Wang and his wife were an older couple, sometimes the tax collectors allowed them to pay less in taxes.

Because tax collectors are permitted to use their own judgment in collecting taxes and other fees, many of them become corrupt. When Wang said that the Chinese tax collectors sometimes reduced his tax, it might have meant that the initial assessment of tax was high and that through negotiation Wang was able to have it reduced. The notorious activities of tax collectors and government officials is discussed further with respect to other personal interviews.

Wang received little education (he only graduated from primary school), but he had some understanding of history and government policy. He remembered that Mao Zedong and Liu Shaoqi had different opinions on the concept of private business. During the early 1960s, there was a popular slogan, "Three Zi and one Bao," which meant more plots for private use, more free markets, more enterprises with sole responsibility for their own profit and loss, and fixing output quotas on a household basis. Deng

Xiaoping followed up with the slogan, "Let some of the people get rich first." During the 1970s and 1980s, it was easy to borrow money from the bank because the government supported private entrepreneurs. But Wang did not want to borrow money from the bank. He wanted to be self-reliant. He was in business because he was retired and had free time, and he did not want to be dependent on his children. He did not want to expand his business. He said:

> During the Cultural Revolution, individual business was repudiated. Now the policy has changed to allow individual business. In my heart, I dislike being an individual businessman so I do not permit my children to do business with me. No, I do not want to make a fortune. I am happy to have ample food and clothing. I only want to keep myself well clad and well fed.

It was not only Wang who did not want his children to take over his business in the future. There were other Chinese entrepreneurs, like Chang, Li (discussed in the next section) and others who wanted their children to get a good education and serve their country. One reason many Chinese entrepreneurs want their children to be well educated is the ever present influence of Confucian philosophy and its emphasis on the importance of education and the relegation of the business person to the lowest end of the social scale. Confucius said:

> Those who are born with knowledge are the highest. Next come those who attain knowledge through study. Next again come those who turn to study after having been vexed by difficulties. The common people, in so far as they make no effort to study even after having been vexed by difficulties, are the lowest.[16]

Confucian economic theory put the businessmen in the lowest strata of society. The peasants and artisans produced food and artifacts, but the nonproductive merchants lived like parasites by selling goods produced by others. The very reason Confucius was against the merchant class was because commerce in China played an important role in Chinese history. In fact, Confucius himself wrote (551–479 B.C.) during a period when the strong merchant class was challenging the establishment of the aristocrats, so his observation was not descriptive, rather, it was normative.[17] The normative principles of Confucius became the norm for Chinese society. As Fairbank and Reischauer put it:

> The growth of production was accompanied by a rapid development of trade and a tremendous increase in wealth. As the Chou period [1122–403 B.C.] progresses one hears more and more of wealthy merchants of all types. This newly risen class proved disruptive to the old

aristocratic order, which perhaps in self-defense, propagated a theory that society consists of four classes: the warrior-administrators at the top, the peasants or primary producers next, the artisans or secondary producers third, and last of all the merchants, whose economic value seemed dubious to the aristocrats. However unrealistic this theory was even in late Chou times, it remained East Asian dogma for the next two millenniums.[18]

A closer look at contemporary Chinese society sheds more light on this topic. In 1987, a fourth grader named Xia Fei had to pay with his life because of unsatisfactory results in academics. Xia Fei was one of the top students in his class, but in exams he received an 82 for math and a 79 for Chinese. He ranked second in math and fifth in Chinese. Knowing very well that his parents would be upset with him, he lied about his grades. Later on, when the truth was uncovered, Xia Fei's father beat him for four hours. He was taken to the hospital, but it was too late to save him. In another case, a three-year-old boy was kicked to death for failing to pronounce a word correctly in an ancient poem. Professor Li Yexian, an expert from Beijing Normal University, said that in the eyes of the parents only children with high grades and the possibility to enter university or study abroad were considered talented. Educationist Huo Maozheng said that because the parents lost so much during the ten years of the Cultural Revolution, they desire to see their children achieve what they could not achieve. On the other hand, others like Nanchang mayor Liu Yun Lai thought that economic development rather than education itself was the primary reason for these kinds of tragedies. According to a survey, in the poor areas, parents and students put higher hopes on high grades and university admission. To students from the poorer areas, institutions of higher learning were the only way out of poverty. Educationist Xu Jialu agreed with Liu Yunlai. Xu observed that the tragedies of parents beating their children rarely happened in wealthy southern China, because the opportunity for prejob training and employment provided another corridor to wealth and social status, regardless of extraordinary grades and higher education.[19]

In another case, Zhou Weibang, a retired cadre, saved a girl from committing suicide in the Yujiang River in the Guangxi Zhuang Autonomous Region. The girl had been strictly rebuked by her parents and relatives for failing to pass the entrance exam for middle school. Zhou reasoned with the girl by telling her that there were other ways of fulfilling her desire of going to school. That incident motivated Zhou to open a private school named Peiren, to cultivate students sound in ethics and intelligence and to educate the students who were left out of the traditional education system.[20] This kind of importance given to education, and complete lack of respect for businessmen is not unique to China. Throughout the recorded history of the Indian subcontinent, the commercial class was looked down on by the elite of the society.[21]

I have an African American friend named Loyce B. who dropped out of school when he was in the eighth grade. He has a good job earning more than $40,000 per year, runs a car mechanic business, and does other handyman jobs. He is entrepreneurial in nature, always looking for opportunity, and has great wisdom. He has raised five children, has almost paid off his mortgage, and owns two cars. With a sound economic environment and vocational training, people with talents may leave behind higher education and find other ways to improve their lives. With the economic development of China, the Confucian value on education will fade away and be replaced by a new culture. In the following chapter we will find that the attitudes toward businessmen are already changing in China.

Businessmen like Wang, who still hold tightly to Confucian attitudes about education and social status are a vanishing group. They will be replaced by younger entrepreneurs who take pride in what they do and successfully move China toward prosperity. Already, China is the third largest economy in the world.

MS. LI

Li, an attractive woman in her late thirties, was a victim of the Cultural Revolution. She must have been only eighteen or nineteen when she was sent to the countryside. She was from an intellectual family and after returning home decided to open her own business.

Her family-run business was located on the side of a main street and catered to daily necessities, such as cigarettes, noodles, sweet peanuts, and so on. Every morning Li and her family displayed soft drinks, yogurt drinks, and fruits for sale. At any time of the day, there were at least three family members in the store.

The day I went to interview Li, there were two people managing the store. It was about one in the afternoon—I choose that time because from about one to two in the afternoon the marketplace is less crowded. Li and I became acquainted when I frequented her store to buy instant noodles and peanuts.

I was not sure how she would react during the interview. In hindsight, I should have taken more time to get to know her better, but I did not have the luxury. Initially, Li refused to be interviewed and told me not to take any notes. Perhaps her Cultural Revolution experience influenced her behavior. I suggested that we just talk in a friendly fashion with no notes taken. She agreed and invited me to come inside the store. We went inside and sat in the back of the store. I offered her my cigarettes. She accepted my cigarettes and started talking. After a few minutes, she said that it was her lunch break so she needed to eat while her brother was watching the store. As she was fixing her lunch, I looked around the store. The commodities were very well organized. The store was about 7' by 12' long with a bed on one side and the entrance on the other. Next to the bed was a window. The walls were painted white; there were two chairs.

After Li fixed her lunch, she brought her bowl of noodles and two chopsticks, sat on one of the chairs, and we started to talk. After she ate, I offered her another cigarette. She declined and took her own packet of Chinese cigarettes, filterless, from the table. She offered me one, and I took it graciously. She crossed her legs and I lit her cigarette. She took a long drag, sat back, and let out a long sigh. Then she said, "I was sent to the countryside during the Cultural Revolution."

Li challenged the traditional portrait of Chinese women throughout the ages—a timid individual with bound feet always bowing to the will of men. Li gave the impression that she was her own boss—to rule, not to be ruled. She shattered the impression of

Chinese philosophy, which assigned to women the darkness and cold . . . and language itself, in which the written character used to designate "women" was derived from pictographs signifying a female and a broom, left little doubt about a woman's value and her place.[22]

My Chinese language teacher at Nankai University in Tianjin, explained the female character as a woman having a baby, with the stomach bulging out, meaning a woman's job was to fulfill the reproductive function. My teacher also mentioned how her father used to kick her books away when she studied and scolded her severely for pursuing education.

During the interview Li's father returned to the store and seemed very annoyed by my presence. Li was uneasy speaking in front of her father. After a few minutes, I said goodbye to Li and left. I then recorded the interview from memory. Li's references to the Cultural Revolution, her unwillingness to talk, and her seventy-year-old father's hostile disposition toward me reminded me of the legacy of all the anti-campaigns. From my experience in China with entrepreneurs, I found that one cannot divorce oneself from the continuation and presence of Maoist philosophy. It is in every aspect of entrepreneurial life. Entrepreneurs recognize the everpresent hangman, who is out there with his noose to get them the moment they raise their heads. Their plight and sociopsychological suffering is further highlighted by Chinese traditional culture. Entrepreneurs fear that a day may come when their own neighbors, friends, and kin may turn into hangmen. Luckily for China, things are changing for entrepreneurs and the entire Chinese system.

Li said that the Cultural Revolution delayed her progress in life. When she returned from the countryside, she did not have a job so she had to find something to do to make a living. In her heart she did not want to be a businesswoman, but after returning from the country and coming from an outcast intellectual family, she did not find any opportunities in the public sector. After discarding her Confucian pride and honor, she decided to venture into the business world with determination. Li worked hard because she wanted to save a lot of money so her two children could go abroad for higher education. Li did not want her children to take over her business. Two things played an important role in her plan for her two children. As mentioned before, victims of the Cultural Revolution in China hope to fulfill their lost dreams through their children. What they could not achieve, they want their children to achieve. On the other hand, Li, coming from an intellectual family, still revered the Confucian philosophy about higher education. The irony of Confucian philosophy is that those women who want their children to be educated, accepted, and honored among society are themselves looked down on because they are women.

It was difficult for Li to start her business. She had difficulties in finding an appropriate place and had to go through many steps. To open a business in China an entrepreneur must go through different procedures. When I asked the officials of Tianjin's Business Administration Bureau about the procedure, the reply was that there were three steps. First, the applicant had to go to the bureau with identification, along with permission papers provided by his or her community office. If the applicant had a job, he or she had to resign. Second, the bureau would check the application. For example, if it was a food business the public health bureau would examine the facility. The bureau had the right to approve or disapprove an application. Third, the bureau would issue the license. According to officials, it took one month to get a license, including other bureaus' examination.[23] But if an entrepreneur wanted to open a private enterprise there was a different procedure. The procedural information provided to me by Tianjin's Business Administration Bureau in 1991 mentioned the following requirements (see Appendix B for the translated full text). The categories of people who were residents of Tianjin and could apply for the license included: unemployed individuals; getihu; anyone who resigned from state-owned enterprises; retired people; scientists and technocrats employed without pay; party leaders; and anyone who resigned from work more than two years ago. Each individual had to show evidence of their position in life. Different areas such as industry, building, transportation, business, food, services, repairs, scientific advisory, recreation, planting, breeding, and so forth had to receive permission from the respective departments. Prospective candidates for licenses also had to provide a prospectus for the given business, including funds, rent contract, contracts with employees, and so on.

Li did not elaborate on the difficulties she faced fulfilling the procedural requirements in opening her business. Altogether eight family members worked closely in the store. I am sure that some of the members of Li's family did not quit their government jobs. Li opened the store at about 9:00 A.M. and closed at 11:00 P.M. every day. During the evening, I never saw Li working. Her youngest brother and others worked at that time.

Li was not unhappy with the tax policy. When buying wholesale commodities, Li paid 3.3 percent tax and, after selling the commodity, Li paid tax according to turnover—about 20 to 30 yuan per 1,000 yuan turnover. The rate was fixed. She said that "we never complain about the tax, we complain about the government officials." When the government officials came, she had to give them a bribe. The officials take whatever they like from her store. Li said that she could not account for the exact loss, but it was a sizeable amount. She went on to say, "The state policy is right, but those who implement the policy change it for their own benefit. You must keep a good relationship (*money guanxi*) with the government officials— *popo tai duo* (too many mother-in-laws, which meant too much red tape). She mentioned that the Chinese system was not like the United States. In the United States, as long as one had the ability and was willing to work hard, one could succeed, but in China one may have dreams that never come true. It reflected her fear of the government's whims vis-à-vis policy.

This kind of fear, which has no relationship to economic activities, is detrimental to economic development. This fear feeds the concept of life uncertainty and forces entrepreneurs to limit creativity and the expansion of their businesses, which would increase the wealth of the nation by creating jobs and increasing purchasing power. Because of this fear, Li relied on her inner feelings that told her not to expand her business because it was a lost cause. She again expressed her distress by saying that although the Chinese people worked hard, even during winter outside in the cold while Americans seldom worked outside in winter, their productivity was lower than Americans. This was the reason, according to Li, China was far behind America. I found that entrepreneurs who are knowledgeable look up to the United States as a model, both politically and economically. In general, the Chinese also look up to the United States as a symbol of happiness and prosperity.

At the end of our conversation, and before Li's father returned, Li said that she was talking too much but she had many worries. She said that she was afraid the policy might change again in the future so it was better for her not to express her opinion. I bade her goodbye and hurried to a nearby park to record what I could from memory.

I had a few more chats with Li. I tried to invite her twenty-two-year-old brother to come to my room for tea with the hope of getting more information from him. He always said that he would visit me but never did.

MR. QU

Qu was a young man with a great deal of energy. Every time I saw him, he was lively and happy. We became friends when I bought cigarettes and other small items from him and chatted with him every now and then.

His store was on the side of a main street and was run by the family. The day I went to interview Qu he was attending the store by himself, but he had a friend with him. His friend was active like him. Qu sold his items from inside the store, with a small counter facing the street. Since items had to be purchased from the outside, it was difficult to see inside the store properly. He did not have anything outside on the sidewalk, although I saw him selling watermelons there during the hot season.

I went inside and sat on a chair. The store was dark. There was a bed. When I asked him about the bed, he said that each family member took turns sleeping in the store. During the interview, his friend jumped into the conversation and offered some information. Qu also used his friend to witness what he was telling me. Every now and then, Qu would ask his friend if he was right and his friend would affirm his answer. It seemed that they were good friends and trusted each other. It was the first time I saw an entrepreneur talking in front of a friend (another interviewee talked in the presence of his employee-friend). It was also the first time a friend took part in the conversation. This strong friendship between Qu and his friend was refreshing. Most of the time, Chinese entrepreneurs were in a state of panic during the interviews.

Qu started his business in October 1990, just eight months before I interviewed him in 1991. He previously worked for the government but, since he was earning little money, decided to quit his job and start his own business. He used his mother's name to register with the Industrial and Commercial Bureau in order to obtain the licenses. Why do some Chinese entrepreneurs use their mother's or wife's name to open a business? Retired individuals face fewer problems in obtaining permission to open a business. But why do they use women's names to open a business? The answer might lie in the sociopolitical arena of China. Entrepreneurs still have memories of the *San-fan* and *Wu-fan* campaigns. They understand that if the government reverted to the policies of the 1950s and 1960s, it would be the entrepreneurs who would become the victims of the illogical wrath. However, if an entrepreneur registered under the name of a woman, the woman might ask for, and receive, mercy from the cadres. Whether this is true or not, reflects the constant life uncertainty under which present-day Chinese entrepreneurs must carry on their business activities.

To verify this, I interviewed eight students from mainland China studying in the United States. Their responses were mixed. Some said alternative names were used for safety purposes—the officials could deal harshly with young people but not with old women. Those who were from the south, like Wenzhou or Shanghai, said that it was unknown to them and must be a local phenomenon of Tianjin linked to tax issues, filial piety, or keeping the "iron rice-bowl" and "porcelain rice-bowl" (job in the private sector) at the same time. Perhaps this mixed response meant that China is changing and evolving into something different from the past. China is living in the past and present at the same time. In a changing society like China, past and present can be simultaneously observed, which means that traditional values are very strong and influence the ruled and rulers alike.

Qu started his business with about 1,000 yuan. It was a family-run business, and four family members worked in the store. I only met two of the family members, Qu and his father. Qu's father was a strong man in his late 50s. He did not talk much to me beyond casual greetings. After the interview, Qu's father became even colder toward me and did not like my friendship with his son. Qu's father did not have prior knowledge about the interview and when he found out about it, was not pleased at all. All the family members had good relations with one another and worked hard together. They kept the store open from 8:00 A.M. to 12:00 P.M. Qu said that he did not work hard when he worked for the government because he earned little money no matter how hard he worked. However, to earn more money for himself, he was willing to work hard. When it came to purchasing goods for his store, Qu faced discrimination from the government-run wholesale business. He said that it was easier for the state-owned enterprises to get funds and raw materials than the individual enterprises. However, the latter earned more money than the former.

Qu hoped to get a new license to sell garments, motorcycles, electric appliances, or foreign currency. These kinds of commodities are very profitable, but the government prohibited individual enterprises from doing such business. To open a new business, Qu said that it would take from one to six months. Qu said that in northern China (Tianjin), the state did not permit an individual businessman to change his or her certificate to establish a bigger business or factory after the entrepreneur had accumulated enough funds, but in southern China the policy was more flexible. Qu further said that it might sound easy to open a business, but in reality it was very difficult. He stated:

> First, one has to fill in an application form, second, get a physical check up; third, register with the Industrial and Commercial Bureau. By the time you receive the license, at least one month has passed. Different departments charge different kinds of fees. The distances between departments are great and we Chinese do not have cars. We can only ride bicycles. Beside this, the government officials work at a low efficiency. Sometimes they create troubles for you. So to do something is more difficult than saying. If you do not believe, you can try for yourself.

Qu might not have been aware of the problems faced by entrepreneurs in Tianjin previously. It used to take about one year, or in some cases, several years to set up a shop, and entrepreneurs had to go through several administrative departments to get the stamp of approval.[24] Compared to this, Qu was lucky in his dealings with government officials.

However, Qu found it very difficult to deal with government officials and tax collectors. He said there was a saying that, "The Guomindang has more meetings, and the Communist Party has more taxes." There were different kinds of taxes he was required to pay, such as a bicycle riding tax, a bridge building tax, a tree planting tax, and so on. He also mentioned that when he faced any difficulties with the officials in any department, he would give money to the officials so the problem could be solved more easily. Susan Young made a similar observation in Chengdu. In Chengdu, business people said that it was important to have good *guanxi* with government officials in order to do business. In the beginning it was difficult, but doing business became easier once *guanxi* was established. One factory owner said, "In the beginning, it was hard getting people to buy from me. I had to spend a lot of money taking people to dinner and giving presents."[25] When the government officials came to buy something, Qu never dared to ask them to pay. Even if they offered money, he never accepted it because it might cause him trouble in the future. Moreover, the money government officials offered was a small amount of the original price. For example, a carton of Kent cigarettes costs 50 yuan, but officials would only offer 10 yuan.

Qu's experience is not limited to China. In the former Soviet Union, entrepreneurs in cooperatives used bribes to lessen the tax burden imposed on them by the government. It was reported that a bribe of 2,000–3,000 rubles would help to reduce the tax by 10 percent.[26] In Hungary, the bureaucrats in the first economy (government-run enterprises and agencies) exploit the weak position of the second economy (private entrepreneurial activities) by taking bribes from entrepreneurs in return for goods and services.[27]

Toward the end of our conversation, Qu reflected on one aspect of entrepreneurship in China. He said that those people in China who were interested in opening up their own business liked entrepreneurs like Qu, but those who could not do so were jealous. During my interviews with entrepreneurs in Tianjin, I discovered that there were different views about entrepreneurs in society. Some said that they were admired, some said they were looked down on, and some gave a mixed response. Present-day culture and entrepreneurs in China are in transition, and it is quite natural to have mixed messages about a single topic. It will take some time to receive a coherent message about the position of entrepreneurs in Chinese society. According to Qu, to change the economic system of China for the betterment of the country, Jiang Zemin should reform the Chinese economic system. While Qu was talking about Jiang, his father walked in and he instantly stopped talking. His father told me that they were glad that I came to visit them but I must leave immediately. After that, I met Qu and his father several times but talked little with Qu. My last purchase from him was two small watermelons, but he neglected to give me my usual discount. He did make sure, however, that I got two good watermelons by tapping on the fruit with his finger and listening to the sound. If the sound was hollow, it meant that it was not a very good watermelon.

MR. MA

Ma was a relative of one of my friends; my friend arranged the interview. Ma sent his Toyota van to pick us up at my friend's home. My friend, his wife, and I went together to interview Ma. My friend's wife wanted to visit with her relatives because she had not had the opportunity to visit for a long time and did not want to miss the convenient chance to visit and improve the relationship. Ma and his family lived on the outskirts of Tianjin city.

It was late afternoon when we reached Ma's house, which was surrounded by big walls. Someone opened the front entrance for us and we went inside. It was a big house with four or five rooms. We went into the living room, which contained a big sofa and small couches. There was a big coffee table in the middle of the room. There were two packets of Kent cigarettes on the table. There was a big refrigerator in a corner of the room. Ma welcomed us and asked us to sit down. He offered us something to eat, we declined but after a few minutes several sweet items appeared along with hot tea. He then asked someone to bring us soft drinks. When the refrigerator was opened, I could see a shelf full of foreign brand soft drinks. It crossed my mind that this display was a way of conveying one's status and wealth.

Ma was in his mid-forties. He was tall, strong, and had a pleasant personality. Ma used to work for a steel plant, which was a collective enterprise, where he earned 57 yuan per month. When his supervisor left the plant, Ma wanted to leave with him, but instead was transferred to a trading firm jointly managed by Tianjin's North Suburban district and Beicang town. He worked there as an assistant manager, and through his efforts the trading firm was able to make a profit of more than 100,000 yuan. Two factors played important roles in his decision to quit his job in pursuit of something new. First, the pay was very low. Second, there was internal conflict between the district and town leaders, and between the managers. In 1986 he quit his job and returned to his village to look for a job on a farm. The village head man looked down on him and regarded him as a loser. It was very degrading and humiliating. To save face, Ma decided to strike out on his own and work hard. He made up his mind to prove that he had the ability to be successful. Ma found another job with a government-run electric machinery company that dealt in transporting, storing, and selling motor vehicles for the government. He was paid 90 yuan for transporting one vehicle from Beijing to Tianjin. During 1986 to 1987, Ma delivered about 1,000 vehicles and gradually saved a large amount of money.

While Ma was employed at the government-run company, he discovered that he only earned 90 yuan for delivering a single vehicle, but the company earned a profit of 1,000 yuan. He decided to go into business for himself, and with the necessary investment in hand he ventured into private business in 1988.

Ma said that he did not need a bank loan. Moreover, he said, banks did not give loans to private individuals and it was even harder for a village enterprise like his to borrow money. A bank would only give a loan to a business if it was sure that the business had the ability to pay back the loan.

It was easy for Ma to obtain his license for the motor vehicle business. The person who was in charge of issuing the license to Ma was the husband of an employee who once worked under Ma. Ma approached the employee to persuade her husband to issue the license to him. When Ma found out how easy it would be to obtain the license, he immediately decided to open his own business. Here the concept of *guanxi* played a very important role in favor of Ma. If Ma did not have a good friendship and good working relations with this woman, things would have been different. In China, *guanxi* or personal connection, plays a very important role in the decision-making process and also in obtaining favors. It is an obligation to another person. It can make the difference in obtaining bank loans, and utility and tax waivers. *Guanxi* in many cases is more important than rules. As one entrepreneur in Tianjin said in response to a question about bank loans, "[It is] not very easy [to get a loan from the bank]. You must have a relationship with the bank. In China, relationships are more important than knowledge or ability."[28] If a person knows someone personally and fails to meet the *guanxi* obligation, it is assumed that the person is shameless and does not honor the *guanxi* obligations. "Thus the exchange of favors allows each ally to demonstrate his interest in the alliance and his willingness to make sacrifices for his ally."[29]

Ma was glad that he had the *guanxi* to help him to obtain the license. Since then, life changed for Ma. He used to make 57 yuan per month in his old job and 90 yuan per vehicle in his second job, but by working for himself he earned more than 1,000 yuan per month. He worked hard along with his sixteen employees, 10 hours a day, from 7:30 A.M. to 5:30 P.M., seven days a week. He had fixed assets of 400,000 yuan, excluding circulating funds, in 1991. His transaction value was 10,000 yuan per day, and he was planning to expand his business in other areas, such as foreign trade. There are entrepreneurs like Ma and Qu who are willing to take risks and expand their businesses. An entrepreneur named Cao, a native of Shanghai, fell into this category of daring entrepreneurs who are willing to expand their business. Cao said that "[he] expects to become China's biggest private businessman in ten years."[30]

While China's reform is in transition, entrepreneurs receive mixed messages from the government and decide to expand or curtail their businesses accordingly. Ma was satisfied with the government's treatment of his business. He had good relations with the government officials. When asked how society viewed him, he replied:

> The tax bureau supports me because I send calendars to them every year. The Industrial and Commercial Bureau and Price Administration Department are good to me. Nowadays doing business is honorable because we have to invigorate and develop our economy. People advocate that I do individual business. No matter how the others treat me, I will work hard and accept the experience and lesson in the course of operation. Career is never smooth sailing.

Ma believed that private businesses had more freedom than before and the trend was toward giving more freedom to the private sector by the government. In return, the private sector contributed to national economic growth by paying taxes. Ma paid 3.24 percent of transactions in taxes, about 324 yuan per day out of 10,000 yuan worth of transactions. He also paid 55 percent in income tax. As Wang Zhongming, director of the Individual and Private Economy Department of the State Administration for Industry and Commerce, said:

> It [the individual and private sector] has enlivened China's planned market economy and accumulated sizable funds, while statistics show that from 1981 to 1988 its total tax turnover to the state reached nearly 31 billion yuan.[31]

Ma elaborated on the positive role of the private sector by stating:

> [It plays] a positive function. Private enterprise has more advantage than the state-owned enterprise; they can make decisions by themselves and quickly enough to take advantage of business opportunities. It is not like the state-owned [enterprise], where permission has to be taken through layers of authorities. In my own business, I have the final say, so I can deal with matters efficiently.

Ma did not take his success for granted. He remembered the current government policy and kept his business activity in proper perspective. He did not anticipate any problems that might arise in the near future because of government policy, but he could not speculate what it would be like in ten to twenty years. He functioned within the limits prescribed by government policy and did not take bigger strides that were not within his control. Being a practical person, he saw corruption in the form of bribes as a necessary evil:

> Though I am against [corruption], sometimes to get things done, you need to present some gifts to persons concerned. However, it takes

only a small percentage of the profit, that is, 1 percent or less. The purpose of doing this is to solve some problems and get help. It is worthwhile. Besides, presenting gifts is a common practice. I cannot escape from this atmosphere.

The two characters *ren qing* in the Chinese language literally mean human feelings, human sympathy, or human relationships. But if we add *song*, which means "send," it means "deliberately do somebody a good turn [sometimes by stretching a point] to curry his favor," or simply it means sending a gift. Nowadays in China this gift does not only mean gift but most often is translated as cash. A nine-year survey of rural Tianjin found that the amount that an ordinary farmer sends as gifts increased by 23 percent annually. A survey of 3,000 rural households in Zhejiang Province found that in 1991, on average, each household spent 610 yuan ($105), ranging from 285 yuan ($49) to 1,850 yuan ($319) on gifts, even though this expenditure was far beyond the capacity of most rural families. Some people do not send gifts just "for face." They select their targets and choose those in power who may be able to return favors for gifts. A factory worker said that when a daughter of a factory head got married, almost everyone gave money as a gift. It was not because they were all close friends of the factory head but because some day in the future they might need his help. "Such 'gifts' seem to be no different from bribes. But investment' is the word preferred by most people."[32]

Besides presenting gifts to make life easier, Ma also understood his position as a businessman in Tianjin. At the end of the interview, Ma said that as a Tianjiner, he had to be careful and follow the direction presented by Beijing. Unlike in Guangdong, the business people in Tianjin had to take careful, small steps in the business world, because if any change of policy occurs, it will be the Tianjiner who will face the consequences long before Guangdong. According to Ma, all business people like him can do is to just step on the rim of the policy boundary and do economic activity—one cannot make a breakthrough. By the time the interview was over, it was dark. After the interview, Ma, my friend, and I shared Kent cigarettes offered by Ma and talked about trivialities. He expressed an interest in establishing some kind of business connection with me in the future, and I returned his interest. We bade goodbye and headed for home.

MR. YE

Ye and I became friends when I would develop and buy film at his store. I also helped him find new customers. Every time I recruited a new customer from the international students, I made certain to take them personally to the store. Ye was very happy with my assistance and would entertain me every time I went to visit him. I used to offer him my cigarettes, but most of the time we smoked Ye's cigarettes.

When I asked Ye if I could interview him for my research, he replied positively. I went to his photo store one afternoon for the interview.

Ye was a tall, handsome fellow with a strong build in his mid-twenties. He was only a high school graduate but was quite knowledgeable about many things including the United States. His shop was about 15' by 10' in size. There were not very many things in the shop: a small counter with a camera on a stand, a few chairs, a stool, and a few powerful lights. The floor of the shop was cement, but there were a few holes here and there. The walls were painted white but needed to be painted again. Ye had his workshop in a different place. He went back and forth between his shop and his workshop.

While I was interviewing him, his employee, who maintained the shop while he was gone, was also present. During the course of the interview, Ye left once to go to his workshop but returned shortly. Ye was the second entrepreneur I saw speaking in front of a friend or employee. During the interview, a few customers entered the store. Ye was always very polite with his customers. One lady customer came in, gave Ye her receipt and received her pictures. After looking at the pictures, she complained that she was not happy with the outcome of the passport-size picture. Ye told her very politely that she could have those pictures for free and if she wanted to take a picture of herself, she was more than welcome. The woman said that she would return later and left with the free pictures. I was very impressed with Ye's treatment of his customers, and I was very sure that it was a product of private entrepreneurship. If it had been a state-owned store, the shopkeeper would have said: "Tough! Take it or leave it."

Ye used to work for a metallurgical industry until he became sick and took a sick leave. During his sick leave, he thought of starting his own business. In 1988 he started his business, and when I interviewed him in 1991, he was still on sick leave. Since Ye liked photography and knew the techniques of photography, he opened his own photo studio with an initial investment of about 20,000 yuan. His investment was a combination of his own savings and a loan from the bank. Even though he was an individual businessman, he did not have any problem obtaining the loan. Government policy at that time stipulated that loans would be given to enterprises that had fixed assets. Ye had none but he did have *guanxi*, which enabled him to get the necessary loan.

Ye, along with his seven employees, worked hard. They worked ten hours per day, from morning to night. Through his hard work he had accumulated enough capital to expand his business. Ye started his business in 1988 and by the summer of 1991, he planned to expand it and establish a big photo studio. He had accumulated enough funds on his own to expand his business, and did not need any loan from the bank. Given the right opportunities, Chinese entrepreneurs are capable of hard work and money management. They take their business matters seriously and are willing to expand their businesses. They also keep relations with customers in proper perspective, because a business exits for its customers. Chinese entrepreneurs are no less capable of doing business and making the right decisions than entrepreneurs in the United States. It is the matter of government policy and the treatment of entrepreneurs by bureaucrats that make the difference. If the Chinese government stays out of the decision-making process and other aspects of business, Chinese entrepreneurs will prove to be successful.

The government is slowly moving away from microcontrol of the economy and is letting the market determine the entrepreneurial activities. In return, entrepreneurs are contributing in a positive way to China's economic development, which reduces the fear of the past and the life-uncertainty factor, and helps the reform-minded Dengists carry on with the reform program. This policy is also having an impact on traditional cultural attitudes by slowly accepting profit-making ventures as an honorable occupation.

Two things motivated Ye to work hard—he was young and he wanted to make money. He felt that he supported his country by paying taxes. In addition, the government policy encouraged him. He paid 10 percent of the turnover as tax (about 400 to 500 yuan per month). He believed that paying taxes was the responsibility of every citizen, but he was not happy about the tax system. In addition to the 10 percent tax, other taxes made his tax rate much higher; tax collectors did not consider problems such as broken machines, when assessing extra taxes. As Ye himself said:

> Although the [Chinese] government policy is good, there are all kinds of rules and regulations and they cannot be implemented. The relationship between human beings in China is very complicated. We have different kinds of relationship. It is not like America, so long as you have ability, you can go to work for any company. In China changing jobs is very difficult. The leader (manager) will cause problems for you.
>
> Corruption cannot be solved in China. The ordinary person has no power. Only those who have power can become corrupted. In America, presidents are changed every four years, while in China it is permanent—no different from the emperor. I think that is the fundamental reason of corruption. People whether they have ability or not, can be the leader.

In spite of the problems faced by entrepreneurs in China, Ye was happy with his position in life. His previous job in the metallurgical industry was hard and the pay was low. Ye acknowledged, however, that working in a state-owned enterprise was a stable job and there is no such certainty in individual business. Fortunately, Ye managed to overcome the fear of insecurity by 1991, when he had earned enough money to feel that his future was secured. What are the consequences of this factor of insecurity in the private sector or feeling secure in a government job? The result is stagnation in the economic realm and the fear of insecurity in the private sector that could hamper the progress of entrepreneurial activities. Hence, there is a strong opposition to change. As the saying goes in China: "Before liberation we had a clay rice bowl. Then Chairman Mao gave us an iron rice bowl. Deng Xiaoping poked a hole in it." Another worker in her mid-forties said that she had a "porcelain rice bowl." "A porcelain rice bowl looks rather elegant, but it's no more sturdy than one made of clay."[33] In state-owned enterprises, employees feel secure because they are assured their wages and other benefits regardless of job performance. Public servants in China are like the emperor's daughter whose marriage is guaranteed regardless of her beauty.[34] In Poland, like China, the government is facing opposition to reform from parties afraid of losing the benefits they enjoyed during the communist era.[35]

Like government employees who are opposed to change, there are other people in Chinese society also opposed to change. According to Ye, some people were jealous of his success, and others admired him, but he wished he had more education, reflecting the continued power of Confucius in Chinese society even after more than 2,000 years. Ye was more concerned about economic freedom than political freedom. Ye said, "To those politicians, political freedom is more important." He went on to say:

[Economic freedom means] buying and selling things which fall in the scope of the government policy. Political freedom helps the economic freedom. We need a four-year election system. During our election, we are allowed to choose the person who is already appointed by the government. Election is a facade. This is not a true democratic election. Politicians only think about their own political power. They never think how to improve the people's living standard.

The comments demonstrate a trend among entrepreneurs. A new culture demanding freedom in both the economic and political realms is not only evolving among the intellectuals and students, but among entrepreneurs as well. With the freedom to make economic decisions, entrepreneurs in China are beginning to understand the benefit of free thinking. As one entrepreneur I interviewed said, "I think individual businessmen should join together to pursue a political career."[36] The evolution of a new culture takes time. It takes a long time to extinguish old habits and paradigms and replace them with something new. The less the observer is aware of this extinction process, the safer the process is from active opposition by groups with the most to lose. Because about 80 percent of the Chinese population lives in rural areas and their main concern is economic freedom and the well being of the family, it will take a long time for this population to become socially and politically aware. With economic freedom, political freedom will eventually come, but patience is needed. Economic freedom has started to give birth to a new culture:

> [E]conomic development is making centralized repression more difficult. . . . Talk radio, on which listeners complain about everything from adultery to housing, local officials and shoddy products, has taken off in Shanghai and Beijing. Newspapers are beginning to experiment with political stories.[37]

Ye and other Chinese entrepreneurs represent a significant part of this evolving culture. After the interview, I visited Ye several times and was struck by how he appeared to be an evolving and maturing entrepreneur, but culturally a different breed, compared to other ordinary Chinese. Entrepreneurs are slowly moving away from the past, removing the shackles of Maoist rule and desiring new cultural attitudes about the marketplace to replace Confucian attitudes about profit-making ventures.

CONCLUSION

From all the interviews, including those presented above, I learned that most private entrepreneurs and *getihu* are determined and strong individuals. They are not only willing to be entrepreneurs as defined by Joseph Schumpeter, but are willing to take the kinds of risks described by Frank Knight in the face of uncertainty. What makes Chinese entrepreneurs even more dynamic, compared to entrepreneurs in the West, is that they are willing to venture into new projects in the face of life uncertainty. Life uncertainty, no doubt, hinders the entrepreneurs' ability to grow and exhibit their talents and innovation to the utmost. Coupled with this, the government's uncertain policies, the abuse of power by officials for personal gain (like unfair taxing and collecting high fees), and cultural disdain all contribute to the uneasy state of affairs for entrepreneurs. From my interactions, I found that Chinese entrepreneurs are patriotic and willing to contribute their talents to building a strong economic base for China. With a sound political and economic environment, which may help to reduce the legacy of the past and change the cultural attitudes in favor of entrepreneurship, I am positive that Chinese entrepreneurs will reveal superb entrepreneurial skills, no less than those of the Schumpetarian entrepreneurs of the West.

Chapter 4

China's Entrepreneurs
and the New Economic Culture

Chinese culture, both traditional and communist, has greatly impacted
the society. The entrepreneurs are the products of this culture. This
chapter analyzes two aspects of Chinese culture that play a major role in
the lives of entrepreneurs and the quick revival of entrepreneurship in Deng
Xiaoping's era. I also analyze the evolving economic culture that is influencing the way society views entrepreneurs, and how traditional cultural
values about women are returning due to the decline of communism. This
is notable because under communist rule the women of China gained social
status vis-à-vis job opportunities, personal relationships, and the division
of labor.

It is important to note that the role of Confucian authoritarianism plays
a vital part in Chinese society. The citizens of China are overly dependent
on culture for direction in life. This makes the Chinese susceptible to any
change of authority or policy. The rulers and their policies can be a
blessing or a curse on the people, depending on the desire of the rulers.
Traditionally, Chinese entrepreneurs have maintained a tenuous position
in society, thus giving rise to the life-uncertainty factor. This no doubt
contributes toward a lack of initiative and creativity among entrepreneurs
and slows down economic growth. With this in mind, we now turn to the
role of traditional authority and entrepreneurial culture in the lives of
Chinese entrepreneurs.

CULTURE AS A CONCEPT

Culture has been defined in many ways, and many different subcultures
have been identified. But whatever the definition of culture may be, it is a
dynamic concept. Culture constantly changes by accepting something new,

rejecting something old, or reincorporating something old that might have been given up willingly (or unwillingly) by certain groups in the society. Usually major changes in culture follow the introduction of new technologies or ideas.[1] Albert A. Segynola, in his study of the Bendel State of Nigeria, defined culture as the dynamic ways of life, religion, and laws.[2] To Clyde Kluckhohn, "Culture consists of traditional (i.e., historically derived and selected) ideas and especially their attached values; culture systems may, on the one hand, be considered as products of action, on the other as conditioning influences upon further action."[3]

To study Chinese culture, Richard Smith, in his article "The Future of Chinese Culture" (1989), viewed culture as, "A system of interrelated perceptions, beliefs, values, and institutions that together shape the conscious and unconscious behavior of that system's constituent members."[4] According to Lucian Pye, political culture is a "[A] set of attitudes, beliefs, and sentiments which give order and meaning to a political process and which provide the underlying assumptions and rules that govern behavior in the political system."[5] Almond and Verba described culture as a "psychological orientation toward social objects." To Almond and Verba political culture is the same as religious culture or economic culture.[6]

ECONOMIC CULTURE DEFINED

I agree with Almond and Verba that just as there is political culture, there is also economic culture. My observation of entrepreneurs in Tianjin, China, convinced me that China's entrepreneurs and the Chinese society are undergoing an economic cultural change. This new economic culture, a continuing process in the contemporary economic life of the citizens of China, began in the late 1970s. Old economic habits and beliefs are being slowly replaced through social mobilization by new economic habits and beliefs. The old and new economic cultures are antithetical, so a rise in one reflects a decline in the other. There is no amalgamation of the old communist economic culture and the new authoritarian–capitalist economic culture. However, there are elements from both the old and new cultures that can be observed during this transition period.

Social mobilization is a process wherein citizens of a system slowly give up major clusters of old sociopsychological and politicoeconomic beliefs and open up to new values and ideas through assimilation.[7] Since a society is made up of different constituent groups that represent the culture as a whole, a major change (e.g., Mao's revolution or Deng's revolution) affects almost every group. To illustrate, economic culture lies on both ends of the spectrum, and social mobilization is the process by which the population moves from one end to the other to start the journey again (see Figure 4.1).

Figure 4.1
Process of Social Mobilization

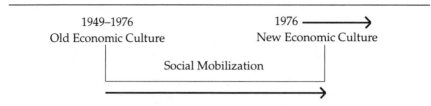

To understand those concepts, a definition of both old and new economic cultures is needed. The old economic culture created by China's communist regime may be defined as a set of values, commitments, and attitudes of the citizens of China toward the economic life of the system. The citizens expected, and to some extent received, the benefit of economic security by accepting allocated jobs, medical insurance, housing, education, and food stamps through a process that was more or less egalitarian. The values, commitments, and attitudes that characterize the new economic culture, on the other hand, reflect an acceptance, to a certain extent, of loss of job security,[8] privatization of education,[9] profit and loss in the private sectors,[10] incorporation of many aspects of capitalism, such as using beautiful models in advertising,[11] acceptance of foreign and domestic competition by public ownership,[12] the fading away of egalitarianism,[13] and the slow acceptance of private entrepreneurship as a respectable occupation. As one entrepreneur said:

> Nowadays the people look highly upon an individual businessman. Nowadays a businessman is considered to be a strong and able person because a common person would not have the courage or ability to do business. Nowadays a lot of university students sell newspapers and do part-time jobs, but they could not do this in the past. Now the values have changed. After opening to the outside world, status depends on money. So, you can marry easily with your girlfriend if you change your occupation and become a businessman—no problem.[14]

COMMUNIST ECONOMIC CULTURE

Social mobilization in China is regulated to a great extent by government policy. During the rule of the CCP under Mao, the government's economic policies were directed toward creating a new Communist Man under the leadership of Mao. Mao followed the doctrine of Marx and Engels very closely. As Marx and Engels said:

[W]ith the abolition of the basis of private property, with the communistic regulation of production (and, implicit in this, the destruction of the alien relation between men and what they themselves produce), the power of the relation of supply and demand is dissolved into nothing, and men get exchange, production, the mode of their mutual relation, under their own control again. . . .

[F]or . . . this communist consciousness, . . . the alteration of men on a mass scale is necessary . . . [and] it can only in a revolution succeed in ridding itself of all the muck of ages and become fitted to found society anew.[15]

For Mao, revolution or class struggle was a continuing process and through this class struggle a Communist Man is born to give new meaning to constituent groups of the system, thereby the culture. As Mao said:

Fight, fail, fight again, fail again, fight again. . . . This is another Marxist law . . .

Classes struggle, some classes triumph, others are eliminated. Such is history, such is the history of civilization for thousands of years. To interpret history from this viewpoint is historical materialism; standing in opposition to this viewpoint is historical idealism.[16]

Mao's Communist Man[17] is a selfless individual who sacrifices his interest for the greater interest of the people and the country. He is not driven by the forces of profit but by the force of self-satisfaction he gained by contributing to society in an unselfish fashion. He is a different being compared to the feudal Chinese. Liu Shaoqi quoted Mao in his work: "At no time and in no circumstances should a Communist place his personal interest first."[18]

What Communist Mao said, and Communist Liu agreed with, was, in many respects, nothing but Confucianism in the guise of communism. This concept of class struggle became the law of the land. Mao used class struggle as a weapon against his opponents and suppressed any movement toward a profit economy. This "continued class struggle—became the predominant features of what we now call Maoism. Thus Maoism . . . became itself a dogma."[19] Maoism produced communists like the martyr Lei Feng, who followed Mao's thought and became an example of selflessness. "He was the embodiment of traditional Chinese virtues—simple, honest and kind-hearted."[20] He "knew how to love the people ardently and hate the enemy. He never forgot the class hatred of the old society where people perished and families fell apart." He was perpetually politically and socially aware, "never forgetting the pain when the scars were healed."[21]

The process to create communist men like Lei Feng to fit into the communist economic culture resulted in a great disruption of Chinese society, both socially and culturally. As it was stated by Marx and Engels,

"The Communist revolution is the most radical rupture with traditional property relations; no wonder that its development involves the most radical rupture with traditional ideas."[22]

Was communism able to destroy the traditional values and ideas of Chinese society? I believe the answer is no. The economic culture of Chinese society was established a long time ago, even before Confucius. Regardless of what Confucius said about the status of entrepreneurs in Chinese society, entrepreneurs played an important part in the economic life of China during the imperial period.

During the rule of the CCP, from 1949 to 1976, the role of private entrepreneurs in the economic arena became almost nonexistent. However, entrepreneurial activities have reemerged under the leadership of Deng. Policymakers in China realized that Maoism did great damage to the economy. They hoped that the country would be transformed into a market economy by Deng's efforts to open up China. It was a choice between the political and economic death of the CCP and China or its continuity. A byproduct of Deng's economic reform was the revival of *getihu* and private entrepreneurship, which had been almost completely eliminated from China during Mao's rule.

The rapid and successful return of entrepreneurs in China may be viewed in two ways. One is that government policy, which can destroy or build Chinese entrepreneurs, made it possible for this evolving new economic culture to become a reality. The other emphasizes the successful entrepreneurial culture of Chinese business people, embedded in the history of the imperial period. An explanation of both of these factors begins with an examination of the cultural aspects of entrepreneurs, and the Chinese people as a whole and their relationship to authority.

CONFUCIAN AUTHORITARIANISM

Confucian teachings and the concept of authority in China have always been intertwined. Since its appearance, traditional Chinese culture has never been immune from Confucian thought. Even during the Maoists' regime, the communists used traditional cultural concepts of loyalty, obedience, selflessness, and diligence to control the Chinese masses.[23] As Lucian Pye wrote, "For both Confucian and Communist Chinese, ideology has been important, not only as a guide for action, but also as a way of making the moral claims associated with leadership."[24]

Confucian philosophy not only guides the behavior of the ruled and ruler, it gives meaning to the Chinese system. Even during communist rule, Confucian philosophy guided the system and Marxist-Leninist-Maoist ideology, as evidenced by the rapid discarding of communist ideas by society as alternative opportunities presented themselves. Chinese traditional culture is exerting great influence on contemporary Chinese society and its institutions, thereby giving new meaning to its constituent groups. New ideas are evolving among the constituent groups in the system, exerting great pressure for institutional change.

The central theme of Confucius's philosophy are rites which give meaning in the Chinese context to the highly hierarchical structure of society, where each finds his or her place in governance, facilitating stability and maintenance of the status quo. The finding of one's place in society is a product of five critical kinds of relationships—parents and children, elder and younger brothers, husband and wife, friend and friend, and prince and minister (or, some say, master and follower).

Lee Kuan Yew of Singapore, claimed in 1990, that Singapore, with a 75 percent Chinese population (mainly from southern China), is governed by, or follows, the five relationships. In Singapore, Confucianism acts as the guiding principles for the society.[25] Agnes Syu observed in her study of Taiwanese business enterprises that the Chinese society of Taiwan is also governed by the five relationships of Confucianism. Syu used master-follower or father-son relationships to explain the behavior of Taiwan's government and its employees in state-owned firms.[26] The following illustrates what Confucius said about the parent-child relationship and ruler-ruled relationship.

> Tzu-Kung asked, "What must a man be like in order that he may be called a true knight [of the Way]?"
>
> The Master said, "He who
>> In the furtherance of his own interests
>> Is held back by scruples
>> Who as an envoy to far lands
>> Does not disgrace his prince's Commission
>> may be called a true Knight."
>
> Tzu-Kung said, "May I venture to ask who would rank next?"
>
> The Master said, "He whom his relatives commend for filial piety, his fellow-villagers, for deference to his elders . . . "
>
> Tzu-Kung said, "What would you say of those who are now conducting the government?"
>
> The Master said, "Ugh! A set of peck-measures [mere thimblefuls], not worth taking into account."[27]

Respect for people in authority is mandatory in Chinese culture, and this breeds stability in society. Confucius looked down on business people who challenged the authority and vyed for power. On the other hand, during his own life Confucius did not feel it was worth talking about the decaying government. What allows a government to run a system is not only ideology, but institutions that are able to give meaning to constituent groups in society. From time to time, the rulers of China took shelter under the authoritarian philosophy of Confucius and created institutions to give meaning to constituent groups and thereby govern the system.

My own experience in China confirms that Confucianism is very much alive today. Many Chinese still revere Confucius. Qufu, Confucius's birthplace in Shandong Province, is visited by people from all over China. When I visited Qufu, I saw literally hundreds of Chinese straining to look at the statue of Confucius; many of them were bowing and praying to the statue. They expected the spirit of Confucius to help them. In fact, the role Confucius still plays in China is beyond measure. In a sense, Confucianism depicts the essence of Chinese culture.[28] China's rulers used Confucian philosophy to set up authoritarian institutions to rule over the people, whether effective or not. The following section examines the role of this authoritarian concept as it was used during both the imperial and Maoist periods to create institutions to rule the system.

AUTHORITARIAN INSTITUTIONS—A HISTORICAL PERSPECTIVE

Confucian "China is like a household in which old people rule, middle-aged people operate things, and the young stand aside and watch."[29] This Confucian concept was passed down over the generations from the Han dynasty to the present. As Von der Gabelentz said:

> If we are to measure the greatness of an historic personage, I can only see one standard applicable for the purpose: the effectiveness of that person's influence according to its dimensions, duration, and intensity. If this standard be applied, Confucius was one of the greatest of men. For, even at the present day, after the lapse of more than two thousand years, the moral, social, and political life of about one-third of mankind continues to be under the full influence of his mind.[30]

The Han dynasty adopted Confucianism as the state ideology and ruled China from 202 B.C. to A.D. 220. Emperor Li Shi-min (600–49), founder of the Tang dynasty and posthumously known as Tai-zong, governed primarily through Confucianism.[31]

The Song dynasty ushered in the period of neo-Confucianism. Under the emperor Shen Tong (1067–1085), a Confucian reformer named Wang Anshi was appointed chief councilor in 1069. Wang proposed a fifteen-point program of new laws (xin-fa) "that brought about institutional changes" to govern the system. Wang's laws, promoted between 1069 and 1073, dealt with economics, fiscal administration, the military, education, and personnel recruitment. They advocated a greater role for government to control the system.[32]

Of all the fifteen new policies advocated by Wang under the protection of Confucianism,[33] the *baojia* (an administrative system organized on the basis of households, where each *jia* was made up of ten households and each *bao* included ten *jia*), as an institution, survived the test of time by proving Confucianism's hierarchical rule.[34] Through the institution of *baojia*, the central government was able to facilitate census taking and the collection of taxes, and help reduce tax evasion. It was reported that the institution of *baojia* was so effective that it almost eliminated robbery in the capital district, whereas before, an average of 200 cases of violent crime occurred every year.[35]

Ming Tai-zu, the first emperor of the Ming dynasty, used the concepts of *li* (rules of ceremonious behavior) and *fa* (law) as *li-fa* to centralize his government. The *li-fa*, in turn, derived its meaning from two interlocking factors of sociomoral principles. One factor was the Three Bonds and Five Constants (*San Gang–Wu Chang*). The Three Bonds were ruler-subject, father-son, and husband-wife, and the Five Constants were benevolence, righteousness, decorum, wisdom, and reliability. The remaining factor was the sixfold hierarchy of occupations, beginning with the gentry class, followed by farmers, artisans, merchants, and, finally, the Buddhist and Taoist clergy.[36]

The institution of *lijia* was very close to the *baojia*. Under *lijia*, families were organized into groups of tens and hundreds for local self-governance. The Qing dynasty also followed the institution of *lijia* to collect taxes. The Qing also introduced the old institution of *baojia*, "inherited from Sung; the system had the characteristics of police-like mutual surveillance."[37]

The Chinese government used the institution of *baojia* to control the people. Political institutions of traditional China in every dynasty were autocratic; it was the will of the ruler whether to use them despotically. There were no concepts of checks and balances to control the power of the emperor. Each individual at every level exerted power despotically, all the way down to the village level, to please the Confucian despot at the top of the hierarchy.

Did the Communist regime of Mao Zedong also use the concept of *baojia* to control the people? The answer is yes. From the time of the Shaanxi period, the CCP, under the leadership of Mao Zedong, established the groundwork to penetrate the peasant household at the village level. The structure of representative government began with the village soviet (the smallest unit), the district soviet, the county soviet, and the provincial and central soviets. Each village elected delegates to the higher soviets and also elected delegates for the Soviet Congress.[38]

The CCP knew that without the universal support of the villages, it could not win the revolution. To win the support of the peasants and to give that support continuity, the CCP organized the Chinese peasants at the village level.[39] Thus, organized peasants were willing to listen to the CCP for direction in their life, making them fertile ground for sowing the seeds of social control and enabling the CCP to reach the highest plateau of social control in China. Two institutions played a vital role in this process of social control—the people's commune (*renmin gongshe*) and the work unit (*danwei*).

Renmin Gongshe

The level of participation by the people in the communes from village to household level was unprecedented in the history of the world. The masses came out in the millions to fulfill the order of the government. However, this does not mean that the masses had control over the government or the institutions. In fact, both constitutional democracies and communist dictatorships are participant polities.[40] As Rousseau said, "A citizen owes the state all the services he can render it as soon as the sovereign requests them. But the sovereign, for its part, cannot impose on the subjects any burden that is useless to the community."[41]

When the orders from the government become a burden on the masses and the masses cannot react openly, authoritarian control is manifested. While the Chinese masses participated in great numbers during the Great Leap Forward, it was a participation from without and not a participation from within. Participation from within means that the citizens are involved in the decision-making process through their representatives in the Senate or Parliament. The legislative body must reflect the opinion of the masses. If it does not, the masses have the right, protected through written law and agreed upon by the majority, to throw their representatives, or even the head of state, out of the government.

Participation from without means that the masses do not have any role in the decision-making process, but they can participate under the auspices of the government and its institutions. This might be voluntary—through persuasion or under a covert or overt threat. Whatever the reason for participation may be, the masses do not have any right to hold the government accountable even if the government dictated burdens that are worthless to the population. The greater the possibility of participation from without by the masses in a system, the greater the social control and the more authoritarian the government will be (see Figure 4.2). There is a direct correlation between the possibility of participation from without and the degree of control the government has over the masses.

When we analyze the people's commune (*renmin gongshe*) in China vis-à-vis social control, we should keep the concept of participation from without in mind. This helps to understand the magnitude of social control through the Maoist institutions imposed on the Chinese people who were traditionally used to authoritarianism based on Confucian imperial power.

Following the tradition of Confucian authoritarianism, the CCP, under the leadership of Mao, established institutions to control the masses in the rural areas at the lowest level of the hierarchy, the villages. The villages were divided into *xiang*, which was a collection of actual villages. In the cities,

Figure 4.2
Level of Social Control

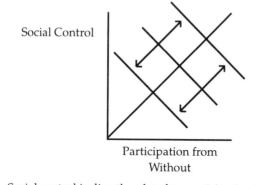

Social Control

Participation from
Without

Social control is directly related to participation from without.

urban residents committees encompassing 100–600 households were set up for the same purpose.[42]

The role of Confucian Mao in the social control over the masses was very powerful. During the Cultural Revolution, children were taught their role in filial piety—they were urged to rebel against their parents if their parents' position did not synchronize with the thoughts of Mao Zedong. It is consistent with Confucian teaching that the position of parents should reflect the emperor's wishes. Moreover, the Red Guards' slogan "Long Live Chairman Mao," appears to be Confucianism revisited. The characters that represent *Wan Sui* (Long Live), literally means ten thousand years. This slogan was used by the Chinese when saluting the emperor in ancient times. The Japanese also used the same term, pronounced *banzai*, in saluting emperor Hirohito.[43]

"Immaculate Mao" in Confucian China was the symbol of authority to whom the Chinese people looked for guidance and direction. As the famous writer Dai Qing said: "For years, I was a good girl for the Party. I used to think Mao Zedong was a god. Later I found out he was just a person. When I realized he could make some mistakes, I knew I had to speak out."[44] Another seventy-three-year-old, physicist Xu Liangying, who spent twenty years exiled on a farm said: "I worshipped him. Whatever Mao said, I believed."[45] So when Mao called for agricultural cooperation for 500 million peasants in 1955, the seeds for the people's commune were sown.[46] The commune was created to cover almost every aspect of daily life.[47]

The urge to move the Chinese toward egalitarianism did not make the cadres and villagers immune from Confucian symbols of authority. Local cadres in the rural areas started to carry flashlights and pens, and smoked cigarettes instead of homemade leaf tobacco. The peasants associated these symbols with the cadres' authority, and the idea was enforced by work teams sent down from urban areas. The higher a cadre's rank, the bigger the flashlight he carried. "The Party secretary would have a flashlight with four D-size batteries while a team leader felt it wisest to use a less powerful one with only two batteries. This was not codified but everyone knew the rules of the game,"[48] which had been implanted in the minds of the Chinese masses from age-old practice during the imperial period. In other words, Communist China was not exempt from Emperor Ming Tai zu's Confucianism.

The establishment of urban people's communes was also tried without much success, and the effort was abandoned in 1959. This does not mean, however, that urban populations were immune from the power exercised by the CCP. The *danwei* played the role of commune or ancient *baojia* for the urban population.

Danwei

Regardless of Mao's rejection of the Confucian philosophy of a hierarchical relationship between all people, Confucianism dictated the relationships between all people in the post–1949 era. Dependence on authority for guidance in the daily activities of life and finding a place in society was never really eliminated. In fact, the Confucian way of life was enforced with more effective coercive processes by the CCP. Instead of creating a new way of life based on egalitarianism, the CCP continued to rule China based on "hierarchical authority relations and paternalism . . . [in] almost every unit relationship."[49]

Hu Min, a professor of social psychology at Nankai University said that without *danwei* permission, an individual cannot marry, go abroad, find a job, or move. In one sense, you can't do anything. But as a *danwei* member, if the professor wanted to buy a house from the *danwei*, he might have to pay 20,000 yuan, whereas a private business person would have to pay 150,000 to 200,000. "Though one's *danwei* benefits a person, the main purpose is total control." In particular, "*danwei* in some aspects represent a tragedy for intellectuals. There is no free thinking, and intellectuals cannot move freely to enhance their talents and research. My salary, position, and sometimes my fame and recognition are provided by *danwei*. If one wants to marry a women one loves, one needs to get *danwei* permission, which may be denied on grounds that the woman is from a 'bad family background' (*jiating chushen bu hao*). Danwei control[s] not only an individual's life but also the family members'. If I don't belong to a good [rich and politically strong] *danwei*, my son has no good future."[50]

Danwei as an institution literally controls almost every aspect of life from cradle to grave. The following case in Beijing helps to illustrate the point. A teacher who took part in the democracy wall protest in the late 1970s, during the post–Mao era, was laid off from his job by his *danwei* because of this action. Later, he was offered a job as a janitor in the same school where he had taught. To the *danwei* committee members, this was not enough. The students were encouraged to spit on the ex-teacher while he was at work. "They were still doing so when he committed suicide. No one was allowed to go to the cremation except the family, because the *danwei* decided anyone who had advocated democracy should receive the minimum of mourning."[51]

Perhaps the officials in Tianjin chose to ignore my research activities because it was not against the government's position. Or it may be that the *danwei* and other methods of social control have become weaker due to economic reform, which might have reduced their will to exercise power. On the other hand, because of economic freedom the Chinese masses have learned to ignore free housing, medical care, the retired "nosey" men (those who spy on others) and women, and so on. Some might even be able to afford to rent a private residence and arrange for their own medical treatment and education for their children. "Suddenly that stick, and the *danwei* Communist Party secretary who wields it, does not seem so threatening." This led Dai Qing, who was jailed in 1989 because of her prodemocracy involvement, to say, "In the past, the [*danwei*] used to give your housing, your salary, your medical treatment. Now this in no longer true. This is the greatest achievement of the reforms."[52] Another former official who worked for the Communist Party Central Committee, said, "The party can't control anything outside of politics these days. It's just like the Qing Dynasty before it collapsed."[53]

The institutions of *baojia*, the commune, and *danwei* illustrate clearly China's historical influence by Confucianism. This traditional dependency on authority breeds life uncertainty. For the entrepreneurs, it is worse. In addition to the historical forces and recent politics that dictate their behavior, entrepreneurs receive scorn from many sectors of society, including the supporters of Maoism. This makes the position of entrepreneurs in Chinese society very unstable; thus, both socially and physically, entrepreneurs are unable to contribute fully to the economic development of China. Entrepreneurs simply cannot escape the life-uncertainty factor. In China, any deviation receives harsh punishment, which makes it even more difficult to ignore authority. A look at the Chinese system vis-à-vis the role of authority may help to understand the concept of social control.

The Chinese System

Confucianism also influences the government's behavior in ruling the masses through organized institutions that in turn affect the constituent groups of the system (see Figure 4.3). In spite of Mao's effort to eradicate Confucianism, even he succumbed to its pull and used it to give authority

Figure 4.3
Work of Authority in Confucian China

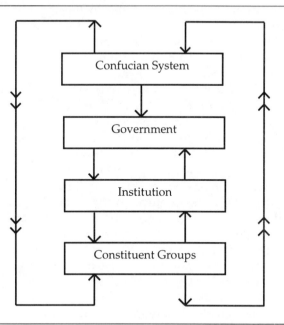

to communist ideological rhetoric. On the other hand, constituent groups are able to influence the Confucian system to adapt to new ideas and thoughts. These groups are also able to influence institutions and thereby the government, making them very dynamic.

The relationship between ruler and the ruled is dictated by economic survival. Any policy implemented by the ruler through the country's institutions that becomes a burden on the constituent groups will push the system toward economic death, threatening economic survival and ultimately the ruling class. This happened during and after the socialist transformation, when the constituent group composed of entrepreneurs became an economic liability. Thus, when constituent groups become a liability for the ruling class, thereby threatening their survival, the government and its institutions change. Constituent groups in China, thus, are both able to influence and be influenced by their institutions and the government. As the famous political thinker and poet Su Dong-po (1035–1101) said, no one can oppose the trend of the times (constituent groups) effectively, not even a cruelly tyrannical ruler or a sage, and therefore laws and institutions follow changes in customs.[54]

In any society rulers base their power on two things—the belief that they are a representative of God with a God-given right to rule, and the belief in their place in the economic order of the society.[55] As a result of the CCP victory, the government owns most of the economy and has extraordinary political and economic power.[56]

When this economic power is threatened by the inability of constituent groups to produce positive economic results in a communist economic system, the institutions and government change in order to survive. This is how constituent groups in Confucian China were able to influence the government (and its institutions) to change.

But just how are constituent groups able to influence the Confucian system? Today in China professors are participating in business, students are working part time, business people are respected, government officials are openly involved in business, and vocational training is sometimes substituted for formal education. These factors are putting pressure on the traditional Confucian society to accept new ideas and to change.

The contemporary Chinese are changing and incorporating new ideas, thereby influencing both the Confucian system and the government and other institutions. This does not mean that the Confucian authoritarian system will disappear in the foreseeable future. An inherent pattern of complete authority, whether by virtue of a mandate from heaven or due to strong military power, along with centuries-old Confucian morality and filial piety, have caused the Chinese to respect and fear men of authority. The government will continue to wield tremendous power and influence the behavior of the constituent groups, including entrepreneurs. As one entrepreneur said, "First the reform and open policy gave me everything. The government gives us a lot of support."[57] This suggests that entrepreneurs will continue to look up to reform-minded officials in the government who made it possible for them to revive so rapidly after a lapse of thirty years, thereby giving rise to a new economic culture. However, any sign of reversal of the reform policy will likely make the entrepreneurs withdraw from the economic arena. However, in addition to government policy, the historical entrepreneurial culture during the imperial period is the other factor that facilitated the rapid comeback of entrepreneurs.

ENTREPRENEURSHIP DURING THE IMPERIAL PERIOD

Entrepreneurs played an important role in economic activities during the Song period; the Ming-Qing and republican eras were no exception. Marco Polo, who visited China during the Yuan dynasty under the rule of Kublai Khan, remarked on the merchants trading gold, silver, and food products with paper money. Under Kublai Khan's domain, no one dared to "refuse to accept [paper currency] in payment."[58]

The merchants of the Ming-Qing era were no less remarkable than the merchants of the Yuan era. To clarify the position and achievements of merchants in the economic arena during the late Ming era, Fairbank and Reischauer distinguished between the imperial rule and the country as a whole. A look at the late Ming economy as a whole revealed "much evidence of growth in almost all its aspects—population, area of cultivated land, volume of foreign trade, production of handicraft and industrial goods, and even, perhaps, in the use of money."[59] The volume of internal trade was so high during the late Ming and early Qing periods, it left a deep impression on the minds of the Jesuits.[60] Du Halde, a Jesuit, said, "The inland trade of China is so great that the commerce of all Europe is not to be compared therewith; the provinces being like so many kingdoms; [that] . . . plenty reign in all cities."[61]

The economic activities of Chinese business people went on even after the end of the Qing dynasty. Chapters 2 and 3 have pointed out how the economic activities of the private sector survived until the Cultural Revolution. In the late 1970s, the private sector was able to revive again with the approval of the government. The Mao Zedong era was too short to break the chain of the Chinese people's entrepreneurial culture. Ten to fifteen years of disruption was not enough to erase the memory of entrepreneurial activities.

RUSSIA IN COMPARISON

Russia, formerly a communist country, is not doing well with its economic reform movement. Unlike China, in Russia those who are

> [u]nder 45 and above 75, the "children" and grandfathers, as it were, were generally in favour of cooperatives [private entrepreneurship]. Between 45 and 60 opinions varied and were generally less emotional, but [of] those between 60 and 75 years of age 80% were categorically opposed to cooperatives. . . . [T]he "children" are open to change and have a high demand for services while "grandfathers" have pleasant memories of their own enterprises in the 1920s. The opposing "fathers," on the other hand, discard cooperatives as unnecessary [and are actively involved in local affairs]. Thus, they have a greater proportionate influence on "public psychology" than the "children" or "grandfathers."[62]

This may help to explain why entrepreneurial activities are not flourishing in Russia, in spite of the similar historical experience between Russian and Chinese entrepreneurial activities and a strong cultural belief in authority. The Russians had a system similar to *baojia* termed *mir*, and communist collective farming, as well as city and village soviets, "[encompassed] virtually every activity of every citizen within its hierarchy."[63]

As for entrepreneurial activities in imperial Russia, Arcadius Kahan discussed in great detail the activities of Russian merchant-entrepreneurs during the eighteenth century in areas such as silk, linen, artillery and munitions, paper industries, brick, cotton, and others.[64]

The success of Russian entrepreneurs ushered in the nineteenth century. Heinrich Storch, a famous Russian economist during the rule of

Alexander I, said this about the native businessmen who started as peddlers and ended up millionaires: "The numerous instances of the rapid success of such people almost exceed description."[65] This reflection of entrepreneurial talent and practice was candidly captured by Dmitri Mendeleev when he reported on Russian industry for the World International Exposition of 1893 in Chicago: "Moscow . . . now concentrates so many enterprising people and forms such an advanced economic center that it will long remain at the head of the extensive manufacturing development destined for Russia."[66]

But, unlike China, Russia has a longer history of communism and the number of private entrepreneurs who were alive in the 1920s is very small. Moreover, Mikhail Gorbachev's *perestroika* (restructuring) resulted in a coup, and President Boris Yeltsin's experiment with private ownership resulted in a shootout in the Russian White House between Yeltsin and Vice President Alexander Rutskoi, leader of the hardliners. The resulting level of uncertainty, which has no relation to pure economic activities in the United States, undermines entrepreneurial activities. In China, by contrast, Deng's government provided a protective umbrella over the country's contemporary entrepreneurs and opened up opportunities making it possible for entrepreneurial activities to flourish again.

China's entrepreneurs have two characteristics deeply rooted in tradition. First, the Chinese entreprenuer looks to authority for direction and security; second, is the intrinsic entrepreneurial culture. When Deng's institutions created an environment for these two factors to come together, it produced positive results, thereby giving the new economic culture a chance to evolve. Not all of the new economic culture is really new, however; rather the Chinese are discovering what was buried in the past or what they had to give up under communism. To the Chinese, who were able to retain their traditional culture for more than 5,000 years, thirty years of CCP chaos is just a small dent in traditional values. Paradoxically, the CCP in many cases advocated traditional values in the guise of communism. Accordingly, the new economic culture simply means letting the Chinese be Chinese. Before examining this evolving new economic culture, there is one important factor that distinguishes individuals in China today, including the country's entrepreneurs, from the imperial Chinese or Mao's Chinese—the emergence of a "fax culture."

Fax Culture

The Chinese of Deng's era can readily obtain more information than was possible in the past through the foreign mass media, such as videotapes, radio, magazines, and even textbooks. Apartment buildings all over China are equipped with satellite dishes, which broadcast MTV and British Broadcasting Corporation television news programs. Although the satellite dishes are nominally banned, even state-owned stores sell them.[67] Present-day Chinese are coming into contact with foreign business people, students, and tourists. Rural-urban interaction also occurs on a daily basis. Whether in Qufu, at the Great Wall, or elsewhere, Chinese from all over the country visit in the thousands. They are interacting not only with each other but with foreigners, thereby injecting more new ideas into their own system. The *danwei* is losing control over the people, and the Chinese are slowly giving up the old culture of the "iron rice bowl." In other words, the Chinese nation as a whole is changing and the government will have to accommodate the changes. Young Chinese talk about politics, religion, and freedom, and modern technology is feeding that flame.

In one case, after a painstaking lecture on international relations to 200 students, a teacher was shocked by the students' questions. The teacher was asked, "What brand of cigarettes do Americans smoke?" One student asked if the teacher "liked the American way of life!" The teacher complained, "These kids are really off the track."[68] Perhaps they are just in a transition, moving toward something new and different from their communist past and giving rise to a new economic culture.

NEW ECONOMIC CULTURE

The previous discussion pointed out how two forces worked together to undermine the social status of entrepreneurs. One force was Confucianism, which looked down on business perople as parasitic but continued to allow entrepreneurial activities. To make the situation worse, the second force, Marxism, emerged and terminated entrepreneurial activities in the private sector. Under a heavy barrage of government-sponsored propaganda against the private entrepreneur, citizens learned to despise private ownership and become dependent on the government, to embrace the "iron rice bowl." Accordingly, when private entrepreneurial activities were allowed in the late 1970s, it was not welcomed by many facets of society. It took a long time and considerable governmental persuasion to convince the masses that private entrepreneurial activities were good for the nation.

The following section analyzes how the status of entrepreneurs is changing in a positive direction because of changes in Chinese society. Also, the reform-minded leaders, with the approval of Deng Xiaoping, are advocating private entrepreneurship and encouraging citizens to view entrepreneurship as beneficial to society. This is helping entrepreneurs to overcome the fear of life uncertainty.

Status of Entrepreneurs

A letter to the editor from Xiao Lingling in *Beijing Ribao* on August 18, 1980, caused quite a lot of excitement among readers in China. She wrote:

A small-time premise today may well expand into a big one tomorrow. While capitalists of the old days are still living, new ones will before long come on the scene, with so many people intent on money-grubbing and so many small shops and roadside stalls cluttering the streets and compromising the good name of our capital city. . . . Socialist civilization and science—that's what we are after, not all these things which are quite out of place in a socialist country like ours.[69]

The threat reflected in this 1980 letter was still felt by entrepreneurs in 1991. As one entrepreneur in Tianjin said:

It is very difficult [to do business] in China because in history such individual businessmen were looked down upon and Western concepts of entrepreneurship were just imported to China. China pays more attention to equal pay and does not emphasize personal development.[70]

In some cases, private ownership brought active opposition by the masses against successful entrepreneurs. Guan Guangmei, a successful middle-aged woman entrepreneur from Benxi city, Liaoning Province, leased eight shops through public bidding and made a handsome profit. This caused a sensation in Benxi, and Guan was accused of exploitation and following the capitalist road. Nonetheless, the Benxi government came to her rescue. She was later elected to be a delegate to the 13th Party Congress. However, Han Wenguang of Tianjin, another successful entrepreneur, did not fare well with the officials. His application for CCP membership was canceled on the grounds that in addition to exploitation in hiring workers, he engaged in hiring ex-prisoners and "organizing a 'dare-to-die corps.' In fact, Han [had simply] offered these workers a job which nobody else was prepared to give them."[71]

The sentiment conveyed in the letter to the editor and feared by entrepreneurs was quite common in the early days of private entrepreneurial activities. Even the word nongovernment would provoke controversy, and private businesses were considered to be the "hot bed of the middle class and capitalism."[72] It took a strong stand by the government, and national leaders like the late Hu Yaobang and Deng Xiaoping had to come forward in public to change the minds of the people, including entrepreneurs, about private ownership. In addition, the government used editorials by citizens to face the conservative forces. As quoted earlier, "To be paid for your work is a socialist principle. It has no relationship with 'money-grubbing.' "[73]

The stand against private entrepreneurial activities was not limited to China. In Russia, "the first private taxis were greeted with comments such as 'fetch the police' or 'look at that impudent privateer!' Occasionally the new entrepreneurs even face active resistance from the population."[74] Culture was one of the reasons for Russian opposition to private entrepreneurial activities. Marxist ideological influence on the masses and officials was heavy, resulting in mistrust of private enterprise.[75]

It was not only that the masses and officials felt negatively about the rise of the private sector; entrepreneurs themselves were ambivalent in the beginning about their own activities. One entrepreneur in China wrote to *Jingji Ribao* (*Economic Daily*) in 1987:

> Since I started out in private business, I've been very depressed, and wanted to talk about my feelings. . . . [W]herever I look, there are only white eyes and red eyes [disdain and envy]. In the last few years, not only have I borne the physical burden of labour, but also a spiritual hardship which is difficult to describe. It's true! I now have money, my material life is very rich. . . . You would think I would be satisfied. But I am actually more and more unhappy and dread my leisure, because as soon as I stop work a voice appears in my mind: "individual businessman—second-class citizen."[76]

One entrepreneur, when I asked him why he did not want to continue his business, responded, "I have earned enough money to get married and my parents want me to improve my social status (because in some cases business perople were still looked down upon, according to the interviewee). At first it was a temporary step, but now I do not have the desire to continue."[77] But another entrepreneur answered in quite a different way. He supported the proposition that China is in transition, and that many entrepreneurs are feeling good about themselves and discovering hidden talents. When asked about the traditional attitude of contempt toward entrepreneurs, he replied:

> I don't think China has such a history [of looking down at individual businessman]. I think individual business is the reflection of my interest and personality. It is a formal profession. I also hope my friends and my children join with me. At first, I started my business for money. Money was everything at that time. But now I think I am young and my personality and ability is fit for doing well in individual business. I really wish I could make China's economy more dynamic and I would make people lead a better life.[78]

As time passed, the scorn for private business diminished. A survey of young people reflected that they would prefer to be entrepreneurs, while "national government work ranked 8th out of 16 choices" on the list.[79] With this enhancement of the image of entrepreneurs, some entrepreneurs in Tianjin and other places in China are feeling good about themselves,[80] and feel that they can contribute to society. This fosters an attitude that to function well in society, an individual needs not only a favorable environment but to feel good about him- or herself. As one entrepreneur said, "In spite of earning a lot of money, one should be happy to do business."[81]

Two other college graduate entrepreneurs went into depth to express their feelings. The first one said:

> I think people in the world should work hard. Yes, they should work hard. Yes, I want to work hard, to do something useful, make our country strong and make our people have a better life. Everybody can have a good education. I like to help my country, to build a new country.
>
> [Society] admires [an individual businessman]. Friends admire you if you open a private company. They think you can do everything even if it is difficult, because it is difficult to open a company. In China it takes a lot of courage and ability to open a new company. I do not know [what will happen if I fail]. Maybe it is a problem. Yes, it is a problem of losing one's face. I do not think it is important whether you lose face or not. It is important for us to build a good company and to make it run, to gain experience and ability. These are important. I do not want to hear about common people's opinions. I want to know the opinion of a wise man. Common people will admire [me] if I succeed but they will laugh at me if I fail. So I care about the opinion of the wise people.[82]

The second entrepreneur expressed similar sentiments. He said:

> Money is not everything for me. The first thing is social responsibility. China has many problems, and as a Chinese intellectual, as a Chinese college student just graduated from Nankai, I do like to combine my own fate with China and devote myself to the Country and the people.[83]

Some Russian entrepreneurs convey a similar attitude. As one Russian private manager-entrepreneur said, "Just running a company and making a lot of money isn't enough. My goal is to do something to help revive Russia's economy."[84]

Many entrepreneurs are positive about their profession and the government played an important role in this turnaround. Entrepreneurs witnessed the government's attitude toward them changing from "severe ban to reluctant tolerance and finally to encouragement."[85] This government support for economic development through private ownership is encouraging others to speak up in favor of reform in a manner that would have been unthinkable in the Mao era. The following statement made by the chairperson of the JinBei Automobile Shareholding Company, Zhao Xiyou, would shock Lenin and Mao. After hearing reports from top executives of the company, many of whom were CCP members, he responded, "Learn from

General Motors and Toyota, not Lenin and Mao. Don't waste your time on theory."[86]

The active recognition of private entrepreneurial activities by the government is also helping to change the minds of people in the society. This is often reflected in statements given by entrepreneurs. One said, "I think this phenomenon [of looking down on individual business people] has changed a lot. With the reform and development, more and more Chinese admire rich people and realize the importance of money."[87] Another said, "Lots of members of society like my success and very few do not. Nowadays, people think it is all right to do business and make money."[88] This new phenomenon of admiring entrepreneurs, which is occurring slowly in Chinese society, is not a one-way process. Value must be given in order to receive something in return. As one entrepreneur put it, "They [society] think that I bring convenience to them. At the same time I earn money. Yes, they [others] praise me and admire me a little. Now the society has changed. Those who work hard and earn more are admired and aren't looked down upon any more."[89]

Government officials and Chinese newspapers are providing reinforcement for this improvement in the status of private entrepreneurs. Minister of Commerce Hu Ping stated that people from all walks of life are involved in private economic activities. "The traditional idea of looking down on business people has been discarded."[90] It was reported in *China Daily* that a successful entrepreneur once "believed himself inferior to the white-skinned, blue-eyed and high-nosed foreigners," but after visiting Russia on a business trip, he felt good about himself and expressed that, "It was the first time that I realized I was considered rich in some foreigners' eyes. Being able to go abroad, I feel, small-scale business people are gaining social status."[91]

This gradual gain of social status by private entrepreneurs, however, may reflect a loss of status for government officials and academics. Workers were another group that enjoyed the ideological favor of the CCP. A 1987 survey of attitudes among the residents of thirty-three cities, where N = 2,348 (total number of subjects), found that 71.6 percent of workers felt that their social status had fallen. When asked what they wanted from reform, 40.2 percent said they wanted to see an increase in personal income; 24.4 percent said a complete legal system (which may indicate that the Chinese are not satisfied with their present legal system); and 25 percent hoped for higher personal social status.[92] In spite of their diminished social status, some workers have no complaint about their economic well-being. As one worker in a private company is reported to have said, "What exploitation? Here they pay us 200 yuan for one month's work. In the state factories you get at most 60 yuan for subsidiary work. You tell me who's exploiting who?"[93]

The social status of private entrepreneurs is improving, even in the midst of some contempt for their activities in Chinese society. This contempt for private profit-making may be understandable, however, if we apply the concept of jealousy in Chinese society. This helps to clarify the extent to which it is philosophical or ideological to dislike private entrepreneurial activities. As one entrepreneur in Tianjin said, "Those who also want to do business like us, admire us, but those who cannot do so, are jealous of us."[94]

Contempt or Jealousy

Jealousy, which the Chinese call *hong yan bing* or red-eye disease, may be viewed as a phenomenon of relative deprivation and may not have a strong link with philosophy or ideology. The group that does not benefit from the reforms used to enjoy the security of jobs, housing, and other social welfare, and may still be doing so. But the gap between the income of entrepreneurs and government employees has become so great that the social security, which was once enjoyed in the pre-Deng era, is be negligible at present.

A survey of 2,400 urban residents in forty-five cities found that 51 percent "felt at a loss in the face of rapidly changing social values." Fifty-six percent complained that they have had problems adjusting to the new values and expectations since the reform started. Sixty-three percent said that a person should work hard to succeed in his or her career, but 55 percent felt that "a safe and sound life surpasses all happiness." Seventy-nine percent expressed a desire to experience diversity in life, 82 percent expressed a desire for a tranquil life without too many changes, and more than 80 percent preferred job security over promotion. Their views on the suggestion to break the iron rice bowl, iron wages and iron post, once again reflected their "contradictory psychology."[95]

In this new environment created by the reform movement, many Chinese do not feel comfortable or have the desire to venture into entrepreneurial activities. When they see the huge income gap between workers, teachers, and government officials on the one hand, and private entrepreneurs or *getihu* on the other, they feel abandoned by the communist system. The result may be similar to the psychological phenomenon where the father hits the child, the child hits the dog, the dog chases the cat, and the cat catches the rat. In similar fashion, the Chinese people and the bureaucrats may target private entrepreneurs as the source of their misery.

An entrepreneur named Guo Chunmei, fifty-five-years old, experienced physical damage to her property because of jealousy. Guo ran a business renting innertubes to tourists and others at the Beidaihe seaside resort in Hebei province. Some people who envied her success tried to destroy her business. She said with tearful eyes, "Only jealous people would have done this. The other day, . . . scoundrels broke into my basement and pricked holes in my inner tubes and slashed my only sun umbrella."[96]

In Russia, entrepreneurs are earning huge amounts of money compared to most citizens. Some Russian entrepreneurs may earn $10,000 per month, while average workers may earn the ruble equivalent of $25 a month. Some Russian entrepreneurs also spend their money lavishly, for example, buying $50,000 apartments and $40,000 Mercedes cars and blowing "thousands of dollars at . . . favorite haunts." This kind of life-style and income gap draws the envy of the common Russian.[97] It was also reported in 1990 that Viktor Kuzmin, a successful entrepreneur, drew the envy of the authorities in Vologda because he held no official position to allow him to live in grandeur.[98]

Under such pressure from ideology, philosophy, and envy, some entrepreneurs in China spend their money as fast as they earn it on expensive parties, burial ceremonies, and other luxurious ways of life. It is reported that "millionaires vie with each other to spend more—one threw a 350,000 yuan ($60,900) banquet to outdo a peer."[99] On the other hand, some rich entrepreneurs follow traditional ways of Chinese life, showing kindness and generosity to keep trouble at bay as long as possible. There are many reports of entrepreneurs donating large sums of money or making contributions to society to earn good names for themselves. One example is Wang Mingxing, a native of Qintang Village of Gangtou Township, Fuqing in Fujian. Wang donated over 2 million yuan ($367,000) to good causes and received the recognition of the community and officials alike.[100]

Chinese entrepreneurs are still unsure about their status in society. Entrepreneurs are not sure if they want to save money and invest, become popular philanthropists, or spend money freely to enjoy it while they can, like many entrepreneurs of the 1950s. In fact "China is moving backward, forward, sideways, all at once. It is much more porous, mobile, corrupt and cosmopolitan than it has ever been before."[101] In this atmosphere of transition where a new economic culture is evolving, almost everybody is affected. Both academics and women are being affected significantly and are adjusting to the new evolving culture.

Academics

Confucius said, "Teachers are the prop of society." For Zheng Xiao, a sophomore at Beijing Normal University (BNU), the experience is different. She always wanted to be a teacher. Her dream was to get a teaching position in Beijing after graduation. But with the evolving new economic culture, teachers are losing their status in society, particularly in the big cities where there is more vigorous private economic activity. For this reason, Zhong decided to return to her small hometown in Gansu Province, where she felt that people still respected the teaching profession of Confucius dating back 2,500 years ago. She lamented that when she introduced herself as a student in a teacher-training school, people looked at her with such a strange expression as if she was suffering from a mental disease. Zheng is not alone.

Lan Mei, twenty-two, a graduate from BNU who earned 280 yuan ($46.70) per month, felt that her future was deadlocked. She said that money was secondary to her. What really disappointed her is that people paid less and less respect to teachers.

With reform came other opportunities to earn a living, thereby resulting in this phenomenon. People are no longer restricted to jobs provided by the government. "For many, teaching is one of their last choices."[102] College graduates, intellectuals, and artists are discarding the idea that "[m]en of letters should not involve themselves in business, while office bureaucrats should not deal with accounting."[103]

The increasing tendency of Chinese graduates and intellectuals to venture into private economic activities and not worry about losing face did not happen overnight. In fact, the phenomenon mirrored the changing status of business people. In the beginning, the government and proponents of reform strongly advocated removing the shackles of tradition and Confucianism to persuade intellectuals to get involved with private economic activities. Economist Cai Beihua, an early proponent of the reforms, proposed in 1980 that China protect its entrepreneurs socially and economically.[104]

Realizing the important role that Chinese rulers play in shaping and reshaping the thinking and behavior of the people, the present rulers came forward to convey the message to college students to work hard. Students in most parts of China took the call seriously and worked to earn money. In contrast to earlier periods, about 70 percent of students in Beijing stayed in the capitol during the summer of 1992 to do various kind of jobs. A son of a rich *ganbu*, who did not need to work, worked during the summer to prove to his friends that he was not rich and lazy. Another student with rich parents worked in construction, over his parents' objections, to prove to his peers that he too had the ability to earn his own living. He was proud to show off his tanned body with broadened shoulders by unbuttoning his shirt. In other cases college students are working as shoeshiners in tourist spots[105] or cleaning and polishing cars "to raise some income for the coming school year."[106]

It was reported in September of 1992 that most of the household services companies (more than twenty in number) were run by college graduates and that nearly 90 percent of the employees had university or technical background. The companies did almost everything needed to make life comfortable for their customers, from cleaning drains to helping people move. A 1986 Beijing University graduate name Chen Shu quit his state-run magazine job and joined a household service company to build a better future. He said, "A man who expects to realize his self-value should do what he wants to do first."[107]

Such developments make it clear that the old thinking about manual work or any kind of profit-oriented work is changing in China. Students are creating peer pressure to discard their image of ivory tower intellectuals and realize the reality of economics. In fact, "this trend of highly-educated people opting for physical work in households [and other areas] confirms a trend in social development. It reflects the change in values of many young intellectuals."[108]

Interestingly, Mao also tried to pry intellectuals and students out of the ivory tower. At the end of the Cultural Revolution, when the Red Guards became a liability to Mao and his interests, he directed the Red Guards and intellectuals to go to the countryside and learn from the peasants about the Maoist way of life.[109] And for an educated youth who wanted to prove to others that he or she was a good Maoist, he or she had to return "with a dark skin and a red heart."[110] Similarly, after the June 1989 Tiananmen Square massacre, Deng directed students to work and earn money and be good Dengists with tanned bodies and golden hearts.

Chinese parents used to be embarrassed if their children took part-time jobs, but times have changed. The parents themselves are competing for second jobs and react positively if their children subsidize their limited income. In fact, during this time of transition, parents are unsure how life will be for their children in the future.[111]

In spite of the traditional Confucian culture and philosophy that dictates the behavior of learned people, in many cases basic microeconomic needs compel them to reevaluate their positions in Chinese society. A rational creature, if left alone in a free market economy, will venture into economic activities to meet his or her basic needs and try to gain maximum satisfaction from any given economic interaction with the society. In this process, the individual will not only contribute to the economy as a whole but will also influence the social values and thinking of the rest. For the rest of society to survive in a free market economy, they will have to emerge from their Confucian and/or communist shells. However, if individuals try to retreat into their shells in the future, they might find a decomposed shell waiting for them.[112]

Whatever their intentions might be, many professors and CCP officials are venturing into economic activities that might have been viewed in the past as degrading to their prestige and status in society. With government encouragement, officials at all levels are plunging into the sea (*Xia hai*)— slang for going into business. The only restriction the government imposes on officials is not to participate in illegal business. Factory workers and students are also venturing into private business, and professors are working as private consultants.

In fact, professors and teachers are venturing into many kinds of money-making activities on their own. They have even been seen peddling goods in markets. "A noted professor was spotted peddling pancakes. He was seen selling them on the campus of Beijing Normal University."[113] Officials from the State Education Commission are coming forward to shield the professors from any kind of criticism by society. They are stating that professors who hold a second job benefit the economic growth of the country because intellectuals from higher learning institutions will be able to contribute their knowledge toward scientific and technological development, perhaps by working for the private sector in research and development. However, some critics are objecting to this phenomenon feeling that the problems far outweigh the benefits. One such critic said, "After all, school is a place for education and a teacher's primary care should be the students, not money."[114]

Nonetheless, the critics at this point are losing to the forces of microeconomic needs. The intellectuals are not listening to the critics; economic survival is dictating their behavior, just as it has dictated the country's rulers'. They are leaving their government allocated jobs in great numbers, creating a talent gap in the public sector. In 1991–1992, many scholars left government research and teaching jobs. About 7,000 teachers in Hunan Province left their jobs between 1990 and 1992, and most of them were less than forty-five years old. Li Hongjun, vice-president at the Educational Commission of Liaoning Province, said that it was difficult to project how many intellectuals at universities have left for business but commented that intellectuals were leaving in large numbers. The same is true at institutions of higher education throughout China. The consolation to critics is "that the brain drain seems inevitable but that the solution is to let the market completely redistribute talented workers, putting them into jobs that give them the best opportunities to use their abilities."[115]

These events should not lead to the conclusion that the value of education or respect shown to intellectuals will diminish in China. Intellectuals will still be an important part of Chinese culture. As one entrepreneur said,

> Everybody should pursue something. I admire those who have knowledge, higher education. But the time for me to go to college has passed. What I am able to do now is to earn more money. I have already earned [saved] 20,000 yuan. I can live a better life depending on the interest. Now I work for self-satisfaction and fame.[116]

Another entrepreneur, a high school graduate, said, "Some are jealous of me and some admire me. I wish I had more education."[117] But with the evolving new economic culture, values and thinking will be adjusted and put into proper perspective. In this respect, some parts of China are moving faster than others. It is reported that scientists [intellectuals] in the northern and inland regions are refusing to accept awards for their hard work, or if they do accept awards, they share their bonuses with colleagues. By contrast, in the coastal and southern areas the rewards are accepted with "ease and pride, signifying that the thinking pattern that has influenced the Chinese for more than 2,000 years is undergoing a subtle change. Individual talents are gaining more recognition than before."[118] One Japanese executive, addressing the difference between northern and southern Chinese, said, "Well it depends. If you prefer their style, you can say that northerners are more principled; if not, you might find them a bit too stubborn and disputatious. Southerners are just the opposite. They are more vicarious, if you want to put it nicely."[119]

With the advent of private ownership, private and nondegree schools are coming into existence in China. Those who could not or will not be able to go to public school can try their chances with private schools or vocational training—nondegree schools with specialty fields such as cosmetology, secretarial skills, languages, restaurant management, and so on. One businessman who quit school at the age of seventeen, returned to a nondegree school ten years later to learn English. He said, "I felt pressure to learn a foreign language since more and more foreigners are coming to visit Beijing. If I can speak English, I won't appear so clumsy in front of foreigners and I can attract more foreign customers." Another woman enrolled in a cooking school with the hope of opening a Chinese restaurant in Japan.[120] These developments suggest that there will be more and more skilled people in China, although China will have to redefine its concept of academics and scholars to accommodate the new talents of people who will be demanding respect from society. Related to this discussion is the question of how women are faring in the evolving new economic culture.

Women and the New Economic Culture

Women are a very important part of any economic development because they represent half of a country's labor and intellectual power. From my observation in China, I found the women to be hardworking and talented. Many of them were entrepreneurial in nature, but compared to men most women were careful and seldom agreed to being interviewed. However, with the evolving economic culture and the revival of the old Confucian values in China, many women are losing the ground they had gained during the CCP rule through the mid-1970s.

Before addressing the present, a look at the past is necessary. Fu Xuan, a third century poet, once lamented at the misery of women in China. He wrote, "By her the family sets no store."[121] The fate of women in traditional China is also aptly reflected in the following story:

Before one of these houses, many years ago, two little boys sat talking.

"Seng," said one, "what do you think father and mother will do with our little girl-baby? I wish they would keep it, don't you?"

. . . "If we ask father very much, he may let us keep our baby," said Lau, the other boy. "Mother wants to keep it. I heard her ask father yesterday not to have it killed. Why do people kill little girls? Why can they not live as well as boys?"[122]

If a girl were allowed to live, chances were that she would be sold into slavery and then resold into marriage. Then it might have happened that "she may be kidnapped by bad men and sold into a life of shame."[123] The suffering of women in China's traditional male-dominated society lasted until the the CCP came to power. Although the CCP was not able to completely eradicate the traditional life of women, they did greatly impact society with a number of reforms. Due to marriage reform, education opportunity, economic freedom, and ideological commitment, women gained greater freedom.[124]

The *Renmin Ribao* of March 8, 1973, reported that Mao Zedong said, "Times have changed and today men and women are equal. Whatever men comrades can accomplish, women comrades can too."[125] Indeed, during the communist rule women were able to improve their position in society. When I was in China, I saw Chinese women in the urban areas conducting business with great self-confidence. They worked as businesswomen, bus drivers, police officers, and so on. Inside the house, I saw both working husbands and wives sharing the household chores equally, and in one case two adult sons helped their parents with the household duties, even in the kitchen.

Under the CCP, about 30 percent of official jobs are held by women and more than one-fifth of parliamentary deputies are women. But market economy reforms have witnessed the reemergence of some old habits and traditions. Confucian attitudes are present in Chinese society again. A recent survey of 100 women found that 60 of them would be willing to change their sex if they could. It was no surprise when it was reported that from 60 percent to over 70 percent of those fired from 1,175 enterprises were women. Many textile factories no longer hire women over forty, and some factories are refusing to hire women after they have given birth until their child is seven years old. Along with discrimination in jobs, other traditional ways of life are resurfacing in Chinese society. Today, Chinese women with normal feet are serving the desires of Confucian men. Men are keeping concubines[126] and using Chinese women as prostitutes. To meet the needs of men, Chinese women are being abducted and sold as wives and prostitutes. Infanticide, still widely practiced in the rural areas, and abortion have been haunting the female baby since adoption of the 1979 law mandating only one child per family. In the urban areas, ultrasound testing is used to reveal the sex of unborn children; a female fetus often faces abortion. "A conservative estimate of the babies killed [after birth] in the past 12 years [1979–1991] would be 1 million."[127]

If a baby girl survives birth and infancy in a poor family, she might be sold by her father, or tricked into going to big cities by a woman trafficker with promises of a good job and a better life. Women are then often beaten, raped, and sold into virtual bondage—often with the help of local CCP officials. The fact that it is much cheaper to buy a bride than to go through a traditional marriage (2,000 yuan compared to approximately 10,000 yuan), has created additional incentive for such trade in women. Trading in women has become a big business, with operations similar to modern corporations with nationwide networks. This practice is widely accepted because of the prevailing attitude that it is acceptable for men to buy and sell women.

Notwithstanding CCP claims that the sale of women was abolished in their first two decades of rule, with the market-oriented economic reforms, the past practices of treating women as cattle has returned. Abducted women are often locked up and, in some cases, their leg tendons are cut to prevent them from escaping. One student said that her eyes were gouged out. "In 1990, more than 10,000 abducted women were rescued . . . [and] . . . more than 65,000 people were arrested in 1989 and 1990 for trafficking in women and children."[128]

Women in China are facing discrimination and becoming more and more often sex objects in the job market, and in other places, under the new evolving market economy. It is impossible to disregard the connection with the prevailing Confucian view about women that claims women are inherently inferior and should always be under the command of men—father, husband, and sons respectively. This mindset was not eradicated in China by the CCP after 1949. A manager who did not want to hire women, particularly beautiful, talented ones, would likely give the following response to a local personnel bureau asking him to hire a women: "If it really comes to that, then send me an ugly one." In doing so, he would avoid problems related to women and possible accusations of personal sexual favors if he promoted a talented woman. In China, women are either laid off or not hired because factories or businesses cannot shoulder the losses caused by women bearing children.[129] To be beautiful is the ideal in today's society, however, and women are facing growing social pressure to look beautiful. "A young beautiful wife or mistress—called 'modern flower vase'—has become the symbol of a man's social status."[130]

In China, men have been glorified for thousands of years as the focus of the culture. With the advent of the market economy, women are losing ground in the job market. There are reports of women being used increasingly as office ornaments or as bait to attract business. Unfortunately, discrimination based on sex has been brought in by the market economy. With the market economy have come Western concepts of advertisements— beautiful young women—as well as pin-ups and pornography.[131] China's defense industry is also using beautiful women in published calendars, which have "been hot-selling items."[132]

The abuse of women in the new evolving market economy is contributing to the falling status and talents of women in China. In many places, women are underpaid or are being fired. Factory managers in Beijing and Shaoxing, due to market competition, are less willing to hire women in order to avoid loss. Income figures obtained showed that women were paid on average 71.7 percent of what men were paid.[133] In one Shanghai district, of 155 employees fired, 135—about 90 percent—were women. Those who were not fired received 70 percent of the average wage, and many were given only part-time jobs. In 1985, unemployed women were 59 percent of the total unemployment figure, rising to 62 percent in 1986 and 83 percent in 1989.[134]

This phenomenon of disrespect toward women and the use of them as sex objects is no less harmful to economic development than looking down on men who venture into business. This traditional attitude about women is a waste of human resources and it is hindering women from using their entrepreneurial and managerial talents for the economic development of China. In this electronic age, it is not a question of using muscles in the grain field, but of using brains to develop an economy. The earlier the Chinese realize this and allow women to take part in the country's economic development, the better it will be for China and the rest of the world.

In other former communist countries, the status of women is also declining. The introduction of a market economy seems to exacerbate female poverty. In Russia, women are also treated as sex objects in the job market.[135] With the introduction of market economy reforms, women are losing their jobs. Of the total unemployment figures in Russia as of August 1993, 70 percent were women, of whom about three-fourths were college or university graduates. Businesses do not conceal their attitudes about women in Russia. Advertisements convey the message that older women need not apply for certain jobs and candidates for jobs "will be expected to extend sexual favors."[136] Polish women are no better off than Russian or Chinese women. Even though Polish women gained status during the communist rule, "women's rights are often perceived as politically suspect and are frequently rejected along with the rest of the communist past."[137] Women have also been abducted in Russia, Bulgaria, Poland, and other Eastern European countries and forced into prostitution. Organized gangs have set up networks to bring women from former communist countries into Western Europe for sex.[138]

V. I. Lenin said, "Bourgeois democracy is the democracy of pompous phrases, solemn words, lavish promises and high-sounding slogans about freedom and equality, but in practice all this cloaks the lack of freedom and the inequality of women."[139] Lenin's words suggest that the economics of feminist poverty will be a growing part of a new market economic system. Unless an economy develops quickly along with pure democracy, where government and representatives will be truly accountable to the public, the economics of feminist poverty will continue in China, Russia, Poland, and other former communist countries.

However, for any economy to develop, cooperation between entrepreneurs, consumers, and an accountable government is necessary or an economy will eventually stagnate. This marriage of parties in a polity is not a simple process of uniting because of economic needs. It is a complex process in which politics or power struggle, often dictate the economic outcome.

Chapter 5

The Political Economy of China and Private Entrepreneurship

To appreciate the role of entrepreneurs in the economic development of China, it is important to also understand the political economy of China in the post–Mao era. The reason for bringing political economy under consideration is simple: economic development does not occur in a vacuum. Particularly in the case of China, political decisions made by leaders, or a single leader for that matter, always have great impact on the private and public sectors, thus affecting economic outcome. Entrepreneurial activities create a market dynamic by filling gaps in the economy and creating new jobs, increasing consumers' purchasing power of both durable goods and services. Acknowledging this factor, China's reformers made the political and ideological decision to release the people's productive forces. It is not only the privatization of rural and urban production that contribute to economic development but also the entrepreneurial talents of individuals. So, with Deng's economic reform, private entrepreneurs and *getihu*, as a natural phenomenon, came into existence in China regardless of the intentions of the policymakers.

In this chapter I discuss the struggle between the different factions in the CCP and how it affects the entrepreneurial activities of private citizens. The struggle between different factions sometimes accentuates the life-uncertainty factor and sometimes helps to reduce it, depending on who the struggle is favoring—hardliners or reformers. In response to the perceived outcome entrepreneurs react by increasing or decreasing economic activities, thus directly affecting the economic development of China. The hardliners try to establish greater control over the economy and push for a socialist model for China's economic development under the leadership of Chen Yun. In some cases the followers of Chen try to revive Maoism to justify their cause. The reformists, under the leadership of Deng Xiaoping, advocate a market economy and prefer private entrepreneurship over a state-run economy. To protect Dengism, the reformists (with the approval of Deng) discredit Mao and his economic principles, creating a power struggle in the CCP. Thus far the reformists have been able to keep the hardliners at bay but they pay a heavy price from time to time. For example, the removal of Hu Yaobang and Zhao Ziyang was a heavy blow to the reformists. In order to understand the political economy of China in the post-Mao era, we must first understand who Deng Xiaoping is and what he stands for.

DENG XIAOPING

Deng Xiaoping was the most important supporter of the reform process. When Deng came to power in 1977–1978, the economy of China was falling apart. By the end of the Cultural Revolution, political persecution and disarray had bulldozed China to the brink of bankruptcy. China's national income was 138,700 million yuan in 1965 and 394,000 million yuan in 1981. The missing link between 1965 to 1981 indicates the curse of the Cultural Revolution, which the Chinese people endured under the leadership of Mao Zedong (see Tables 5.1 and 5.2). When Deng came forward with his reform plan, it was a matter of China's economic and political survival; failure to institute reform might have brought about the country's disintegration. Deng not only had a vision for the economic survival of China, he also was prepared to use any means necessary to preserve his reform plan.

For much of the post–1949 era, China's political economy was implemented by Mao's mass campaigns. These campaigns were mostly coercive in nature and executed through the institution of *danwei* to produce both political and economic results. Mao said, "Political work is the life blood of all economic work. This is particularly true at a time when the social and economic system is undergoing fundamental change."[1]

Under these conditions where politics were in command over economics, Deng Xiaoping came to power to change China through private economic activity. Although he became the most powerful person in China, he never held the official position of president, chairman or general secretary of the CCP, or premier of the State Council. Instead, he served as general secretary of the Central Committee, chairman of the Central Military Commission (CMC), and vice-premier of the State Council. Deng ruled China through a network of faithful followers, thus exercising tremendous power and influencing the post–Mao era with Dengist ideology. The more power a policymaker has to make decisions in the state and a country, the fewer people above him there are to make decisions in the state and bureaucracy. Moreover, the less defined the role of the policymaker, the greater the chances are that his personal thinking or ideology will influence the decision-making process.[2]

Table 5.1
Main Indicators of the National Economy

Items	Units	1952	1957	1965	1981	1982	1983	1984
Year-end total population	million	574.82	646.53	725.38	100,072	101,541	102,495	103,604
National income	mil. yuan	58,900	90,800	138,700	394,000	426,100	467,300	548,500
Revenue	mil. yuan	18,370	31,020	47,330	109,000	112,400	124,900	146,500
Total volume of retail sales	mil. yuan	27,680	47,420	67,030	235,000	257,000	284,940	335,700

Source: Statistical Yearbook of China, 1985. Compiled by the State Statistical Bureau, P.R.C.

Table 5.2
Output of Major Industrial and Agricultural Products

Items	Units	1952	1957	1965	1981	1982	1983	1984
Coal	100 mil. tons	0.66	1.31	2.23	6.22	6.66	7.15	7.72
Electricity	100 mil. kwh	73	193	676	3,093	3,277	3,514	3,746
Crude oil	10,000 tons	44	146	1,131	10,122	10,212	10,607	11,453
Steel	10,000 tons	135	535	1,223	3,560	3,716	4,002	4,337
Grain	10,000 tons	16,390	19,505	19,455	32,502	35,450	38,728	40,712
Cotton	10,000 tons	130.4	164.0	209.8	296.8	359.8	463.7	607.7
Oil-bearing crops	10,000 tons	419.3	419.6	362.6	1,020.5	1,181.7	1,055.0	1,185.2
Output of pork, beef, and mutton	10,000 tons	338.5	398.5	551.0	1,260.9	1,350.8	1,402.1	1,525.0

Source: Statistical Yearbook of China, 1985. Compiled by the State Statistical Bureau, P.R.C.

A higher position might have put a limitation on Deng's power. Instead, Deng was able to intervene in any organ of the government, and the officials, bureaucrats, and the masses accepted the intervention in the belief that Deng was truly powerful and in command. By not holding a higher official position, Deng could avoid accountability for any actions taken, thereby making the act of decision making easier. This gave Deng tremendous power to move rapidly toward economic development of China.

Deng was born in Guang'an, Sichuan Province in 1904, the eldest son of a well-to-do landowner. At the age of sixteen, he went to France under a work-study program. There he became involved with the Chinese Socialist Youth League in 1922 and won the admiration of his peers while working as a mimeographer for the *Red Light* journal. In 1924 he joined the CCP.

Deng later told Edgar Snow that he simply worked as a laborer and had not studied while in France. After studying for several months in Moscow, he returned to China in 1926. His first position was as an instructor in the political department of the Xian Military and Political Academy. With the split of the GMD and the CCP, all Communist cadres were removed from Xian Academy. Deng went to Shanghai to work in the CCP central organization. In 1931, he had the opportunity to work in the Ruijin CCP central organization headed by Mao Zedong and was assigned the editorship of a Red Army journal. In 1933 he was purged but was rehabilitated in 1934 during the Long March. During the 1937 war with Japan, Deng became the political commissar of the 129th Division of the 8th Route Army.

At that time, Deng revealed his understanding of the concept of incentive in the process of economic development. He experimented with his incentive theory in 1943 by starting a campaign called the great production movement to raise local harvests. This was accomplished by "rewarding the hardworking and punishing the lazy," that is, model producers received bonuses. He also introduced contract work (another feature of Deng's 1980s rural program), where farmers worked on public property and, after meeting their production quota, were allowed to keep the rest.

This was the beginning of Deng's movement toward private entrepreneurship. He realized during that time the importance of profit in the process of economic development. Thereafter, from time to time, he expressed his political and economic thoughts openly in a hostile environment created by Mao and his wife Jiang Qing.

In 1961, Deng and President Liu Shaoqi openly advocated private farming plots, peripheral industries like hog raising, and extensive free markets. In industry, experts, such as managers and technicians, would be in charge, instead of party bureaucrats. These programs foreshadowed Deng's second revolution.

The wrath of Mao and Jiang fell on Deng during the Cultural Revolution. Just before his purge, Deng confessed with the hope of avoiding the decreed fate. He said that his recent errors were not accidental. They had their beginnings in a particular way of thinking and a particular style of work which had developed over a period of time. This statement reflects the fact that Deng already had a blueprint for the economic development of China, although the nuts and bolts were still missing.

After Deng was rehabilitated in 1973, he helped Zhou En-lai design the four modernizations program (agriculture, industry, national defense, and science and technology), which was announced in January 1975. With the death of Zhou, Deng stood unprotected and was removed from his offices. The subsequent death of Mao and the arrest of Jiang Qing and her gang members paved the way for Deng's return. Confronted with demands for a letter of contrition, he signed it in order to speed up the process for his rehabilitation. "Deng is a man who knows when to bow and bend."[3]

After coming to power, Deng removed the "two whatever" faction, which had obeyed Mao's orders without question and believed in whatever Mao said. According to Deng, Mao had repeatedly acknowledged the error of some of his statements. Nonetheless, in order to give legitimacy to his demands, Deng took shelter under Mao's image. During the Central Committee plenum of July 16–21,1977, he resurrected Mao's 1942 slogan, *shi shi qiu shi* (seek truth from facts or arrive at the truth by verifying the facts).[4] In reality, the main truth and fact was the politicoeconomic survival of China and the CCP depended on reform. As Deng said, "This [capitalism with Chinese characteristics] is the only road China can take. Other roads would only lead to poverty and backwardness."[5]

Deng's decision to follow the reform path for economic survival was a purely political decision in order to survive both politically and economically. When his political prestige was threatened by the 1989 Tiananmen Square student-led demonstration, Deng lashed back with a vengeance to protect his, and the party's, power. However, when he sensed that the hardliners were about to take control of the pace of economic development, slow down economic activities, and cut foreign investment, Deng took the famous train tour of the south in early 1992 to assure private and public sector entrepreneurs, reform-minded officials, foreign investors, and Chinese consumers that there was a difference between his power, the party's political power, and China's economic development. After all, as Deng's famous saying of 1962 goes, "It doesn't matter if a cat is black or white, so long as it catches mice." Deng has continued to maneuver to insure the continuity of his political and economic agenda. This is reflected in his close friend's removal from a position of power and, it is reported, the removal of his daughter's father-in-law, Yang Shangkun, and his half brother, Yang Baibing, who, according to reports, planned to "reverse the verdict" on the Tiananmen massacre by blaming Deng after his death.[6]

POLITICAL ECONOMY DEFINED

In a transitional communist country like China,

[t]he systemic transformation is not an exercise in applied economics or in applied political science; it is a process which involves human beings, which affects their day-to-day life, which creates new groups of gainers and losers, which changes the relative political and economic strength and standing of different socio-economic groups and which, therefore, destroys the original political, social and economic equilibrium. The communist system was characterized by its own, peculiar, relatively stable equilibrium. Whether the new equilibrium and especially the path from one equilibrium to another becomes stable or unstable depends upon the [political and economic factors] interplay.[7]

Thus political economy is the interplay of powerholders, goals of the powerholders, and the whole system of exchange relationships (economics). This interplay of political power and economics is largely responsible for the continuing survival of inefficient institutions. A wasteful enterprise, which mainly produces inadequate outcomes, cannot survive in any human society until and unless force is used to hinder the advent of efficient organizations.[8] Political economy is "the interaction between a political system (a structure of rule) and an economy (a system for producing and exchanging goods and services)."[9] To understand the interplay of political and economic factors in China, we must define politics and economics as they relate to China and describe how the political economy is manifested.

In China, politics may be defined as the machinations adopted by individuals to obtain power to implement their ideology and achieve goals or hinder the progress of the opposition's ideology and goals, thereby taking the chance of enhancing or decreasing their power and bringing possible downfall to the self, others, or or even engaging in a life-or-death struggle. Economics may be defined as the capacity of the system to use its constituent groups to produce and distribute wealth to meet the various demands of the constituent groups within the system. The use of political power, which enhances or disrupts the capacity of the system, to produce and distribute wealth to the constituent groups, is called political economy. The private entrepreneurs and *getihu* directly benefit or lose with the manifestation of political economy in China.

DENG XIAOPING AND CHEN YUN'S TEMPORARY COOPERATION

In July 1977, Deng Xiaoping returned to power after the fall of the Gang of Four as a deputy chairman of the CCP and a vice-premier. Whatever arrangement was made between Deng and Hua Guofeng, Deng was not prepared to accept anything but the supreme leadership of the CCP and China. However, early in 1980 during the 5th plenum of the CCP 11th Central Committee, with the help of Chen Yun and Hua, Deng successfully removed from a position of power Wang Dongxing, the head of the "two whatever" faction and his followers Ji Dengkui, Chen Xilian, and Wu De, known as the "small gang of four."[10] But for all practical purposes, the matter was already decided during the 3rd plenum of the 11th CCP Central Committee meeting in late 1978. The "two whatever" faction was severely criticized by the group headed by Chen Yun, general Xu Xiyou (who had sheltered Deng in Guangzhou after his downfall in 1976), Wan Li, and others. The reformer's philosophy that practice is the sole criterion in finding the truth was established, meaning that Mao's words were not the sole criterion of testing truth. This was the beginning of demaoisation. In fact, Chen Yun attacked Mao's reputation and his achievements as the CCP's leader during the meeting.[11]

Besides consolidating his power through purges and putting his trusted followers and comrades Yu Qiuli, Qin Jiwei, Wang Zhen, Yang Dezhi, Yao Yilin, Hu Yaobang, and others in powerful positions,[12] Deng implemented his plan to emancipate the minds of the people through reform and liberate their productive forces. Deng's call for modernization and good livelihood (economic prosperity) was laid down during the 5th National People's Congress on March 5, 1978, when it adopted in the constitution the legal status of individual entrepreneurs. The 3rd plenum of the 11th Central Committee in December 1978 put its authoritative stamp on the process (see Chapter 2). After that, the official newspapers of the CCP, both central and local, published a series of articles to persuade private individuals to become active in the reform movement and try to change the impression of private capitalists lingering from the 1950s and 1960s. *Renmin Ribao* reported that China needed the participation of the private capitalist to recover and develop the economy.[13]

With the fall of the small gang of four and continued support for private entrepreneurship in the early 1980s, Deng's article of January 16, 1980, said that socialism did not mean poverty. The article further called for developing production and improving people's livelihoods and put forth the proposal of reward and incentive for hard work.[14] On February 10, 1980, Deng further revealed his views of economic policy by saying that China needed to expand the role of the market economy and urged former Chinese capitalists to invest their money in China.[15] Due to this kind of persuasion, entrepreneurs were able to overcome, in some fashion, their fear of life uncertainty for the first time since the *San-fan* and *Wu-fan* campaigns and the Cultural Revolution, and China saw a rapid growth in private entrepreneurship. In 1981, the number of individual entrepreneurs doubled from the previous year (see Table 2.5 in Chapter 2).

Demaoisation

The relationship between politics and economics in China suggests that in order to establish political and economic policy, it is necessary to discredit any other existing or possible counterforce. Deng understood this very clearly. Although he did not want to discredit the concept of a traditional paramount leader deeply rooted in Confucianism, Deng was adamant about discrediting Mao in the eyes of the CCP members because of Mao's complete contradiction to Deng's position. If Mao wanted continued class struggle, redness of the cadres, egalitarianism, self-sacrifice, and collective initiatives, Deng wanted emancipation of the mind, experts,[16] glory in getting rich, and individual initiative for profit and self-gain.[17] Because these two ideologies could not coexist, demaoisation became imperative, both politically and economically. This effort was accomplished by attacking Mao as a person, his economic policy, and his political stand against the so-called rightists (the rehabilitation of the CCP members purged during the Cultural Revolution).

The demaoisation effort started in the late 1970s simultaneously in all of the above mentioned areas. The internal criticism of Mao also coincided with a covert external one. The frequent use of references to Lin Biao and the Gang of Four in the mass media in conjuction with China's shortcomings could be interpreted as synonymous with the phrase "down with Mao Zedong." With this subtle attack on Mao came the rehabilitation process for the comrades who fell during Mao's era. The posthumous rehabilitation of Qu Qiubai in March 1980, following the rehabilitation of Liu Shaoqi and Peng Dehuai, was viewed as "another slap in the face for the late Chairman Mao Zedong."[18] The effect was multiplied by rehabilitating hundreds of purged victims. Reports from every corner of China talked about the miscarriages of justices during the Cultural Revolution by Lin Biao and the Gang of Four (i.e., Mao) and how the victims were rehabilitated.[19]

Liu Shaoqi's rehabilitation was of particular importance. He had, after all, been characterized as the number one power holder taking the capitalist road when Deng was designated the number two power holder taking the capitalist road. The concept of losing face is very important in Chinese power politics, and the culture in general. Deng's rehabilitation of Liu Shaoqi constituted a slap in the face of Maoism, thus elevating Dengism and Deng himself.[20]

The CCP continued the demaoisation process while denying it was doing so. In Guangzhou, for example, portraits of Mao Zedong and Hua Guofeng disappeared from the airport. When AFP correspondent Francis Deron asked an employee at the airport about the disappearance of the portraits, the employee acted as if he did not know what Deron was talking about. The conversation went like this:

"When were the picture of Mao and Hua taken down?"
"I don't know what you mean."
"Well, the portraits were up until recently weren't they?"
"Is that so?"

The employee refused to say anything further.[21]

Demaoisation Through Dazhai

Deng also attacked Mao by attacking Dazhai. The Dazhai brigade of Dazhai commune in Xiyang county in Shanxi Province was a pet project of Mao's. He wanted to propagate his idea of an ideal communist society based on the practice of Mao Zedong thought—hard work, ideological chastity, and political awareness of Maoism. After Deng's ax fell on Chen Yonggui (who had been credited for the success of Dazhai and rose to power with the agricultural success of Dazhai),[22] the criticism of Dazhai began. Through political and economic criticism of Dazhai, Mao's economic principle of "taking grain as the key link" (agriculture was the foundation of Mao's economic policy, and he dictated the mandatory cultivation of basic foodstuffs) was rejected. This made room for advocating for rural individual entrepreneurs to engage in production of other agricultural and non-agricultural products, such as raising farm animals and handicraft projects, for profit. An article in *Guangming Ribao* denounced Lin Biao and the Gang of Four for using an anti-Dazhai movement to attack cadres. It condemned using Dazhai as the model "advocated by Chairman Mao" and encouraged people to take an "all-round" approach to development.[23] In addition to criticizing Dazhai, the CCP mass media advocated the implementation of scientific methods to increase production in agriculture.[24]

By discrediting Mao's previous activities, particularly during the Cultural Revolution, and by removing the small gang of four and rehabilitating the victims of the Cultural Revolution, Deng and Chen undermined Hua. Hua was removed from power by mid-1981 on the grounds that it was wrong for him to take sole credit for overthrowing the Gang of Four. He had put forth the "two whatevers," later developed into a theory by Wang Dongxing and others, and favored ultraleftist views. After coming to power, Hua did not try to rectify the errors of the Cultural Revolution, instead he stated that it was an ongoing process. He wanted to be addressed as the

Wise leader Chairman Hua, similar to cult personalities. As CCP chairman and premier of the State Council, Hua had to take responsibility for the economic failures of 1977 and 1978. Finally, his political, ideological, and organizational capabilities were not adequate to lead the CCP.[25]

The removal of Hua, however, was not easy for the Deng-Chen faction. The People's Liberation Army (PLA) did not view the removal positively. Most of the PLA forces were of rural origin, and the CCP under Mao had definitely helped to liberate the rural areas from the traditional oppression of imperial times. Moreover, the PLA had positive feelings for Mao and his designated successor, Hua. According to some senior cadres in the army, Deng Xiaoping and his group were not pursuing Marxism-Leninism. *San zi yi bao* (fixing output quotas for each household) and other incentive concepts based on market economy were "capitalist and revisionist stuff."[26] The strong superstitious belief in Mao on the PLA's part, a growing power in the political economy of China, was manifested during the war of the pen in 1981 between the CCP central authority and PLA writers and advocates of Maoism. While the Deng-Chen faction was advocating the elimination of leftist thinking, the PLA and its supporters were advocating the propagation of the four cardinal principles—that is, upholding the socialist road, the people's democratic dictatorship, the Communist Party's leadership, and Marxist-Leninist and Maoist thought.[27] The process of implementing the four principles in an overbearing way could easily become "four sticks," because at that time the most serious problem was in the army. For many years under Mao's rule, the army was plagued with the leftist "disaster."[28]

With common enemies removed from power and the task of rehabilitating Cultural Revolution victims (who were either mentors or protegees) completed, the common ground between Deng and Chen Yun, who had been characterized by China observers as monolithic,[29] began to give way. The result was the birth of the hardliners led by Chen, and the reformers led by Deng.

HARDLINERS AND REFORMERS

A clear line of demarcation between the hardliners and reformers is not always apparent. First, the CCP is one party, and the interest of the major players, such as Deng Xiaoping, Chen Yun, Wang Zhen, Deng Liqun, Peng Zhen, Yang Shangkun, Bo Yibo, Li Xiannian, Hu Qiaomu, Deng Yingchao, and others, lies in defending the party's survival. Second, each group has its own members on the other side. Third, the leading members have close, sincere friendships dating back to Shaanxi times. Fourth, both groups overlap with each other on the concept of reform and economic survival of China.[30] There are also other groups that exert pressure on both the hardliners and the reformers, including the bureaucracy, local cadres, the PLA, and, recently, foreign investors (see Figure 5.1).

Figure 5.1
Dynamics of Hardliners and Reformers

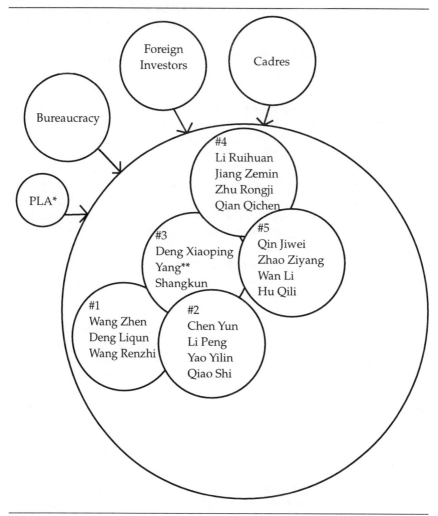

#1 Ideologue tending toward Maoism but under control of #2.

#2 Go slow on reform with hard rule.

#3 Reform and hard rule.

#4 Conformist under control of Deng.

#5 Reform and soft rule. Though they do not have real power, their ideas are still alive.

* At present PLA is proreform but believes in hard rule.

* *At present Yang might advocate group #2.

Hardliners and reformers are constantly playing tricks on each other, like the eunuchs of imperial times. Sometimes Deng appears to be the chief eunuch, and sometimes the emperor. Deng himself agreed while complaining about the rivalry between Zhao Ziyang and the hardliners. While visiting Shanghai in early 1989, Deng said in support of Zhao during the Shanghai Municipal CCP Standing Committee meeting that it was all right to complain about Zhao but it was not good to play tricks. In this tug of war between the hardliners and reformers, Deng sometimes appeared to be as weak as the chief eunuch and sometimes strong as the emperor. His supposed weakness was manifested when he sacrificed Lei Yu,[31] Hu Yaobang, and Zhao Ziyang. However, this was simply a tactic to gain advantage and mute criticism. Previous chapters discussed how Deng's power was manifested when he steamrolled over Gao Di, Wang Renzhi, Yang Shangkun, Yang Baibing, and others. One should not look at the extent of Deng's power lightly. Observers must remember his control over the PLA and his network of subordinates in both civilian institutions and the PLA, who owe their positions to Deng and are, therefore, loyal to him. Deng also has the support of constituent groups that have no option but to support Deng's reform policy because the alternative would be Chen Yun's method. Deng's word is absolute and to oppose him is to take the chance of stern castigation or the muting of that opposition.

In the political struggle for power and survival of the CCP and China, both Deng Xiaoping and Chen Yun realized that they needed to reform the Maoist economic and political policy. The group led by Chen Yun, which consisted of Deng Yingchao (Zhou En-lai's wife), Wang Zhen, Peng Zhen, Hu Qiaomu, Deng Liqun, Yao Yilin, and others, advocated a strong stand on communist ideology, less reliance on foreign investment (thus preventing spiritual pollution through Westernization), and a slower pace in economic reform by keeping the state-owned sector as the mainstream of economic development and allowing the private sector to complement it. Like Deng Xiaoping, Chen Yun had his mind set about economic reform and the development of China. His stand on economic reform was nothing new. In 1956, shortly after the socialist transformation of the private ownership of the means of production, Chen Yun, perceiving problems due to the government policy, put forth the economic policy called the three principals and three supplements, at the Eighth National Congress. Chen said that the state-owned and collective economy was the mainstream and the individual economy was its complement; planned production was the main pillar and free production was its complement. Likewise, the state-controlled market was the main organ of distribution, and the free market was its complement.[32]

Deng Xiaoping and his associates, Hu Yaobang, Zhao Ziyang, and others were willing to let the reform process take its own course. Hu and Zhao were willing to take radical measures (with Deng's tacit blessing) in both the political and economic arenas, such as price reform, structural reform, the use of high consumption to boost production and employment, and allowing inflation to take its own course by stimulating production and thereby profits, reinvestment, and increased job opportunities until settling down under market conditions. They opened the window to joint ventures, accepting the risk of Western pollution entering China and allowing different views and ideas to be aired.

These measures led the Chen and Deng factions to go in different directions. Although Deng from time to time changed hats as a reformer and hardliner, particularly in the areas of ideology and CCP absolute rule, he never compromised his economic policy. By maintaining a balance between the two factions, Deng became indispensable to both sides. With the downfall of Hua Guofeng, economic and political reform started to accelerate in both the public and private sectors and, interestingly, in the PLA as well. The PLA has become a maturing actor whose blessing is sought by both factions to further their goals. So far, however, Deng Xiaoping is the only one who has been able to channel the PLA's blessing according to his wishes vis-à-vis economic reform, thus keeping his ideology alive—reform through party leadership and Deng's communist ideology.

Through 1981, 1982, and part of 1983, the private sector received support from the government to develop rapidly. In the official newspaper *Renmin Ribao*, private industry was highly praised because of the contribution it made to the state and the economy by using small investments and quickly producing positive results.[33] The PLA also joined in the process of economic reform by producing civilian goods for profit. By 1980 the PLA, through use of its strong organization and technology, produced more than seventy kinds of products for civilian use, including consumer goods, medical equipment, engineering machinery, and printing machines. In 1980 the output value of civilian goods use topped 1979 by 84 percent. In the late 1970s and early 1980s, the PLA established connections with local buyers and sellers for marketing their products, thus establishing a base to further develop their interests.[34] This monetary interest of the PLA based on the market economy became a blessing in disguise for the economic reformers and the private entrepreneurs, if not for the political reformers. With the growth of the PLA's civilian sector economy, the advocates of civilian production by the PLA became more vocal. In 1983, Defense Minister Zhang Aiping called on all departments of military science and technology and the defense industry to help develop China's economy by supporting both military and civilian objectives and strengthening the military industry to support national economic development.[35]

The hardliners took notice when they observed the rapid growth of the private sector economy and entrepreneurial activities, the participation of the PLA in the reform process by producing civilian goods, the rise in antiparty sentiment, the spiritual pollution of Maoist ideas due to the rising crime rate, political freedom and thoughts, and the use of pornographic elements. With the call for retirement of the old cadres[36] and Deng's call for structural reform during the 12th CCP National Congress, it was time for the hardliners to take action to stop the pace of reform. During the second plenary session of the 12th CCP Central Committee, Deng again called for structural reform in light of the 12th CCP National Congress. But this time he put forth the idea of combating spiritual pollution because of the spread of corruption in the realm of ideology, as reflected in the growing crime rate among young people.[37] This gave the hardliners a weapon and with it they attacked. The reformers reacted with their own defense of structural reform.

ANTI–SPIRITUAL POLLUTION MOVEMENT AND ENTREPRENEURSHIP

News of the anti–spiritual pollution movement and its activities were like a virus spreading over China. In some places it took a serious turn and in some areas, like in Guangdong, it only received lip service. With the campaign of party rectification proceeding at the same time, it was like the *San-fan* and *Wu-fan* campaigns revisited, but on a smaller scale. History came back to haunt the entrepreneurs, who were just recovering from the wrath of Mao and still hoping to overcome their fear of life uncertainty. Mass campaigns (*yundong*) in China typically had not been limited to the goal of the campaign but easily rolled over to microeconomic aspects of life, thus making life miserable for private entrepreneurs and consumers alike. Moreover, local cadres who had lost power and privilege because of the private economic freedom enjoyed by both buyers and sellers, often had their own agendas, motivated by jealousy.

Four officials, with the blessing of Chen Yun and possibly even Deng Xiaoping, led the charge against spiritual pollution and private economic interest. The four were Wang Zhen, politburo member and president of the central party school; Peng Zhen, chairman of the National People's Congress; Hu Qiaomu, a politburo member and a leading ideologist; and Deng Liqun, a member of the secretariat of the CCP Central Committee and the director of the propaganda department of the Central Committee. Deng Liqun's August 20, 1983 speech on spiritual pollution was the precursor of the entire campaign. In his speech, he criticized art, literature, and theoretical circles that were willing to introduce new ideas not on par with Maoism.[38]

From October 1983 to the beginning of 1984, the war of words between hardliner advocates of the anti–spiritual pollution campaign and advocates of structural reform continued in the mass media.[39] The targets of the anti–spiritual pollution movement were radical reformers and the reform policy itself. The death of the reformers would be the death of the policy and private sector entrepreneurs (who look to the reformers for protection). This is a classic example of political economy. A Deng Liqun victory would mean the downfall of Hu Yaobang and his reform ideas. It was the major

move by the hardliners to undermine the reformers in the post–Hua Guofang era.

Unlike during the Cultural Revolution, the constituent groups did not
support the movement at all. This gave the reformers the confidence to
try to stop the anti–spiritual pollution movement. Hu Yaobang, Zhao
Ziyang, and Wan Li became active and vocal against the movement and
wrote a letter on its elimination to Deng Xiaoping. Under pressure from
both inside and out, the CCP Central Committee Politburo held an
enlarged emergency meeting in November 1983. Hu and Zhao stressed
the need for eliminating the anti–spiritual pollution movement and continuing with party rectification. At the same time, the CCP Secretariat
issued a document entitled "Report on the Investigation of the Enlarge-
ment of the Scope of the Work of the Elimination of Spiritual Pollution."
The document reported that women were denounced for keeping their
hair long and wearing makeup and/or earrings. In some areas, individual
businesses were banned and all-round responsibility contracts were destroyed. Bank deposits of households with 10,000 yuan were frozen. In
Sichuan, a peasant entrepreneur committed suicide because he was unable to pay to execute his all-round responsibility contract as a result of
the bank freezing his deposits. Actions were also taken to restrict the
personal choice of army cadres with regard to their engagements and
marriages.[40]

In Guangxi the campaign was carried on against bookstores operated by
collectives (which includes private entrepreneurs) and getihu on the
grounds that they were selling harmful materials to consumers.[41] Before the
reformers could aid private entrepreneurs and getihu, the campaign had
already disturbed economic reforms. It hindered the normal practices of
using foreign capital and the importation of advanced technology, and the
implementation of enterprise reform in the state-owned enterprises. Rich
peasant entrepreneurs were harassed by local cadres. They were very
scared and their enthusiasm was dampened. The campaign denounced
entrepreneurial scientist-teachers who had started technical schools as
"putting money above everything else" and as victims of "decadent bourgeois ideas."[42]

Due to the negative effect of the movement on private entrepreneurship and the reform efforts, the politburo called for an end to the campaign. The official newspaper began to publish articles about the positive
aspects of becoming rich and having a life full of variety to encourage the
private entrepreneurs and getihu to overcome the fear of life uncertainty.[43]
The effort to eliminate the movement received support from different
parts of China, such as Henan, Guangzhou, Shanghai, and other places.
Tianjin's radio service and newspaper criticized "some comrades" for
following "old ways and conservative ideas" and not pioneering a new
cause.[44] It should be noted that Li Ruihuan, a reformer and member of
the Standing Committee of the CCP Politburo, was mayor of Tianjin at

that time. Opposition to the anti–spiritual pollution movement was also demonstrated in places in northern and interior China, such as Jilin, Hubei, and Guangxi.

In China the process of establishing power and ideology against opposition brings the downfall of the individual or the party. The collapse of the anti–spiritual pollution movement meant victory for the radical reformers led by Hu Yaobang. Hu's party advocated radical reform and vigorously charged Deng Liqun's group, bringing about the beginning of the end of Hu Yaobang. With the collapse of the anti–spiritual pollution movement, the position of the PLA in the reform process became clear. The PLA became the guardian angel of the economic reform movement and whatever happened—dislike for leaders, collapse of ideology, civil disharmony—the PLA would carry on the economic reform movement. On July 28, 1984, *Guangming Ribao* reprinted an article from *Jiefangjun Bao* titled "Questions and Answers About Thoroughly Negating the Cultural Revolution, Eliminating Factionalism, and Strengthening Party Spirit." The PLA's article blasted the leftists, under the pretext of negating the Cultural Revolution, and charged the hardliners with obstructing the reform process in all fields. The PLA had tasted the fruits of a market economy and wanted more. Deng Xiaoping and the economic reformers had gained a vital ally, which had guns to support the political and economic policy of Deng.

THE FALL OF HU YAOBANG

One after another, reformers presented their plans to reform not only the economy where private entrepreneurial activities can flourish, but also the political structure of China. On October 4, 1984, the State Council approved and disseminated "Some Provisional Regulations on Improving the Planning System," formulated by the State Planning Commission with the approval of top reform-minded leaders. It was a comprehensive plan to reduce the authority of the central planning system, which might be viewed as a threat to the hardliners' hold on power. A circular was issued by the State Council directing all localities, ministries, and commissions at the central level and their direct subordinates to follow and implement the regulations. The circular stated that the rigid and overcentralized planning system should be changed and replaced by the law of the market, which should also regulate grassroots functions of private entrepreneurs and *getihu* in the areas of catering, the service trades, and small commodity producers. The state would control the macroeconomy and individuals would control the microeconomy according to the law of the market.[45]

With the passage of these regulations, some state-owned small enterprises were allowed to be run by collectives (private entrepreneurs) and *getihu* under the pretense of changing the hands of the operation only, not ownership. The political and ideological decision made by the reformers to distance themselves from Maoist ideology resulted in economic gain for both the state and its citizens. In Harbin, for example, the economic result was dubbed Triple Happiness, when sixty-two small state-owned stores with new entrepreneurial mangagers were able to make a profit, customers were satisfied with their services, and workers received higher salaries.[46]

This initial success, coupled with the hardliners' lack of active resistance to the provisional regulations, led the reformers, with Deng's blessing, to put forth a comprehensive blueprint for both economic and structural change during the third plenary session of the 12th CCP Central Committee on October 20, 1984. As a result of the government's policy of persuasion and the failure of the anti–spiritual pollution campaign, the number of private entrepreneurs jumped tremendously (see Chapter 2). The blueprint for comprehensive economic change articulated a preference for experts over communists and meant a loss of power for the hardliners. The enterprises under the workers and staff members were responsible for paying taxes to the state, shouldering their own gains or losses and managing the enterprise based on "ever-changing" local needs and demands.[47]

Deng Xiaoping personally went to the PLA as the chairman of the Central Military Commission (CMC) on November 1, 1984, with a blueprint for the PLA's role in the reform process. Deng knew that the PLA's patronage was vital to his political and economic reforms and wanted to make sure that the PLA supported his comprehensive reform plan, which was crucial for the continuity of the reform process and thereby Deng's survival. To accomplish this, Deng wanted to get the PLA deeply involved in the economic development process by making it dependent on the civilian market. A crash in the civilian sector would hurt the PLA so badly that it would no sabotage Deng's reform movement but instead would protect it wholeheartedly. Deng called on all branches of the PLA—the Air Force, the Navy, and the Commission of Science, Technology, and Industry for National Defense—to get closely involved with the economic development of China and told the PLA how to do so. The Air Force could develop civil aviation, the Navy could use its harbors for civilian use, and the national defense industry could produce civilian goods. He also called on the PLA to train qualified personnel for both civilian and military purposes and for the rejuvenation of the PLA. Deng was planting the seeds of entrepreneurship and profit-making in the fertile soil of the PLA.[48] The PLA responded positively by calling on all parties to resolutely execute the Central Committee's decision to reform the whole economic structure centering on urban reform.[49]

With their success in derailing the anti–spiritual pollution movement and the initial success of the comprehensive reform plan, the radical reformists headed by Hu Yaobang fired Deng Liqun from the post of director of the central propaganda department. The removal of Deng was a setback to the hardliners led by Chen Yun,[50] but this victory by the reformers was short-lived.

As a precursor to the reorganization of the central leadership of the CCP, rejuvenation was first carried out throughout the country. It was reported that 74 percent of the governors and provincial CCP committee secretaries should be under the age of sixty, and that 15.5 percent of those under sixty should be under the age of fifty. The average age of provincial CCP committee secretaries should be fifty-eight, and that of governors should be approximatley fifty-five. This would make them seven and four years younger respectively, post rejuvenation. In the PLA, they would be seven years younger.[51]

September 1985 saw the next major aspect of the rejuvenation program. During the 4th plenary session of the 12th party Central Committee, 131 leading CCP members submitted their resignations. Sixty-four older cadres resigned from membership or alternate membership in the Central Committee. Among the retired members were Ye Jianjing (marshal and vice-chairman of the Central Military Commission) and a member of the Standing Committee. Those resigning from the Politburo were Deng Yingchao, Xu Xiangqian (marshal), Nie Rongzhen (marshal), Ulanhu (colonel-general), Wang Zhen (colonel-general), Wei Guoqing (major-general), Li Desheng (major-general), Song Renqiong (army general), and Zhang Tingfa (major-general). Thirty-seven older cadres resigned from the Central Advisory Commission and thirty from the Central Commission for Discipline Inspection.[52]

These resignations and personnel changes in the politburo and the Central Committee sharply diminished the leverage of the military in the party. It was also considered a loss of face, and therefore, culturally a great setback for the party elders, whose ranks included PLA veterans. They might quietly accept demaoisation, the economic reform process which was becoming increasingly beneficial to the PLA, and the defeat of the hardliners during the anti–spiritual pollution movement at the hands of the reformers. However, it was almost impossible for the hardliners and veteran PLA members to accept all the resignations, because in China political power creates privilege and honor. It was time for PLA and non–PLA veterans to join forces and take revenge. Since it was Deng Liqun, Chen Yun's spokesperson, who suffered humiliation after the anti–spiritual pollution movement, it was natural that to get back at Deng Xiaoping, the target should be Hu Yaobang, the outspoken advocate of rejuvenation of the party and the PLA.

However, judging from the economic activities and reports about reform and the reformers, it appeared that the reform process was moving smoothly, and Hu Yaobang was ascending to ultimate power. On September 23, 1985, the PLA newspaper *Jiefangjun Bao* published an article titled "Comrade Hu Yaobang and the Political Work at the 18th Army Corps." The article praised Hu, accentuated his political work in the Army, and paralleled his teachings with those of Mao Zedong and Deng Xiaoping. The article also called on those in the army to study the works of Mao, Deng, and Hu on the army. This was the first step to consolidate Hu Yaobang's power in the army. Other articles were written praising reformers in both the public and private sectors by calling them the heroes of today, but they also candidly pointed out that there were people who were obstructing the reform process and doing wrong to the reformers—that is, to the entrepreneurs.[53]

The official news media—*Renmin Ribao*, Xinhua News Agency, and *Guangming Ribao*—conveyed viewpoints favoring the reform process through structural change and called on everyone to reinvigorate the economy. At the same time, the reformers pushed for good news in the media about private entrepreneurship to highlight the good points of the reforms and to discredit Maoist ideas by discrediting Dazhai. Xinhua and *Ta Kung Pao* (the reformers' mouthpieces) praised the private entrepreneurs and *getihu* for their achievements and contributions to society. They not only made life "more convenient for consumers" but also provided jobs for unemployed youths and payed taxes thus contributing to "social stability."[54] *Renmin Ribao* printed an article on Dazhai criticizing the past practices there. The article lavishly praised Deng Xiaoping, raising him to a status higher than Mao. The article quoted people from this mountain village as saying, "We are free now, we can go to the fields to work any time we want." A woman named Lu Xiying reportedly said, "Deng Xiaoping is great. He can even emancipate people like us women."[55]

During that time, Deng Xiaoping and Hu Yaobang also defended their reform plan, which was being attacked by the hardliners. Deng and Hu said that the reform process was not following capitalism or advocating democracy.[56] This acknowledgment reflects some recognition that the hardliners were getting ready to strike back, but now with collaboration from the PLA.

It is not clear why Deng Xiaoping used Hu to remove powerful PLA elders and theorists from the party through retirement, particularly from the Central Advisory Commission, which was dominated by powerful individuals. Of all people, Deng Xiaoping should have known the power of *guanxi* held by the party patriarchs, particularly those in the PLA. As a powerbroker, Deng should have known not to go after PLA elders and CCP theorists at the same time. But Deng was getting old, and he knew that if he was gone, others would have the power or prestige to bring about changes; the patriarch rule would thereby prevail for a long time, threatening the reform process. This is the most plausible reason why Deng and Hu did not want to delay the process of structural reform of the central authority. Deng wanted to bring things under control before Hu took charge. This led some observers to say that after September 1985, everything would be settled and the reformists would have everything under control.[57]

In retrospect, it was a serious mistake, at least on Hu Yaobang's part. No doubt, good news about economic and structural reform was pouring out from all sides, and private entrepreneurs were enjoying some stability, but the proliferation of good news simply meant that the reformers were in control of the party propaganda machines and had macrocontrol over the state of affairs. It did not mean that grassroots and top-level CCP members opposed to the reforms were sitting idle.

The success and credibility of reform depended on the cooperation on the economic front by the urban enterprises whose primary responsibility was industrial production and construction, and commodity circulation. China in the mid-1980s had more than 1 million urban industrial, building, transport, commercial, and service enterprises, with a total work force of more than eighty million.[58] The *danwei* had great capacity to enhance or jeopardize the reform process. Unfortunately, the actions of many *danwei* leaders jeopardized China's efforts to reform the economy. At a time when China needed the support of the working masses to change its economic fate, the *danwei* leaders began plundering China under the pretext of helping China to change its old system through structural and economic reform. In the name of upgrading enterprises, some leading cadres abruptly increased salaries and spent money lavishly on travel, dinners, presents, and buying "expensive consumer goods at public expense." Some embezzled, evaded tax payments, and randomly increased prices, thus threatening the interests of the state, the reformers, and the consumers.[59]

This led Hu Yaobang to lament that unlike the early 1980s, when grassroots peasants and top-level leaders (mostly in the reformers' camp) were euphoric about reform but the middle-level bureaucrats were not, the mid-1980s was the opposite. At this point it was the grassroots *danwei* and top-level leaders (hardliners) who were passive toward reform.[60] This inability on the reformers' part to get immediate positive results from the urban enterprises made Hu Yaobang an easy target for the hardliners, which now included leading PLA veterans.

How did PLA veterans and non–PLA hardliners come together as a team? No doubt, they all knew each other quite well, but a look at the personal relationships of two old leading cadres will help put things in proper perspective.

Wang Zhen, a career soldier, played a major role in protecting Deng Xiaoping. He also criticized Hua Guofang heavily and was not unhappy to lose his position of power in the politburo. Moreover, rejuvenation of the PLA meant that a large number of old generals were forced to retire. These individuals were looking for revenge and a scapegoat—this turned out to be Hu Yaobang. Deng Liqun was also unhappy with Hu because of his defeat during the anti-spiritual pollution movement. As a result, neither Deng Liqun, Peng Zhen, Chen Yun, Wang Zhen, nor the old generals wanted Hu to become chairman of the CMC. At this point, Deng Liqun and Wang Zhen became the centripetal force that brought the parties together. In 1950, Mao Zedong tried to bring Xinjiang under CCP control by using Deng Liqun as his special envoy to Xinjiang. It was then that Deng Liqun met Wang Zhen. When Xinjiang was taken over by the CCP, Wang Zhen became the secretary of the CCP Xinjiang bureau and the commander of the Xinjiang military region; Deng Liqun became director of the propaganda department of the Xinjiang party bureau. Since that time, the two men maintained a good relationship. With Hu as the common enemy who caused both of them to lose face, it was natural for them to come together to destroy Hu and what he stood for—private entrepreneurship and political reform. It was reported that the military was very tense at that time, a signal that something might have happened.[61] It was the student movement's demands for greater freedom that gave the hardliners and Deng Xiaoping a legitimate reason to call for the downfall of Hu, thus relieving them of the burden of doing it themselves.

THE RISE AND FALL OF ZHAO ZIYANG

Hu Yaobang had a vision for changing China's collapsing system in which many party cadres were living off the subsidized economy like parasites because they did not have the courage or entrepreneurial skills to survive in a competitive world. Hu Yaobang wanted to improve the enterprises and advocated the development of production by stimulating consumption. But instead of increased production, many government employees increased their wages and went into high consumption and importation of foreign goods. Naturally, if enterprises do not produce enough, and wages and consumption go up, there will be a shortage of consumer goods resulting in inflation. At the same time, the common people, peasant entrepreneurs, and *getihu* were already suffering from life uncertainty. As mentioned before, many CCP members created additional burdens for private entrepreneurs and *getihu*. As a result, even if private entrepreneurs earned a lot of money, they did not have the courage to invest and expand their businesses to produce and create jobs, thereby circulating money and increasing purchasing power. In this unusual situation, the potential private investors did not have much choice but to join the spending spree phenomenon created by the CCP members and their ilk. Private entrepreneurs could have saved money but low interest rates and inflation (which erodes savings) coupled with the threat of the hardliners' ax made them fearful (like the "tadpoles" of the 1950s) that the government might confiscate their money and their property. So why not, like the 1950s, spend money while they were able? To blame the reformers or private entrepreneurs for inflation and the dislocation of the economy is groundless. Moreover, the hardliners were not willing to lose their power base by giving autonomy to state-owned enterprises or the private sector. Soon after the student movement started in December of 1986, China observers predicted Hu's downfall due to rising inflation and the unhappiness of the PLA and old cadres.[62]

Deng Xiaoping did not want to squabble with the old cadres and the PLA over Hu Yaobang. Hu's official resignation was announced by Xinhua on January 16, 1987. Deng Xiaoping had also expressed contempt for the student movement and complained about Hu's failure to handle the student crisis properly. After all, it had been students who threw Deng's son out of a window during the Cultural Revolution, resulting in his paralysis. It had also been students who harassed Liu Shaoqi, (Deng's mentor), put him through interrogation, and dressed his wife as a whore in public. It is no surprise that Deng is paranoid about student demonstrations. Deng's political stand against student movements is better understood by keeping in mind the above experiences along with other factors such as Leninism. It certainly helps explain Deng's role in the downfall of Hu and, later, Zhao Ziyang.

With the downfall of Hu Yaobang, the hardliners were quick to get even with him. Liu Binyan, Hu's protege, a special correspondent for *Renmin Ribao* who wrote an investigative report to expose the party's corruption and ill use of official power for personal gain, and Fang Lizhi were expelled from the party. Zhu Houze, another Hu protege and a reformer and director of the propaganda department under the CCP Central Committee, was replaced by Wang Renzhi, a hardliner. This was a major victory for the hardliners. Deng Xiaoping and Zhao Ziyang tried to slow down the triumphant march of the hardliners by declaring that, in spite of recent events, the reforms and the open policy would continue.[63] However, the hardliners, who were under the protection of the old generals and basking in their recent victory over Hu, were eager to reap the rewards from their victory. Hu Qiaomu, Deng Liqun, Wang Zhen, PLA newspapers, local supporters, and others led the charge against the reformers under the pretense of opposing bourgeois liberalization.[64]

The movement against bourgeois liberalization did not garner enough support from the masses, many of whom had supported Hu. On January 29, 1987, Zhao Ziyang, acting general secretary of the CCP Central Committee and premier of the State Council, with the approval of Deng Xiaoping, called on the CCP to limit the movement against bourgeois liberalizationonly within the party.[65] Along with the political measures adopted by the reformers to combat the hardliners' anti–bourgeois liberalization campaign, the reformers reassured private entrepreneurs that their economic activities would be protected by the government. By doing so, the reformers not only protected the enthusiasm of the entrepreneurs but also were able to win support from entrepreneurs and other constituent groups, such as the intellectuals, part of the PLA, and some provincial players, particularly from the coastal areas.

Renmin Ribao along with other official media came forward to assess the needs of both public and private entrepreneurs and brought back the subject of enterprise reform, with management based on a responsibility system involving profit, loss, payment of tax, and separation of party and management. *Renmin Ribao* cited examples of successful public and private entrepreneurs by describing their contributions to innovation and salvaging dying enterprises and poor villages. One such private peasant entrepreneur was Ou Yanqi from Bopu township of Wuchuan county. With his creativity and talent, Ou not only became rich but also helped about 240 households in the township increase their income to more than 10,000 yuan per year. Ou Yanqi was praised by the masses, admitted into the CCP, and elected a people's deputy of the county.[66]

To demonstrate his absolute power over the party and oppose the bourgeois liberalization movement, Deng arranged for Hu Yaobang's appearance at the 6th National People's Congress,[67] which was covered by Xinhua on March 24, 1987. Deng had his opinion about the bourgeois liberalization movement published in *Hongqi* in late March or early April 1987. Deng said that the four modernizations would require fifty to seventy years to succeed; therefore, bourgeois liberalization was a slow process and there was no need to take any drastic measures.[68] The PLA took simultaneous action. On April 14, 1987, the PLA newspaper said that the anti–bourgeois liberalization movement should not interfere with the reform and opening up policy because this must be accomplished. The article went on to cite from Deng's work about the defects of the big pot and iron rice bowl system and criticized overconcentration of power with no separation of party and government administration. The article even mentioned the thorny issue of lifetime tenure and retirement.[69]

With a favorable political situation at hand, Zhao Ziyang, then acting general secretary and premier, came out forcefully in support of reform and to combat the anti–bourgeois liberalization movement. He said that adhering to the four cardinal principles and pursuing reform and easing restrictions in China were as inseparable as lips and teeth and criticized those who said that the reform process was capitalistic. He went on to protect the private entrepreneurs—both rural and urban—by saying that elements of society that might help to propel the advancement of the productive forces should not all be judged as capitalist, because China was exploring new ways of reforming and easing restrictions.[70] On May 23, 1987, *Wen Wei Po*, a mouthpiece of Beijing and of Deng Xiaoping, heavily criticized ultraleftism and blamed the leftists for slowing down the reform process,[71] indicating an attack by Zhao's group in an effort to discredit the hardliners. It was also reported that Zhao criticized a few hardliners by name.[72]

THE 13TH NATIONAL CONGRESS AND THE BEGINNING OF ZHAO'S TROUBLES

In the hostile environment created by Deng Liqun and his group, the upcoming 13th National Congress formed an ad hoc committee in charge of producing a plan for future political and economic reform. The ad hoc committee consisted of Zhao Ziyang, Wan Li (a reformer and senior vice-premier), Hu Qili (a reformer and party secretariat member), Bo Yibo (a hardliner and vice-chairman of the Central Advisory Commission), and

Yang Shangkun (a Dengist-type reformer who was a hardliner and a party loyalist).[73] The composition of this committee reflected movement toward a reformist line.

The 13th National Congress in October 1987 put in place the next blueprint for China's economic development, of which entrepreneurs were a vital part, until it was temporarily shattered by the June 1989 Tiananmen Square massacre. Zhao Ziyang's vision about economic and political reform in China was similar to Hu Yaobang's—he wanted to give more power to the enterprise management, separate party and government, and ease restrictions in the free trade zones. Zhao once said, "As a first major step, let us take the coastal areas from Liaoning Province in the northeast to Hainan Island in the southwest—and 200 to 300 million people who inhabit the belt—out of the existing system. Let the coastal economy *guagou* and *hepai* (integrate and march in lock step) with the international economy."[74] Successful implementation of this plan probably would have meant the death of the hardliners.

Zhao's report delivered at the 13th National Congress of the CCP reflected continuity with Hu Yaobang's plan of separating ownership and managerial power, separating party and government, and delegating more powers among lower levels to avoid a concentration of power and bureaucratism. In addition, private entrepreneurship (the next step from the *getihu*), which was already in existence, was legalized (see Chapter 2). These proposals were antithetical to the interests of the hardliners and lower level cadres and bureaucrats who were living off the subsidized *danwei*.[75] Shortly after the 13th National Congress, Zhao Ziyang was elected general secretary of the CCP, and Li Peng replaced Zhao as premier. Zhao Ziyang, Li Peng, Qiao Shi, Hu Qili, and Yao Yilin were elected as members of the Standing Committee, Deng Xiaoping remained as chairman of the Central Military Commission, and Chen Yun was elected to replace Deng as chairman of the Central Advisory Commission—a hotbed of hardliners.

Following the 13th National Congress, Zhao forged ahead with the reform policy. *Guangming Ribao*, Xinhua, *China Daily*, *Renmin Ribao* and other mass media voiced opinions in favor of reform and the separation of party and government, indicating the increasing power of the reformers. Deng Liqun had not been elected to the politburo of the CCP Central Committee by the delegates, indicating further the loss of power by the hardliners at the grassroots level. Deng Liqun was later elected to the Central Advisory Commission (CAC) but was not elected to its Standing Committee, which may have signaled that party members were tired of him.[76]

With the reformers' success, Zhao wanted to arrange for the end of state-owned enterprises and thus create opportunities for private entrepreneurs to grow in the competitive marketplace. He was reported to have said that the state-owned enterprises would face disintegration under the competition of township enterprises (collective and private sector) if they failed to carry out reform. Responding to the ministers who disagreed, Zhao replied that it was a matter of unprejudiced economic law, and there was no escape from it.[77] With the backing of the reformers led by Zhao, official newspapers resumed publishing news about the success of both private and public entrepreneurs and the problems they were facing from different interest groups in China. In fact, *Guangming Ribao* on August 3, 1988, reported that "[p]rotecting the entrepreneurs [was] protecting the reforms" and thus advancing the reform movement.[78] But the enthusiasm for reform was short-lived. The state sector, which still occupied the major share of production and distribution of resources, continued to show poor results, as expected (see Table 5.3).

Since 1985 the deficit of losing enterprises in urban areas had been increasing. In 1985 the total was 16.2 percent; in 1986 it was 65 percent; and in 1987 it was 14 percent. In the first half of 1987, 7,000 enterprises were running at a loss with a total deficit of 2.56 billion yuan (about $690 million).[79] By the end of 1988, the deficit had risen to 13.6 billion yuan.[80] These losses, along with the *danwei* members' consumption behavior, frustrated workers who started destroying and sabotaging government properties. In Beijing workers used metal to scar newly painted cars at an estimated loss of 10,000 yuan per day. Noodle factory workers threw bits of glass into the flour, causing a disruption in production. The underground pipes of a petrochemical plant were plugged up by workers, resulting in accidents and the disruption of work. The air conditioning system of a cold storage plant was secretly turned off by workers, leaving a large quantity of spoiled provisions.[81]

In addition, the government lacked an adequate system of tax collection from the private sector and had to continue subsidizing failing enterprises due to of worker unrest. As a result, the government started running out of money. At the same time, because of low interest rates, people did not save money in banks and continued to spend money in self-satisfying ways. Accordingly, the government started issuing currency; by the first half of 1988, the amount of currency issued had increased by 35 percent compared to the corresponding period in 1987.[82] At this time, serious bureaucratic corruption continued. The rise in prices, corruption, and the PLA's dissatisfaction with the prevailing situation caused *Cheng Ming* writer Lo Ping to forecast that the downfall of Zhao Ziyang was very near.[83] Zhao's desperate attempt to relax commodity prices, adjust wages, and let the economy develop through inflation was rejected by the provincial and central leadership. Li Peng and Yao Yilin (senior vice-premier), "advocates of go-slow in reform," attacked Zhao viciously. Deng Xiaoping responded, prior to the August 1988 CCP Politburo meeting, that he did not give protection to anyone.[84] This signal was enough for the hardliners to retaliate. Eventually Li Peng and Yao Yilin took charge of economic matters, and along with the Tiananmen Square incident in 1989, Zhao, like his predecessor general secretary Hu Yaobang, was purged from his position of power.

Table 5.3
Value of Retail by Sectors

| Year | Total Value of Retail Sales | Ownership | | | | Retail Sales by Rural to Urban Residents |
		State-Owned Units	Collective-Owned Units	Joint-Owned Units	Individual-Owned Units	
1978	155.86	85.10	67.44		0.21	3.11
1979	180.00	97.18	77.64		0.43	4.75
1980	214.00	110.07	95.49	0.04	1.50	6.90
1981	235.00	117.15	105.06	0.11	3.74	8.94
1982	257.00	125.16	113.14	0.16	7.46	11.08
1983	284.94	133.88	118.95	0.36	18.45	13.30
1984	337.64	153.79	133.72	0.76	32.37	17.00
1985	430.50	174.00	160.03	1.27	66.10	29.10
1986	495.00	195.10	180.40	1.52	80.48	37.50
1987	582.00	224.90	207.96	1.88	101.16	46.10
1988	744.00	293.59	255.79	2.72	132.40	59.50

Source: China Statistical Abstract, 1989. Combined by the State Statistical Bureau of the People's Republic of China. The China Statistics Series. William T. Liu, series editor. Westport, CT: Praeger, 1989, p. 76.

Since Deng's famous southern train trip in early 1992, the reformers seem to have been in practical control (see Chapter 2). As for the hardliners, the PLA is making so much money from the market economy that it would be senseless for them to try to resurrect Maoism. The PLA is becoming China's Mitsubishi, a giant corporation with interests not only in military-industrial products but in almost everything from luxury hotels to pharmaceuticals. It has been estimated that enterprises sponsored by the military generate income equal to the defense budget, which was 42.5 billion yuan as of October 1993. As many as fifteen generals now attend and exert their influence over Politburo meetings to safeguard the PLA's interests. Family members of many high ranking party officials, including Li Peng and Chen Yun, have plunged into the sea of business, and they want to swim at full speed.[85]

Unlike China, Russia, which was once a model for economic development for China, is not faring well. First, Russians do not have a powerful leader like Deng Xiaoping, and Boris Yeltsin was not able to win the support of the army. Hardliners in the Russian government and the Parliament

(Duma) were able to frustrate the reform movement significantly, thus hampering the growth of private entrepreneurship—the key to economic development. This mismanagement of the politicoeconomic factors gave the state enterprises' managers and bureaucrats the opportunities to plunder Russia's resources for personal aggrandizement.[86] It appears that with government control of the economy, the economy will suffer from mismanagement. Even in a society where government is a buyer, mismanagement of the economy happens. For example, in the United States, the Pentagon has been known to purchase toilet seats and hammers from defense contractors for outrageous prices. Government bureaucrats also sell their services to the highest bidders, thus pocketing the taxpayers money in return for lucrative contracts to the defense industries.[87]

THE POLITICAL ECONOMY OF BUREAUCRACY AND ITS IMPACT ON ENTREPRENEURS

In addition to the central authorities, whose activities have a great impact on the reform movement and entrepreneurial activities, bureaucrats and local leaders play an important role in the reform process. They also influence the lives of entrepreneurs directly at the grassroots level and exert a great impact when implementing policy legislated by the central authority. In China, bureaucrats and cadres interact and support each other closely. There are only about 46 million CCP members to control 1.2 billion people. As a result, when talking about bureaucracy and localism, the same concept of political economy used to analyze the central authority in China cannot be applied. The political economy of bureaucracy and localism is based on the personal environment of an individual or the environment in which an individual interacts. As one entrepreneur said, "[If I meet Jiang Zemin], I will say, the government's policy is right but the people who implement the policy do not carry it out well."[88]

Within the bureaucracy, bureaucrats (or cadres) look out for their personal interests and the interests of the organization. The latter might translate in different ways. For example, in the case of the free use of official cars by family members, the more cars an organization has, the greater its flexibility and reduced conflict when it comes to permitting personal use. Big banquets, drinking parties (*dachi dahe*), and other functions can also overlap between personal and organizational interests. As for the local aspects of the political economy, the local cadres (or bureaucrats) give more importance to local environment than do the party or central authority. In the struggle for economic benefits or political gains, the local cadres' decisions are greatly influenced by local conditions. Also, the cadres are not the only winners or losers in the game. Their family members and close kin can also lose face if the cadres fail to produce positive results for the local people. In the interaction of two parties, face is the mutual obligation, honor, or respect that each side expects from, and extends, to the other, and a lack of either of these aspects, will result in loss of face and effective rule over the local affairs.

Bureaucracy

According to Max Weber, legal authority binds the ruled and the rulers, and the apparatus of administration. The bureaucrats, who run the administration, are impersonal. They obey the law and the person in authority only within the prescribed principle of hierarchy in the rational pursuit of interests. They thereby serve only the constituents, not their own private interest.[89]

Of course, Weber's ideal bureaucracy exists nowhere. It is a matter of degree how close a bureaucracy is to the ideal. In his discourse on Chinese bureaucracy, Liu Binyan describes a contemporary bureaucracy that is far from the pursuit of the ideal. According to Liu, today's Chinese citizens have lost the power to change the bureaucracy. Anyone who opposes bureaucratic corruption is subject to merciless and ruthless consequences because Chinese bureaucrats are so engulfed in personal aggrandizement that they fail to understand normal human emotions. Like the central authority, the power struggles at the middle and lower levels in China arise over personal interest, and each faction constantly prepares itself for the power struggle by creating close networks based on an intermarriage of children, common birthplace, schools, and the like. This gives rise to the concept of bureauprotect where individuals are shielded from outsiders, giving rise to tremendous arrogance and leading to disregard of higher officials and law, including the central authority figure. More than once, Hu Yaobang's directives to punish certain individuals for "evil deeds" fell on deaf ears.[90] What is unique about the political economy of the Chinese bureaucracy is that the majority will support any acts that defend their economic interest, because the members of a community or *danwei* have closely knit personal relationships or *guanxi*. This creates a sociopsychological burden to protect each other. As in the case of Daqiuzhuang, a village under the jurisdiction of Tianjin, the villagers banded together to protect local officials who killed a worker for stealing 29,000 yuan when Tianjin police came to arrest them.[91]

In a communist society like China, power is often used arbitrarily by administrators and cadres from the highest level to the grassroots level without any sense of accountability due to the absence of a well-developed legal system. It is not only the ordinary people who lack control over the bureaucrats and the local authorities; even the central authority is losing power over the bureaucracy and local authorities. With newfound economic resources, which have made the bureaucrats and local authorities more independent, matters will likely get worse before they get any better. It remains to be seen whether the new tax system put in place by the central authorities at the beginning of 1994 will help to correct the balance of power.

Bringing any instrumental change to the bureaucracy will be difficult. Chinese bureaucrats can sometimes be parasitic and hate any sudden change that might threaten their secured positions in their organizations and in society. Because failure for an entrepreneur usually means a loss of money, he or she might be able to recover. On the other hand, failure on the part of a bureaucrat due to change will often lead to a loss of his or her identity. Face may be lost in front of both superiors and subordinates, haunting a bureaucrat throughout life. As a result, innovation and change in society are much more likely to frighten bureaucrats than entrepreneurs whose nature makes them more willing to face risk and uncertainty.

The reform movement finds bureaucrats and local cadres trying to find their places. In some areas they support the reform movement and private entrepreneurship, and in others they hinder the progress of reform. Some were initially against reforms but later became proponents, and vice-versa. A number of local authorities have awarded handsome bonuses, such as cars and apartments, to entrepreneurs for their positive contributions to the community.[92] Contrary reports also exist. For example, in Liyang, Jiangsu Province, local authorities ganged up on a small community company, which was salvaged and running successfully, to abrogate its stock distribution within the firm and transfer the company's management to the town, thus interfering with the progress of the firm.[93]

To escape the wrath of CCP members and bureaucrats in China, entrepreneurs use all means necessary to please officials. By using graft, entrepreneurs can actually buy peace and perhaps even thrive. Recently, corruption of officials has become so common that it is almost an accepted way of life. This led an economics professor in Nanjing to preach to his students that, "Corruption is a price that China has to pay for the changes from a centrally planned economy to a market system—it is the grease that can lubricate the political machine in a changing society."[94] Some entrepreneurs, however, do not see bribery as a lubricant. As one entrepreneur said,

> With competition and ever rising prices, it has become more and more difficult to get raw materials and this bribe thing has become worse. Production has gone down and profit has also gone down. Previously, China's officials took money and things from the business people and now business people send them money and officials need not open their mouth. I do not think the problem of corruption can be solved in just several generations. . . . If you send more money to the officials, you will have less trouble; you will need less time to open your business. Officials serve the people for money.[95]

Failing to send money to officials can result in a personal visit to extract economic benefits in some other way. In Tianjin, officials and policemen literally ate a restaurant out of business.[96] This kind of behavior by officials led one entrepreneur to extend the following advice to a prospective restaurant owner:

My most important suggestion (to a prospective restaurant owner) is to tell him how to deal with all kinds of people. For example, he has to build a good relationship with the police station. When troubles occur, the policemen will help the restaurant. He also has to get along well with the food quality-control department. When the officials come, you must treat them well and not ask them to pay; otherwise, they will make trouble for you—that is, punish you.[97]

Another entrepreneur lamented in response to the author's inquiry about the possibility of eliminating corruption in China,

Absolutely not [corruption cannot be extirpated]. In China's history corruption existed during each dynasty. One cannot expect it to disappear in a short period. The United States has fewer problems and that is attributed to its private system. Banks are privately owned with flexible policies and high efficiency. In China all the banks are state owned and individual business people have to deal with government officials with money.[98]

In China, officials use various methods and their positions to extract money from entrepreneurs, thus hampering their progress and, in the process, economic development. In the West, entrepreneurs and the general public take it for granted that such services as public protection, utilities, phone, banking, and licenses will be made available upon payment of appropriate fees. In many developing countries, including China, entrepreneurs often have to pay additional fees regardless of the amount already paid. Bureaucratic corruption employs many techniques, including "manipulating electric power supply, using commodities, or using materials under one's control. . . . The essence of all these cases is that a person uses his functional power or authority for his private gain."[99]

The December 16, 1985, *Beijing Ribao* reported on the corruption of Ma Xueliang, director of Beijing's public utility bureau. Ma accepted bribes and helped set up an illegal gas company. Twenty-two officials, including high-ranking veteran party leaders and young cadres, were involved in the case. The Ma group made a profit of 1.53 million yuan. They spent 400,000 yuan in *dachi dahe* (big banquet and drinking parties), used 130,000 yuan as bribes to coopt others, and pocketed the rest of the money (1.08 million yuan).[100]

While talking about the corruption factor in China, two entrepreneurs put the matter very candidly, as if they had accepted corruption in their business life. One of them said, "I do not think it [corruption] is caused by a certain social system or a certain government. It appears in the human society. Different countries and social systems may have different extent of corruption. The more underdeveloped [a country is], the larger the possibilities are."[101] The other one said, "These [cases of corruption] are normal happenings in the developing countries. Some government officials make use of their working position to do things against the interest of the people."[102] Even the vice-mayor of Tianjin, Ye Disheng, expressed his frustration with the official corruption and hindrance of economic reform and development concerning Tianjin's Tanggu Economic and Technological Zone: "Bureaucracy is the major threat to a favourable investment environment."[103]

Pakistan and India, which share common borders with China, also suffer from bureaucratic corruption, resulting in a waste of limited resources.[104] This waste of limited national wealth drains the savings of a country, thereby depriving potential entrepreneurs of capital to invest in productive ventures that might create jobs and circulate funds.[105]

Corruption in China may initially help things move quicker by reducing the rigidity of bureaucratic institutions. In the long run, however, it leads bureaucrats to hinder any move toward decentralization of power, which might reduce their economic booty. The longer pervasive corruption exists, the stronger "corrupt pseudostructures" will become and the more difficult it will be to change the system.[106] This suggests that what entrepreneurs, and the public in general, need is decentralization of authority to function well in developing societies. This will facilitate creativity and boldness in innovation, knowing that business licenses, telephone and utility services, bank loans, and free public protection are available.

In any event, private entrepreneurs will always be influenced by the actions taken by the central government, bureaucrats, local governments, and other parties like the PLA and consumers in their efforts to challenge the existing semi-socialist economic system to move China toward economic development. In their pursuit of genuine economic development, entrepreneurs, the government of China, and consumers will have to work together to challenge each other with their willingness to take risk with innovation, implement new policies, and try new products. As failed entrepreneurs exit the market and make way for others to move in, similarly, the government and consumers should be entrepreneurial and take chances with policies, abandoning those that become a burden on the process of economic development.

Chapter 6

Entrepreneurs and the Economic Development of China

As a whole, the state firms in China failed to produce and innovate goods and services to meet the needs of the consumers, thereby pushing the Chinese economy toward ruin. However, after the return of Deng Xiaoping and the introduction of a market-based economy, both consumers and sellers found the freedom to interact in the economic realm. One of the positive outcomes of this reform process is the rebirth of private entrepreneurship in China. Nevertheless, the legacy of the Maoist past and recent politics influenced by culture have produced an entrepreneurial class that is aware of its past and is sensitive to any policy change. Because of this the Chinese system is still haunted by the life-uncertainty factor. However, the dynamic entrepreneurs are helping China slowly move toward a more effective system of economic development. Due to positive economic growth, the reformers in the Dengist camp are curtailing the government's role in economic matters and allowing private entrepreneurs and *getihu* to take a leading role in the economic development of China. Reformers are introducing new labor laws, monopoly laws, a new private banking system, ownership laws, consumers' rights, and tax laws. All this progress means that the state sector is losing ground and private entrepreneurs are gaining more access to economic activities and feeling confident that the past will not be repeated. Private entrepreneurs, consumers, and the government are finding common ground as maturing actors in the economy, which may help China to evolve into something new, quite different from the Maoist and Dengist eras. There is also more power at the disposal of entrepreneurs and consumers to voice their opinion in the marketplace.

For approximately thirty years, the CCP implemented a planned economy to develop and modernize China. They calculated the demands of the society and put in place the mechanisms to supply those demands with the hope of developing China's economy. However, one cannot predicate economic development on such static demand and supply notions. Economic development depends not so much on whether existing demands are met as it depends on facilitating new demands. Simply meeting the traditional demands of an economy leads to saturation of the economy, stagnation, and lethargy. For an economy to be dynamic, entrepreneurs must recognize opportunities to create new demands and new supplies. Given the freedom to innovate with available resources and to enjoy the profits or suffer the losses in the market, immune from government encroachment, entrepreneurs are willing to risk marketing new products and create new demands, which translates into new jobs and a fresh circulation of funds. It is the entrepreneur who is the main power behind innovations and drives the economy. As one entrepreneur replied when asked why he decided to go into business:

> It is a kind of work, quite independent. I have working experience of more than 20 years in cities of northeast China and Xian. It is within the limit of the reform and opening policy. I have some relatives abroad who are prepared to invest in China. Thus I have the chance and condition to run a business, a brand new type of business which should be different from the present types prevailing in China.[1]

To create new demands, an entrepreneur needs to look at the existing situation. For example, in a developed economy the demand for automobiles is close to the saturation point, and consumer consciousness of environmental issues and pollution control is putting pressure on decision makers in both government and industry to produce cars that pollute less. At this point, entrepreneurs can enter the picture to create new demands, for example, for solar-battery run cars, by producing and marketing the product. If successful in convincing consumers to buy the car, the entrepreneur not only enjoys the profits, but also helps the economy by creating jobs in the service sector, such as teaching the new technology, and developing complementary industries, such as battery and solar energy receiver manufacturing, and distributing equipment. Consumers will spend money not only to purchase the new cars but also to repair them, to learn about them, and so on.

In the process of innovation and the marketing of new products, an entrepreneur faces the possibility of losing money. To overcome and minimize the uncertainty factor, an entrepreneur always tries to reduce costs and increase efficiency so that if a loss occurs, it will be minimal. This, in turn, contributes to the savings of the nation, thus providing investment capital for other potential entrepreneurs with new ideas. This makes an economy dynamic so that raising the point of equilibrium becomes a perpetual state of affairs, creating new jobs, a fresh circulation of funds, and more purchasing power. Thus, entrepreneurial activities are like infusing new blood into an old body to make it young and vigorous. As one entrepreneur said, "Generally speaking, individual businesses can lower their cost and speed up the circulation of funds. I believe that doing my business well contributes to the country and also promotes the development of state-owned businesses."[2]

Under the leadership of Mao Zedong, China's economy not only became old because of a lack of innovation and creativity, it became stagnant. Deng Xiaoping and his followers found it very difficult to cure China's economy. If they use a market economy and let private entrepreneurship flourish, surely China will develop economically. We now turn Maoist economic thought which was, and still is, trying to destroy China's economy, and propose a new model in which private entrepreneurs play an important role in the process of recovery and development of the system.

A NEW PARADIGM

China's existing communist system finds the country slowly moving toward something new. However, a large part of the old system is still in operation. The successful movement toward a new system will bring economic development to China (see Figure 6.1), but present-day Chinese entrepreneurs, and the entire Chinese system for that matter, are still threatened by the uncertainty factor. The *Beijing Review* reported in 1988 that almost 91 percent of young people were afraid that the reform policy would change in the future.[3] The same perception about the change of government policy lingers among the Chinese people, but at a noticeably lower rate.

A survey by China Survey Research in 1992, found that 37.6 percent of the people thought government policy lacked coordination, and 17.9 percent doubted the credibility of the policy. In particular, private entrepreneurs worried that their property could not be protected under the laws. This leads them to donate money as philanthropists to build bridges, schools, and roads in their hometowns to please the local people and in the future avoid the rage of mass campaigns.

Entrepreneurs' lack of confidence due to the life-uncertainty factor significantly frustrates the spread of economies of scale. Some try to find partners among the state-owned enterprises to expand, but most are not so lucky and end up restricting their production. In Wenzhou, for example, many private firms hire only eight or nine employees and are unwilling to expand even if they are able to do so. This led Zhang Shuhong, an economist with the Institute of Economics of the Chinese Academy of Social Sciences, to say, "They dare not accumulate property to expand production. Discrimination towards the private economy still exists, which is another reason to

Figure 6.1
The New Paradigm

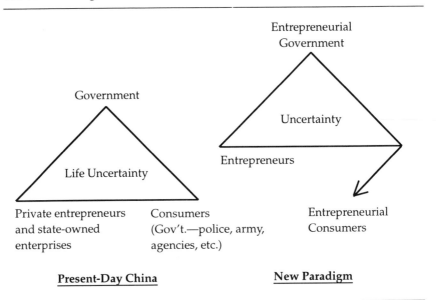

force private entrepreneurs to co-operate with state firms." The survey also found that 53 percent of private firms thought they were in an unfavorable position, compared to public firms.[4]

On one hand, the private sector is suffering from life uncertainty and therefore not functioning at maximum strength; on the other hand, the state sector is not doing well either. The state firms waste resources, both human and natural, in many ways. The deputy mayor of Harbin said that most workers at state-owned firms in Harbin only work productively three hours a day.[5] In 1988, only 50 percent of college graduates hired had jobs corresponding to their education. One unit, which employed 300 college graduates, had about 50 percent working in mail distribution, photocopying, buying office supplies, and cleaning.[6]

All these factors reflect a great burden on the economy. Distinguished professor of economics Li Yining of Beijing University said that in 1989 debts among firms amounted to 100 billion yuan and the central government spent 60 billion yuan, subsidizing unprofitable state-owned enterprises. "Together with state subsidies on prices given to enterprises and foreign trade subsidies, the central government invested 100 billion yuan in state enterprises. This accounted for one-third of state expenditures last year," he said. This led to a 9.54 billion yuan deficit in 1989.[7] In 1992, *China Daily* reported that the Chongqing General Knitting Mill, the largest of its kind in southwest China, went bankrupt. It had a debt of 80.63 million yuan ($15 million), 42.21 million yuan ($7.8 million) in assets, and most of its fixed assets, valued at 23.28 million yuan ($4.2 million), were mortgaged to banks. "Poor management and unwise knitwear marketing decisions incurred losses of more than 20.97 million yuan ($3.8 million) over the past six years."[8]

On the consumption side, the behavior by government agencies and *danwei* forced general consumers to behave irrationally. Unpredictable government policies, which contribute to life uncertainty, also influenced consumers to buy durable goods and spend money as fast as they could, instead of saving.

As for the government, the CCP is ruling China as an authoritarian regime and plans to survive by giving partial economic freedom. But for an economy to develop to its fullest potential, a sense of freedom in all aspects of life is needed—freedom to travel in search of resources and opportunities, freedom to explore new ideas and policies and to reject them when they fail. Along with these freedoms, the government should restrict certain behaviors that are detrimental to economic development, such as monopolies or oligopolies, pollution, and a strong tendency toward import-based consumption and development. Some restrictions may be based on law and others based on changes of policy, such as monetary or fiscal policy, tariffs, the money supply, and so on.

If the Chinese economy is governed by a life-uncertainty factor along with the vices of irrational government, irrational consumers, agencies, *danwei*, and the public, why is it that China is one of the world's fastest growing economies, with a 13 percent growth rate in 1993? Consumers are enjoying a better life, both on the dining room table and in the availability of consumer goods. China is slowly moving toward a market-based economy, where usual uncertainty and risk rule and entrepreneurs are able to function properly in the marketplace to meet the demands of consumers. Each party is willing to accept the responsibility of failure that comes with uncertainty in the areas of production, consumption, policy making, and implementation.

In an ideal system, entrepreneurs are willing to produce new products, venture into new markets, create new opportunities, jobs, profits, and provide satisfaction to consumers. An entrepreneurial government is willing to come up with new policies which, if successful, will be supported by consumers and entrepreneurs and, if unsuccessful, will lead to change in policy-making institutions. Entrepreneurial consumers are willing to take chances with new products in the market offered by entrepreneurs and, if dissatisfied, have the right to reject them and challenge the entrepreneurs to produce better quality products. In this process, entrepreneurial consumers take a chance in electing an entrepreneurial government to protect their interests. With good policies, they enjoy the fruits of their efforts, and with the failure of policies they again take a chance with a new government and policies.

In the following discussion about the movement of China toward the new paradigm, these points are analyzed: (1) the changing role of the government; (2) the changing government policy toward state-owned enterprises; (3) private entrepreneurs' role in economic development and their increasing power, which is having a trickle-down effect on consumers; and (4) the role of consumers in the new evolving market economy. In response, the government is introducing a new tax policy to strengthen itself. This new policy is designed to strengthen the central government against provincial power and to counter the power of entrepreneurs, though these factors are related. Consumers are also becoming entrepreneurial by asserting their rights, which in the long run will spill over into policy areas. Entrepreneurs, the government, and consumers in China, knowingly or unknowingly, are moving toward a matrimony to be governed by the usual uncertainties of the market. Any disruption that would reintroduce the life-uncertainty factor into the process will almost certainly give rise to economic chaos, leading to stagnation and possible collapse of the economy. In any event, the result would be a China much different from the one today.

THE CHANGING ROLE OF THE GOVERNMENT

Upon realizing the shortcomings of a planned economy, which were moving China toward economic collapse, the Chinese government under the leadership of Deng Xiaoping decided to push for private entrepreneurial activities. However, due to pressure from the hardliners, the reformers are having a hard time pushing the reform process fast enough. Nevertheless, if the reform process keeps on moving toward the new paradigm and the reduction of the life-uncertainty factor, a day will come when the state sector will collapse under the pressure and challenge of a private sector governed by the uncertainty of the marketplace.

China is very different from other developed countries. Its traditional Confucian values are deeply ingrained in the society; its constituents look to authority for direction in life, and a powerful leader can influence policy outcomes. In China, a powerful leader plays an important role in the policy-making process. For example, during Mao's rule, in many cases he effectively stopped the introduction of policy against his will. When Deng Xiaoping returned to power, he was able to start the second revolution, which is antithetical in many respects to Maoism.

Along with the problem of authority, China has a population of more than 1 billion people, and only 7.2 percent of its total land area can be utilized to feed the population. As a result, whether or not the planned economy vanishes, the Chinese government will play a very close role in many aspects of life, including private entrepreneurship. Because China does not have a well-developed market economy, the government (being a well-developed unit) will exert great pressure on an inadequately developed private sector. The government has the potency to coerce. But as China's reform-minded leaders have already acknowledged, the inherent weaknesses of a planned economy supported through coercion and subsidy, may be reluctant to use any kind of coercion or subsidy in the market that might introduce the life-uncertainty factor, thus making more room for private entrepreneurs to grow.

It is not only an authoritarian communist subsidized economy which results in the creation of parasitic producers and consumers; an authoritarian capitalist subsidized economy can achieve the same detrimental impact on economic development. For example, in his study of Saudi Arabia, an economy heavily subsidized through oil revenue to support an import-based consumption economy, Tayseer Khunaizi found that because of heavy subsidies to the nonoil sector, the country failed to grow with an "autonomous" diversified economic base, demonstrating "the fragility to the Saudi economic structure."[9] The Saudi economy is already showing its weaknesses. In 1994, Saudi Arabia cut its budget by 20 percent, putting great pressure on the system because of increasing population growth, which is expanding by about 3.8 percent a year, one of the highest growth rates in the world. This led an international banker who lives in Saudi Arabia to observe that "subsidies have encouraged people to consume irrationally."[10]

Based on the experience of the CCP's planned economy and its consequences, the Chinese reform-minded leadership, in the process of moving toward a new paradigm, may advocate a model similar to South Korea's 1960s–1970s approach to economic development, where the state directed development and the "principal engine" was the private sector.[11]

As architects of reform policy, and with continuous success in the area of economic development of China for the last seventeen years, the reformers in the CCP are willing to open up more opportunities for private entrepreneurs. The support and opportunities provided by the reformers go beyond the act of entering or exiting a market. Every step in a favorable direction for entrepreneurs is a step away from the life-uncertainty factor and a move toward the new paradigm, which means the creation of new demands and meeting unsatisfied demands.

In many cases, the central government is leap-frogging over southern provinces to adopt policies to implement nationwide. The pressure on the central government to change its policy of a subsidized economy is not only a result of the failure of the planned economy but also because of the tremendous success of private entrepreneurship and the lead taken by the coastal provinces in implementing new policies at the microlevel. For example, the *China Daily* reported that in the beginning of 1992 Guangzhou's city government issued new regulations to facilitate the growth of private entrepreneurship by allowing private firms to engage in foreign trade directly and to go abroad for business purposes.[12] Following this, the central government on February 25, 1993, put forth a package of incentives whereby private businesses were allowed to invest or trade with foreign countries and set up joint ventures with foreign partners.[13]

In other places, both local and provincial governments are pushing for rapid development of the private sector and thereby changing government positions and impressions about private entrepreneurs. In Yunnan Province, provincial administrators are advocating the development of private entrepreneurship, and the private sector is responding to the favorable policies by overcoming the fear of the life-uncertainty factor and opening up new businesses and creating new jobs. As of July 1993, Yunnan had 400,000 *getihu* and private enterprises hiring more than 580,000 people, which was 105 times more than in 1979. Open-mindedness and favorable policies are the main reasons for the *getihu* and private entrepreneurs' success in Yunnan. The provincial circular stated that private entrepreneurship was in the interest of the province, local government, and individuals, because the private sector brought more income, job opportunities, and stimulated the economy.

Due to the change in the government position in Yunnan, private sector output in industrial products during 1992 was worth more than 466 million yuan ($81.754 million), and retail volume was 3.211 billion yuan ($563 million), accounting for 13.68 percent of Yunnan's total retail sales. The private entrepreneurs and *getihu* also donated 5.9 million yuan ($1 million) toward social welfare, bought 8.99 million yuan ($1.57 million) of government treasury bonds, and paid taxes of more than 1.25 billion yuan ($219 million) to the state.[14] A similar success story was revealed in Nanjing due to a positive change in the local government's policy, which helped to reduce the life-uncertainty factor.[15]

Such developments demonstrate that upon realizing the mistakes of the CCP planned economy and after observing the success of private entrepreneurship, the CCP is changing itself, willingly or not, and moving toward the direction of the new paradigm where reformers' successful advocacy on behalf of reform policy is helping to reduce the life-uncertainty factor. The reformers are putting forth policies that are favorable to private entrepreneurship, such as the leasing and contracting of state-owned enterprises, which were considered the basis of the socialist economy. This suggests that China's contemporary leadership as a whole has accepted that the private sector will be the backbone of China's economy in the near future.

Because of the new evolving reality, the Chinese government is accepting its role as a referee rather than a dictator in the economic realm. The proof is in the policy-making process, where new ideas are put forth concerning labor laws, monopoly laws, a new banking system, ownership laws, consumers rights, and tax laws. Laws are evolving to serve the role of a contract among the three parties—entrepreneurs, consumers, and governments—so that they will respect each others rights in a relational situation.

New laws have been passed to regulate the labor market and disputes between parties. One such resolution went into effect on August 1, 1993, addressing both private and public sector workers. It was designed to address "disputes concerning wages, insurance, welfare, training and labour protection," the firing of employees, and the implementation of labor contracts, which were already in effect regarding state-owned enterprises.[16] The *China Daily* (reporting from *China Labour Daily*) reported in early 1994 that implementation of the labor laws was beneficial to the development of a market-oriented labor system. Given the freedom to deal with each other without intervention by the government, employees in about 100,000 state-owned enterprises received floating salaries based on efficiency and expertise. About 55 million workers were affected under the new law, and about 35 million workers signed contracts with their enterprises.[17] The government is responding to the demands of a market economy to protect the rights of employers and employees, which also benefits consumers. An entrepreneur in 1991 expressed his dissatisfaction about labor contracts in the following terms:

There is no protection law about hiring workers. For example, I hired a person; the contract period was one year, but after he worked for a month, he broke the contract and left. This had a bad effect. My uncle established seven branches in Taiwan. They have protection laws, so they do business well.[18]

This discussion suggests that as China moves toward a market economy, all the actors must move toward a system that properly addresses their grievances and interests. The more an economy departs from the new paradigm, the more the life-uncertainty factor will influence entrepreneurs and others, causing the economy to suffer malfunctions and dislocations. The actors in the system will also be divorced from each other, causing disruption in the flow of information and distortions in the system, thus giving hardliners an opportunity to derail the reform process and create more errors like the Tiananmen Square massacre of June 1989. This will, in turn, give the losers in the reform process the opportunity to take shelter in traditional and communist culture and draw on the Maoist past in order to harass or even kill entrepreneurs.

However, after Deng Xiaoping's southern train tour, policy implementation by the government seems to be encouraging entrepreneurs and consumers to overcome their fear of life uncertainty and move toward the new paradigm, thus avoiding distortion of information and weakening the hardliners. If these trends continue, both entrepreneurs and consumers will be able to influence the policy-making process in the long run.

Reformers are also pushing for reform in the banking system. Jing Shuping, a member of the Standing Committee of the Eighth National Committee of the Chinese People's Political Consultative Conference

(CPPCC), has suggested establishing a private banking system to overcome the deficiencies of state-owned banks and help the private sector grow.[19] Because government-owned banks do not care about their losses or gains, instead of giving loans to real entrepreneurs, they give loans to those who most often serve the interests of the bureaucrats. As some entrepreneurs in Tianjin said when asked about bank loans, "We did not try [to borrow money from the bank]. It is complicated to borrow money from the bank, very complicated. So, we borrowed money from our friends. If it is easy, we will borrow from the bank in the future."[20] Another one said, "[It is] not very easy [to borrow money from the bank]. You must also have *guanxi* with the bank. In the Chinese context, relationships are more important than knowledge or ability."[21] Two other entrepreneurs, who had connections with the bank, felt that it was easy for them to borrow money, but both of them said that about 90 percent of private business people did not borrow money from the bank. *China Daily* reported on the difficulties faced by private business people in Shanghai in "raising capital" to expand their businesses because local banks will not lend money to the private sector.[22]

When the government tries to control the flow of money, local banks end up lending off-the-books, thus making any policy ineffective. When the government clamped down on credit in early 1994 to control inflation,[23] it did not mean that the hardliners were refusing credit to private entrepreneurs. It means is that monetary and fiscal policy in China has yet to be developed. Moreover, checking the flow of cash by manipulating interest rates will not work in a state-owned, corrupt banking system. Therefore, it is just a matter of time before we see a private banking system emerge in China.

An important sign that indicates the changing position of the CCP and its movement toward the new paradigm, is the evolving policy toward state-owned enterprises which are, or were, the backbone of the socialist economy.

POLICY CHANGE TOWARD STATE ENTERPRISES

The state-owned sector in China has become a great burden on the economy. In 1991, 40 percent of state businesses were losing money according to official reports, but "in reality two-thirds [were] probably [then] in the red." By the end of September 1991, in the state sector's warehouses, 230 billion yuan ($42 billion), about 12 percent of GDP, worth of unsold and unsellable goods were in stock.[24] *The Economist* reported again in 1992 that "the culprits, as usual, [were] the loss-making state enterprises" because of the loss of 8.2 billion yuan by the biggest companies in the first five months of 1992, which was 20 percent more than in the corresponding period in 1991.[25] At the end of 1993, the state sector's story was the same. "As many as a third of China's state-owned firms may be idle at present, their workers receiving minimal basic wages but sitting at home [or more likely working in private firms on the side]."[26]

Why did the central government allow the state enterprises to be such a burden on the economy for so long during the reform process? Because they cannot suddenly change the system and shut down the enterprises. The central government could have, from the beginning, tried to change the ownership or lease it out to the private sector, however, they had to consider the interests of the hardliners and the ministries of different sectors—coal, agriculture, steel, oil, and so on. Closing enterprises or transferring ownership would not only make managers lose power and privilege, the ministries would also lose power and privileges and, with their constituents gone, the hardliners would have no ground to fight for. Moreover, there would be increased unemployment and political instability.

It was quite natural at the microlevel to hinder any move to bring the state sector under the laws of a market economy. Successful entrepreneurs naturally leave inadequate employees behind who threaten their economic survival. To protect their interests, those who would be adversely affected create hurdles to the progress of entrepreneurship. In some cases they might even be successful in bringing an end to it. In a system where this occurs, the life-uncertainty factor will prevail, thus prohibiting entrepreneurs from venturing into any project that might contain risk and uncertainty. When an economy faces a static equilibrium, only conscious efforts by the policy-makers to encourage entrepreneurship can help to raise equilibrium and make it dynamic.[27]

When the economy was threatened by stagnation due to life uncertainty in the post–Mao era and post–Tiananmen Square incident of June 1989, the reformers, led by Deng Xiaoping, took steps to remove the fear of life uncertainty in an effort to push the economy toward the new paradigm. There was active encouragement by the reformers for the private sector to flourish. At the same time the public sector was being dismantled and replaced by a market economy. Right after Deng's southern train tour, the *Beijing Review* called for an end to the "three irons" (iron rice bowl, iron wage, and iron work post) and suggested that the state enterprises become independent and bear the "sole responsibility for their own profits and losses."[28] During that time, reform-minded leadership, such as Zhu Rongji, Li Ruihuan, and others, was on the rise. *The Economist* reported, "If people like Mr. Zhu are in charge when the brakes next need to be applied, they will at last be in a position to start dismantling the State firms—which are the main obstacle to China becoming the greatest economic miracle ever."[29]

On May 22, 1992, Deng Xiaoping personally visited the Shougang Group (capital iron and steel corporation) and gave his personal stamp of approval for the corporation to have its own banking system and participate in foreign trade. This was the beginning of the dismantling of the state sector.[30] In July 1992, the government put forth a regulation containing fifty-four articles dictating the status of the state-owned firms and gave them freedom in fourteen areas, including imports-exports, labor, employment, investment, pricing, marketing, and the allocation of manpower, funds and materials. The state council economic and trade office, headed by Vice-Premier Zhu Rongji, summoned about 400 high-ranking officials to discuss the implementation of the regulations "to ensure greater autonomy for the 105,000 State-run firms," which meant, "the State [would] no longer take responsibility for related debt problems of those enterprises which [were] oozing red ink," according to Hong Hu, vice-minister of the state commission for restructuring the economy.[31]

The government policy toward the economy is such that privatization of the public sector through leasing, contract, or corporatization is just a matter of time and strategy in taking social, economic, and political issues into consideration. Half of China's small public shops were leased to the private sector; new owners give over a certain percentage of their annual profits to the state. They are managing to compete with the state-run sector quite successfully. In Beijing about 4,000 small shops were leased, accounting for 60 percent of state-owned stores. "Leasing has so far saved the State at least 100 million yuan (about $17 million) in annual subsidies. These subsidies were a must in the past to keep the stores afloat."[32] *Xinhua* reported that state-owned small and medium-sized enterprises were also leased to individuals for management. Tongling in Anhui Province leased out twenty debt-ridden enterprises in August of 1992. By September 1993, they had already improved their economic performance. Their productivity rose by 50 percent and some had already overcome deficits and were making a profit. Beijing, Shanghai, Tianjin, Jiangsu, Hubei, Guangdong, and the Fujian Provinces have also carried out similar reforms and "obtained ideal economic efficiency."[33] The recent news is that government-backed research organizations and officials are calling for the corporatization of state-owned enterprises and the closing of money-losing enterprises. At the same time, the reformers are pushing for fair competition that has the government playing the role of referee rather than babysitter for state-owned enterprises, leaving it to the market to determine which will survive.[34] The government is stepping aside from its role as a micro-manager and letting private entrepreneurs take the lead.

ENTREPRENEURS AND ECONOMIC DEVELOPMENT

The following discussion uses the information gathered during interviews with entrepreneurs in Tianjin. The Tianjin interview data is augmented with additional information about economic advancement and the activities of other entrepreneurs in China.

Aggregate statistics about the economic development of China include the output of the state sectors. However, it is the contribution and challenge posed by private entrepreneurs that made it possible for China to become the world's third largest economy with 13 percent growth in 1993. It is the private entrepreneurs who are catering to the consumers' needs with goods produced by both private and public sectors to make the market more varied and dynamic. As Zang Hongge, director of the Beijing Municipal Commerce Commission said, the rapid development of the private sector has posed a challenge to the state and collective enterprises. "This has forced the State-run enterprises to conduct further reform in their management."[35]

When I asked a young college graduate turned entrepreneur what a *getihu* was, he replied,

> People work hard in an individual company, they do not waste time. They try their best to finish their work. If what he does is good for the company, he will do it. But in the government company, people always have to be lazy because they have no other choice because of the environment, and the policy is not good. Maybe the leader of the government enterprise did not understand the situation. Most of the time they do not make good decisions, and most of the decisions are not suitable. So, some people want to find a new environment to work hard and use their minds. So, I decided to find a new environment, and the individual business environment is a good place. People can put their heart into it. Now the world is changing, so young people want to bring change. They do not want the old structure. Most young people want to have achievement, success, and a better life. They like to go abroad to study the new technical knowledge and whatever. They want to do something for the motherland and make it strong. . . . Now some people are saying that individual businesses are needed. Individual businesses help the economy.[36]

One such young person was Chen Jing from Guangzhou. Chen was only ninteen years old when she left her hometown in 1987 when the hardliners were in power in Beijing. Chen went to Beijing to try her luck in the restaurant business with 9,000 yuan ($1,034) borrowed from her father. She struggled for seven long years and went through failures in two restaurant businesses. Finally, with innovative ideas and hard work, she became successful at the age of twenty-six when she opened a third restaurant with fifty tables. She considered this "her biggest success so far."[37]

The successes of private entrepreneurs in China do not come easily. Entrepreneurs must work hard, dream, and plan for success. They look for opportunities to introduce a new commodity, improve organization, a new technique, raw materials or the development of newly discovered resources. They must coordinate the necessary capital, management, labor, and materials to accomplish their goals. In any economy, the rate of development depends greatly on the supply of entrepreneurs and their ability to function in a given environment. One entrepreneur, who had ability, worked hard with his parents, and planned to expand his ice cream business by incorporating new technology, said,

From my experience as a part-time manager, I think it is difficult to do individual business. My business is connected with the weather. Even if the weather is hot, we work hard. My parents are feeling better by doing business and they are happy. With a big company, life will be much easier, but with more use of brains than using muscles like now. Sometimes I feel pity for my parents because they work hard during hot weather even when it is too hot.[38]

The hard work and desire to break new ground not only brings profits to private entrepreneurs, it creates jobs, increases the purchasing power of consumers, and improves the varieties of goods. In 1992, both *getihu* and private companies in the industrial, construction, and transportation fields produced output in goods and services worth 113 billion yuan ($19.8 billion)—4.1 percent of China's total output. Sales volume in commerce, the food industry, and other services was 195 billion yuan ($34.2 billion), 18.1 percent of total retail sales. By 1991, 89 percent of retail sales outlets—7.72 million—belonged to the private sector and "during 1978 and 1986, the number of individually employed people increased to 18.82 million, without any government assistance. During the same period, however, the State-owned enterprises received 131 billion yuan ($23 billion) in government money for employing 18.82 million labourers."[39]

The private sector's business people are aware of the unemployment problem, and they understand that they contribute to China's economic development and social stability by creating new jobs. One entrepreneur, when asked if individual business helped solve the problem of unemployment, replied, "Yes. Some people can no longer count on the State to give them jobs. Now they can make a living by themselves [and they can also switch occupations]. Now, my relative has quit the clothing business to open a small restaurant, and he can earn more money."[40] The private sector is doing a great service to the CCP and to its survival. A drastic increase in unemployment could result in social instability and a threat to law and order in the country.

No doubt inflation contributes to social dissatisfaction and economic instability, and in general affects all citizens of the country, but unemployment is different. During unemployment, the unemployed masses compare their misery with the condition of others and feel unfairly treated. "When this psychology goes to an extreme degree, it would affect social stability," observed Li Yining, an economist at Beijing University.[41] China has a large population and limited arable land. To raise productivity and avoid the problems of unemployment, it is imperative on China's part to transfer millions of rural residents from the agricultural to the nonagricultural sector.

This cannot be done by the parasitic state sector. The only way China can avoid unemployment is to facilitate the rapid growth of *getihu* and private enterprises, which are the only sectors that can absorb such a large number of workers. In the first half of 1992, about 8 million workers became unemployed, over half from rural areas. Most of the unemployed workers from the urban areas were able to find jobs in township enterprises and the private sector. A survey by the All China Federation of Trade Unions found that about 10 to 15 percent of the 144.6 million work force were unemployed and needed to be resettled.[42]

The entrepreneurs are coming to the rescue of the economic survival of China by creating jobs; officials of the Labor Ministry have confessed to this fact. In 1993, private-owned businesses were creating new jobs while the state sector was laying off its employees. One official said that the private sector, including foreign-invested firms (which may include private entrepreneurs in disguise) increased the number of their workers by more than 300,000 from March through August 1993, whereas the state sector cut their labor force by over 1.4 million. Lower-level state-sector rural township and village-run industries increased their number of employees by three million.[43] Vietnam, a socialist country, also experienced an increase in national wealth and job creation because of active participation by private entrepreneurs in its economy.[44]

Private entrepreneurship, and the freedom that accompanys it, creates room for other entrepreneurs to move in and create more jobs as a complement to the existing ones. This is particularly true for a communist economy moving toward a newborn market economy. For example, in 1991 insurance revenue in China was $32 billion, which was 1 percent of its GNP (while in the United States it was $431 billion, representing 8.9 percent of GNP). Though small, this is the beginning of a new and previously unknown sector in China's economy.[45]

Commercial advertisements in the mass media[46] and the real estate business are becoming part of the communist economy. In 1991, China's income from land use taxes was 3.17 billion yuan, income from real estate transaction taxes was 187 million yuan, and taxes paid by real estate enterprises amounted to 2.045 billion yuan. Altogether the amount totaled up to 2.3 percent of China's total financial income. In 1992, more than 10,000 real estate related enterprises were in existence, with a total of 2.4 million workers.[47] Private entrepreneurs are also pouring money into the economy as philanthropists. In Quanzhou, Fujian Province, local entrepreneurs united to invest 400 million yuan ($46 million) to build an eighteen-kilometer highway, including a two-kilometer bridge. They also plan to renovate Quanzhou Airport.[48]

All of these new activities are contributing to the economy by creating jobs, increasing purchasing power, and circulating money. In the communist system, there were no individual freedoms to expand and take individual initiative to create something new. The communist economy furnished no incentives for anyone to put forth any ideas. Because the economy was artificially saturated by government imposed demand and supply, all sectors of the economy—agriculture, heavy industries, light industries, and service sector—shrank, and the service sector virtually disappeared.

Generally, in an economy, the service sector occupies the majority of economic activities; it is where most jobs are created and the circulation of funds occurs. The durable goods market becomes saturated very easily. In order for consumers to spend money for self-satisfaction, they look to the service sector for variety and proper treatment. The service sector may be "defined to include trade, transportation and public utilities, finance and insurance, professional services, personal services, government, education, and the independent hand trades."[49] In other words, it is often small businesses that create jobs and try to provide maximum satisfaction to the consumers, thus making an economy dynamic. In 1992, the service sector constituted 27.7 percent of China's GNP and workers were 19 percent of the total work force. But in the United States, Japan, and Hong Kong, the service sector accounts for 60 to 70 percent of GNP. In the United States and Japan more than 70 percent of the workforce are involved in the service sector.[50] The Chinese are spending more money and time on the service sector, thus giving it the impetus to grow. In a study of Tianjin's residents, it was found that they are spending an extra hour per day in leisure activities, compared to ten years ago. Spending by Tianjin residents in tourist activities in the first half of 1994 was up threefold, compared to the same period in 1993. With the demand for leisure-time activities, the leisure industry is contributing toward China's socioeconomic development. In fact, during the past few years 839 recreational facilities have been built in the coastal cities of China with a total investment of 3.75 billion yuan ($440 million).[51]

China has more room to grow in the service sector with the energetic involvement of private entrepreneurs or *getihu*. As one entrepreneur said, "It [individual businesses] provides small commodities and strengthens the competition and stimulates the economy."[52] Another entrepreneur said, "The individual businesses will bring prosperity to the economy of the PRC. Individual businesses will become active, doing business so they will have responsibility to run the business well or lose."[53]

Private entrepreneurs must work hard and utilize their resources effectively. Where state sectors waste, private entrepreneurs save. Where state sectors are slow, private entrepreneurs are fast. Where state sectors are unwilling to provide services, private entrepreneurs are willing to provide them. It is a matter of inefficiency versus efficiency. A look at a private entrepreneur who repairs bicycles in Beijing will help make the point clear. The entrepreneur opened his shop intentionally beside a state-owned bicycle repair shop. When asked why did he do so, he replied, "The State shop does not accept any business that might present trouble, or anything urgent or trivial. And the attendants there do not work after hours. So I work more than a dozen hours a day and manage to finish all the tasks I accept on the same day."[54]

It is not unusual at all to find private entrepreneurs working hard and spending long hours on their businesses. All the entrepreneurs I met while in China adhered to this profile. One entrepreneur in the electronics business who worked long hours said, "We work six and a half to seven days a week. Every day we work from 9:30 A.M. to midnight. As a founder, I have to work and stay up late till 1:00 A.M. to 2:00 A.M. the next day."[55]

The government of China is saving both time and materials by letting private entrepreneurs be governed by market law. Under market law, entrepreneurs do not have the luxury of free time, free raw materials, or free goods. They must work hard and utilize time, human resources, and other material factors to the maximum in order to survive in a competitive market and, at the same time, please consumers. An entrepreneurs' offspring and descendants will have to follow this same routine of hard work, innovation, and efficient use of time and resources in order to continue the success of their ancestors. It is the very nature of market law to leave incompetent and idle individuals behind. There is no such thing as a perpetual flow of income. Every venture should be renewed by entrepreneurial labor.

This law of the market is motivating entrepreneurs with a desire to succeed and to find new resources and avenues to offer services to consumers. In a newly developing market economy, a bicycle repair shop, restaurant, eyeglass shop, or grocery mart with good service may not look like a great innovation, but the establishment of such a project, which was not previously available in a communist system, is indeed extraordinary and represents the creation of new demands in their own right. As observed by Peter Morris in his study on African entrepreneurship, "In the African countryside, an innovation may not seem, at the outset, very remarkable—a wholesale business, a restaurant at a crossroad, a bus service, a saw mill. But to achieve it, the owner must have seen what others had missed—an unsatisfied demand, a way of raising money, a source of skilled labor—and put them together."[56] In China, private entrepreneurs are not only meeting the market's demand by providing services, they are also innovative in introducing new findings in science and technology in the marketplace for profit, thus reflecting entrepreneurship as described by Schumpeter, which was missing during the Maoist era.

Many entrepreneurs in China are not only innovative but they are also determined. In the face of problems, they prove themselves winners. One such entrepreneur was forty-year-old Ye Wengui, a native of Jinxiang Town of Wenzhou City, Zhejiang Province. He could not enter a university and later on became a victim of the Cultural Revolution. In 1978, he returned home to Wenzhou. In the early 1980s, he quit his job in a state-owned enterprise and started his own business. By 1992, he had invested more than 5 million yuan ($900,000) in the process of developing an electric car. With cooperative agreements signed with partners in Guangdong and Anhui

Provinces to produce electric cars, Ye planned to produce 3,000 electric cars per year.[57]

Entrepreneurs like Ye are not alone. There are other entrepreneurs who take failures and problems in life and business and turn them into successes because of a strong desire to succeed and, in turn, make life better for others. As one entrepreneur put it when asked if he faced any difficulties in his business career,

> Yes, in one word [I faced difficulties]. I spend more than half of my time dealing with business beyond my own business. When I meet with problems, I regard it as a normal thing that I am sure to meet while beginning and expanding my business. I do not work for money and therefore, I do not worry about problems caused by money very much. I will not stop walking [that is, working].[58]

With hard work, innovative ideas, and tenacity in the face of difficulties (which come from the communist system) entrepreneurs in China are changing economic conditions for the better. They are changing ghost towns into lively places to live. Take Yanghekou, a village in Funing County in Hebei Province, previously known for its backwardness. "An old saying described it as an evil village with an evil smell. Girls preferred to marry out of the village." With the introduction of a free market economy and the changes that come with it, the village is now a prosperous place to live, and most of the 700 families in the village are newcomers. Interestingly, "anyone can get a permanent residence by paying 5,000 yuan ($920) to the local government."[59] In a similar case in Xiaoyuzi village of Pinggu county, men left the village for better earnings, but the women grouped together to save the village and were successful.[60]

With the success of Chinese entrepreneurs, newspapers that were once controlled by the communist propaganda machine are coming forward to analyze the success of private entrepreneurship. *Jingji Guangli* reported in a case study of Baoding City near Beijing in Hebei Province that individual entrepreneurs are motivated by profit-driven ventures. Entrepreneurs offer better services along with extended and prolonged labor time, which is usually ten hours a day and sometimes extends to twelve hours per day. Along with hard work, which increases the intensity of labor, private entrepreneurs offer a good service attitude, smiling faces, and always cater to the customers' needs. The management is also very efficient, and entrepreneurs are sensitive to market demands and are able to adjust to supply goods as the demand changes. During the communist regime the commercial service trades were very limited. Before 1980, in Baoding City there were only six service units for every 1,000 people. "This was far behind public demand." So with the reform policy, private entrepreneurs were able to move in and offer goods and services to consumers, thereby making the economy dynamic.[61]

With the success of the private sector, the hardliners in Beijing and other places in China are taking a back seat in the reform movement while the reformers are heeding the natural law of economics and the call of private entrepreneurs for greater opportunities to expand and help the economy. As one entrepreneur replied, when asked what he would like to tell Jiang Zemin about the Chinese economic development, "I will tell him to give more opportunity to individual businesses because it will help the economy. If some businesses are harming the society, like pollution, I will tell him to stop those businesses."[62]

With renewed support from the government after the fall of Zhao Ziyang, entrepreneurs are responding in a positive fashion and the government is reciprocating. An engagement for marriage between entrepreneurs and the government is occurring as we define the economic roles of the entrepreneur in China. Government officials "based their optimism about the prospects for China's private economy on Deng Xiaoping's South-China-tour speech last year (1992), which gave the go-ahead signals to the sector."[63] A recent nationwide survey of 1,432 private enterprises "found that private entrepreneurs spent most of their profits expanding their ventures rather than squandering them on non-essentials."[64] This is good news for China's economic development. For the first time since the *San-fan* and *Wu-fan* campaigns, China's private entrepreneurs are showing confidence in their system. This renewed confidence means a reduction in the life-uncertainty factor, confidence to start a new chapter on entrepreneurial history in China and create a new culture for the Chinese to respect and honor enterepreneurial talents. All of these factors make the economy dynamic. This is a move toward risk and uncertainty as defined by Knight, leading the private sector and the Deng government toward mutual understanding and respect.

If the Chinese government again betrays this evolving mutual understanding, as it did during the Tiananmen Square massacre, it will have an even greater impact on all aspects of China because more resources and talents are at stake. Moreover, many in government have given up hope of survival for the state sector and have surrendered, in principle, to the private sector.

The government appears truly committed to the privatization of the economy. With the vigorous involvement of the private sector to produce and sell goods to the consumer, more outlets are needed. The government is not only providing these new outlets, but with the increase in the private sector's numbers and capacity, the government is allowing the private sector to take over incompetent money-losing state companies and revitalize them. In September 1992, it was reported that since 1978, the number of cities in China had risen from 192 to 488, due to the increased production of goods and the expansion of markets. Due to the thirteen years of reforms, state planning in the domestic economy has decreased. The government now fixes prices for only 30 percent of goods and controls the flow of only nineteen categories of goods, down from 256 in the past. This led Gao Shangquan, vice-minister of the State Commission for Restructuring the Economic System, to observe, "Wherever local markets play a decisive role, the economy enjoys a faster development; wherever compulsory economic plans rule, local development remains sluggish."[65]

In 1978 there were only 33,300 free markets, and the volume of their business transactions totaled 1.25 billion yuan ($143 million), only 5.4 percent of China's retail sales. By 1993 there were 83,001 free markets with a business volume of 534.3 billion yuan ($61.4 billion), accounting for 28 percent of gross retail business volume. Moreover, today's free markets are not like the traditional markets where the sellers were mostly farmers. They are busy places, and the actors include state-run enterprises and collective units, in addition to private entrepreneurs. The goods for sale include industrial materials and products, not only daily necessities.

Due to all these activities, new doors for employment have opened that were not available during communist rule. More than 470,000 people are involved in transporting commodities to the free market, and it is estimated that 1.06 million motor vehicles and 83,000 ships are involved in transporting commodities.[66] Tianjin has also set up an extensive market system consisting of both national and local markets, spot goods and futures markets, and retail and wholesale markets. In recent years Tianjin's retail sales have increased at a yearly rate of 20 percent, totaling 22.7 billion yuan ($2.6 billion) in 1993.[67]

Due to all the positive results produced by the private sector and the momentum created to expand it, the government is leasing state-owned enterprises to the private sector. They are producing positive results by salvaging dying industries. For example, the Tongling Jinxing Silk Mill in Tongling, Anhui Province, was leased to a private entrepreneur named Si. According to Si, the mill is running successfully with 340 employees and 16 managerial personnel. "As a result, the mill has overcome deficits and made profits. It generated about 1 million yuan ($173,310) in profits and tax payments over the last year (1992) since it was leased to Si's individual management."[68]

In Beijing, about 90 percent of 4,000 street stores leased or contracted to private entrepreneurs are running successfully. Xu, a successful entrepreneur who could not get loans from the government under the contract, but who was responsible for her own profits and losses, was making a profit, and paying leasing fees and "all taxes" on time.[69]

The efficient performances by private entrepreneurs is causing the state sector to curtail their activities. In 1978, state enterprises accounted for 73 percent of all industrial output; collective units accounted for the rest. By 1990, the state sector's industrial output fell to 35 percent, collective units' output fell to 27 percent. In contrast, "real growth had come from foreign-invested and private companies, whose share of industrial output has risen from a zero base in 1978 to 5% in 1985 and 38% in 1990."[70] Because of the rise of market-sensitive firms, China's industrial output by lower-tier governments, collectives, private entrepreneurs, and foreign firms account for half of all industrial output. The government of China expects their share of output to rise to 75 percent by the year 2000, "when over 50% of the country's industrial assets, as well as practically all rural land and most city property, will also be out of the Central government's hands."[71]

With a positive government policy toward the private sector and movement away from the Maoist past, entrepreneurs are producing results. This is reflected in the betterment of consumers' lives and the healthy economic statistics. The Chinese are eating more food per capita than ever before. A report from forty-three big and medium-sized cities stated that since 1992, the consumption of eggs by the Chinese has reached 12.9 kilograms per person, the average in some developed countries. Meat consumption has reached 31.3 kilograms, which is close to the world average, and 180.1 kilograms of vegetables are consumed per person; China has exceeded consumption levels of some developed countries. In 1992, the sales volume of food products was 22.36 billion yuan ($3.86), "46.1 per cent more than 1991 and an increase of 200 per cent over 1988." On average, the Chinese living in cities spent about 35 percent of their monthly budget on nonstaple food in 1992.[72]

The GDP of China rose from 358.8 billion yuan (about $44 billion) in 1978 to 3,138 billion yuan ($404 billion) in 1993. In 1978, yearly per capita income of urban citizens was 343 yuan ($38); by 1993, it had jumped to 2,337 yuan ($262). For the Chinese in rural communities, income rose from 145 yuan ($16) in 1978 to 921 yuan ($103) in 1993.[73]

With the rapid economic development of China, it is expected that the government's reform policy will strongly encourage private entrepreneurship. It was predicted by Yang Dakan of the State Planning Commission's Economic Research Institute that there would be 19 million *getihu* in 1994 (a 12 percent increase over 1993), and they would absorb 32 million workers. The number of private enterprises is predicted to be 370,000, employing about 5 million people. The average assets of private enterprises would be 370,000 yuan ($42,000), with an average output value of 100,000 yuan ($11,500), and a sales volume of 70,000 yuan ($8,000).[74]

Over time, growth of the private sector relative to other sectors means that the power wielded by the others will be diminished. New actors will emerge to fill the resulting power vacuum. One group of potential actors are private entrepreneurs backed by new wealth.

THE RISING POWER OF PRIVATE ENTREPRENEURS

With the progress of the reform process over the last sixteen years and the rapid economic development of China, the control of the CCP over its masses is diminishing. The Chinese people, in many cases, are no longer dependent on the government for a subsidized way of life. More than 100 million people are looking for jobs in urban areas. This suggests that people in China are freer than they were in 1978 and are more in control of their lives. The perpetuation of this trend will lead China and its people toward something new. China's national agenda is not only being set in Beijing but across the country by millions of citizens who are grasping the entrepreneurial opportunities in the free market.

Along with economic reform comes political reform; one is unlikely to occur without the other. It will not be surprising to see different groups in China advocating a legal system to protect their life-styles through new laws. Without such a system, China will not be able to move fully toward the new paradigm. There is also a movement to revert to the policies of the past. It is also possible that a civil war will result if the hardliners try to stop the reform movement.

At best, an authoritarian regime is now ruling a new, evolving China that is heavily influenced by the richer provinces to move the country toward greater economic freedom. This will eventually force China to follow the paths of other successful countries—Taiwan, South Korea, Singapore, and Malaysia—that emerged from authoritarian regimes as freer societies with improved economic development. For China, the move toward the new paradigm is even more crucial because of its historical tendency toward separatism. At present, there are separatist tendencies between the poorer interior provinces and the richer southern coastal provinces. In particular, the centers of economic development in Guangdong and Hong Kong—who have their own customs and whose dialect, Guangdonghua (Cantonese) is different from putonghua (Mandarin)—pose a threat to the central authority.

Private entrepreneurs are one group that may help China move toward economic development and keep it stable. They have already invested resources, both material and emotional, to make life better for themselves and others, thus bringing changes to society, and they are seeking ways to influence their environment. Anita Weiss, in her case study of Punjab, Pakistan, found that entrepreneurs were the vanguard of a new epoch brought about because of economic development and were contributing significantly toward a new culture of development in Punjab.[75] Similarly, Hungarian entrepreneurs offered a challenge to the existing system and were a force to bring "far-reaching" social and political changes to the country.[76]

The case of China is no different. With growing economic power, Chinese entrepreneurs are becoming socially and politically conscious. Before the Tiananmen Square massacre, private entrepreneurs were involved in publishing journals and books. This support by private entrepreneurs was one of the reasons the dissidents were able to be so bold. Repression of the Tiananmen student-led demonstration does not mean that all the apparatus of opposition to the central authority has withered away. Opposition to authoritarian rule will likely raise its head again unless China moves toward the new paradigm and comes to a legal, binding agreement with entrepreneurs and entrepreneurial consumers. "It is impossible to fully repress a minority position since it is a timespirit. . . . A minority may appear to comply, but the group spirit and atmosphere of even a large organization will eventually be ruined by the mood of resentment, mistrust, and hatred."[77]

With the slow movement toward the new paradigm led by the entrepreneurs, China may be able to avoid further bloodshed and any possible separatist sentiments. With the development of private entrepreneurship, where private sellers and buyers are the main actors, government is losing its control over the masses. At the same time, entrepreneurs are moving to accumulate not only economic power but political power because both these factors will help entrepreneurs guide China toward the new paradigm.[78]

With the increase in economic freedom and power, private entrepreneurs are slowly moving into China's national politics. The Eighth Chinese People's Political Consultative Conference (CPPCC), China's top counseling body (considered to be a rubber stamp of the CCP), gave membership to twenty-one entrepreneurs; current membership is 2,095. This is, at least, a beginning and gives the private sector some opportunity to assert its presence in the Chinese economy and also influence the government policy. With their newfound freedom, private entrepreneurs have formed their own organization—the All-China Federation of Industry and Commerce—and have become unprecedentedly vocal in airing their opinions. Xia Shouchun, a member of the CPPCC and a private businessman from Sheyang County, Jiangsu Province, said that the private sector was "a force which [could] not be under-estimated." It has liberated productive forces, created job opportunities, and produced wealth to make life easier for consumers. Xia advocated for private enterprises not to be discriminated against politically or economically by the CCP, and hoped that with the deepening of reform, "China's private economy [would] have more opportunities than difficulties."[79] Rong Yiren, known as a national capitalist from the 1940s, was empowered by Deng Xiaoping to be chairperson of one of China's leading private companies, International Trust and Investment Corporation (Citic) in 1979 to pioneer China's reforms, was elected as vice-president of the state.[80]

Even though private entrepreneurs are able to get some recognition and opportunities in the political realm, in reality, even with economic freedom, there is no real political freedom. China is still an authoritarian regime and viciously quells any political discord. The death of communist ideology does not mean that the apparatus of the CCP to suppress any opposition is dead. All this may be true, but there needs to be a starting point for change. In Russia we saw the beginning of the Duma in Gorbachev's glasnost and perestroika; in Poland we saw the labor unions leading Poland toward greater freedom.

If China wants to move toward an ideal system of economic development, it must provide opportunities to both entrepreneurs and consumers to participate politically. Policymakers must be held accountable for the implementation of policies and the resulting consequences. This accountability means that entrepreneurs and consumers must have legal rights to throw existing policymakers out of office and replace them with those willing to continue the process. If this does not happen, entrepreneurs and consumers will not have the freedom to enter and exit the market at will because the life-uncertainty factor will continue to dictate the behavior of entrepreneurs and consumers alike, which will make them irrational in economic behavior—they will not invest when investment is needed, they will not save when it is appropriate to save, they will consume beyond what is needed. All this means a diminution of wealth and a lack of capital to meet unsatisfied demand and to create new demands. Moreover, in a repressive system, the consumers and entrepreneurs may initially go along with the regime's economic policy but in the long run they will demand their basic human rights and political rights, which may cause chaos in the society, threatening both economic and political stability. For an economy to develop fully, both economic and political freedom are needed.

If this is the case, it would be quite natural for entrepreneurs, consumers, and the government to cooperate with each other through legal institutions to move China toward the new paradigm. Because the government of China is a well-organized unit, it is necessary for entrepreneurs and consumers to also organize and protect their interests, and thus bring a balance of power to the system. Consumers are exerting their rights as buyers and organizing themselves, which may lead to something new.

Entrepreneurs realize that as individuals, they cannot bring about any significant change; however, as a group, they may be able to bring about significant change. As one entrepreneur said, "One individual entrepreneur is too weak [to bring any economic change]. The union of individual entrepreneurs can help China's economic development. The municipal government of Tianjin has such an organization."[81] As if to second this idea of the entrepreneur in Tianjin, an entrepreneur in Anzhou, Fujian Province, named Xu Jingnan, president of the Peak Shoemaking Group and a member of the local entrepreneurs' organization, said, "As a single private enterprise, our strength is limited. But once we unite, we are more able to do what we would like to do."[82] According to a survey, 37 percent of "wealthy, powerful private entrepreneurs" felt that they were contributing in an important way toward their communities. This led Dai Jianzhong, deputy director of the Department of Sociology of the Beijing Academy of Social Sciences, to observe that "private enterprises will ask for more participation in their communities when their business ventures become increasingly successful."[83]

This involvement of private entrepreneurs at the local level, and the decline in power and control over the lives of the citizens by the CCP means that as days go by, private entrepreneurs have an opportunity to become powerful. With involvement at local levels, entrepreneurs should be able to win the support and recognition of the masses as a source of resources beside the CCP. Private entrepreneurs as philanthropists are contributing significantly to their communities, thus making life better for the local people. Because private entrepreneurs are fulfilling some of the traditional obligations of the government, they are becoming powerful in their own right and gaining their own constituents.

The magnitude of private entrepreneurs' potential involvement in their communities and the economy is not truly reflected in the data presented by the Chinese National Information Center, which estimated that in 1991 the state sector accounted for 53 percent of all industrial output; collectives, 36 percent; and private businesses, 11 percent. In the year 2000, the shares would be 27 percent, 48 percent and 25 percent, respectively.[84] The number of registered private businesses is misleading because many private entrepreneurs use the umbrella of collective enterprises, joint ventures, or *getihu* to receive special treatment and retain more profits.[85] According to Thomas Rawski, an economist at the University of Pittsburgh, "tens of millions" of persons employed in the "unrecorded economy" are not reported,[86] both economically and in numbers for the private sector.

The Chinese economy is more dependent on private entrepreneurs and *getihu* than the statistics convey. With the growth of the service sector, which makes an economy dynamic, more economic and political power will be at the disposal of private entrepreneurs.

A close look at one young man's aspirations will help to reveal the sentiments of some of the Chinese people. He was from Anhui Province, working as a waiter in Beijing. When asked if he would ever go back to Anhui, he replied spiritedly, "Well, whether I go there or stay in Beijing, at least that will be my own decision."[87] Is not freedom all about making decisions on one's own? As days roll by with increasingly greater freedom in economic areas, the Chinese will venture into other areas of life where they will have to make decisions about schooling, health and medical care, housing, employment and other daily necessities of life. This means less dependency on the government and a loss of control by the CCP, which, in turn, means a gain in the individual's power to make decisions. The greater the ability to make decisions by individuals, the less encroachment on individuals' lives by the government. The longer the process goes on, the less power the CCP will maintain. The Chinese society as a whole will slowly move away from the life-uncertainty factor (a product of the Maoist past), recent politics influenced by authoritarian Confucian, and communist culture. To balance this new evolving power and properly distribute the wealth to avoid polarization, neither the government nor the CCP has much choice but to move toward the new paradigm by formulating new laws to guide a market economy. One such law is the law of taxation, which may help China to balance its political and economic power.

TAXATION—THE BALANCING FACTOR

With the introduction of a market economy, the CCP had to allow the private economy to flourish, and at the same time free the state-owned enterprises from government control. Direct control over the economy by the CCP is diminishing, and the economy is moving away from the life-uncertainty factor, which has hindered the economic development of China in the past, and is moving toward the new paradigm. If the CCP wants the economy to continue to grow, it cannot use coercive measures arbitrarily to raise money. If these measures are taken, the life-uncertainty factor would once again rise and bring ruin to the economy. In the past, most government revenue came from state enterprises. With the evolution of state enterprises as separate entities not under government control and the rapid development of the private sector, the survival of the CCP and the betterment of the country depends on an effective tax law system that incorporates both local and central actors.

A look at the evolving tax laws regarding private businesses shows that the Chinese government, and the system as a whole, are moving toward the new paradigm by incorporating new tax laws as new circumstances and economic realities arise. Before 1980, private businesses were taxed like collective enterprises, according to the Trial Regulations of the State Council on Adjusting the Industrial and Commercial Income Tax Burden and Improved Tax Collection Method, issued on April 13, 1963. The tax was divided into fourteen progressive rates until the Cultural Revolution began, reaching a highest marginal rate of 86.8 percent on yearly income of more than 5,000 yuan. After the Cultural Revolution, the number of progressive rates was reduced to eleven and in 1980 it was reduced to eight.[88]

China's tax policy and reality are very different from the written laws. "On paper, the system appears almost rational—replete with schedules, adjustments, scales, and detailed regulations. In reality, tax payments are politically negotiated at every level. What you pay and to whom you pay it, depends mainly on who you are."[89] It was reported in *Renmin Ribao* on January 25, 1986, that with the advent of the *getihu*, local officials saw an opportunity to fill their coffers and arbitrarily raised tax rates and fees. This forced many entrepreneurs to withdraw from business and return their permits.[90] In Wenzhou, Zhejiang Province, officials' harassment led some private businessmen to spend money on luxury goods and expensive family burial tombs. Some entrepreneurs quit their businesses or evaded paying taxes by taking advantage of the lack of regulations.[91] In Shanghai, about 86 percent of registered private business people did not pay taxes. "The streets of China's towns and cities are full of unlicensed peddlers" and "probably 100%" of them do not pay taxes. Many private business people simply bribe the collectors in order to feel secure.[92]

From my interviews with entrepreneurs in Tianjin in 1991, I found that few of them complain about tax rates or policy. Most were bothered by the government officials who were in charge of collecting taxes and fees. One entrepreneur said, "After selling, we pay tax according to our turnover, e.g., 20 to 30 yuan per 1,000 yuan turnover. It is fixed. We never complain about taxes, we complain about the government officials."[93] Another entrepreneur said, "The tax is too high [because of officials' harassment and manipulation of money]. I have some problems with the authorities. They sometimes randomly come and take taxes. Sometimes I give them a free hair cut."[94] Some entrepreneurs, who paid monthly fixed taxes or other forms of taxes, were happy about the tax policy, if not the officials. And others felt that by paying taxes, they were helping to support the country's construction. One such entrepreneur said,

> I am satisfied with it [tax policy]. The government's favorable policy toward our high-tech company is to reduce the tax rate by 10% to 20%. As we know, tax revenue is the main source of government income and it supports our government administration. As individual businessmen, we should not try to avoid and evade paying taxes. The tax rates in some developed countries are very high. Therefore, the reduction of tax rates is not the prerequisite of favorable policies. The more important thing to do is to create a taxation environment. There is a lack of education; few individual businessmen have the knowledge of paying taxes. For such people, tax education is necessary.[95]

It has been reported that because of a lack of "standardized laws and regulations on taxation," the state lost more than 8 billion yuan ($1.4 billion) before 1992.[96]

When life uncertainty governs a system, laws are not properly implemented. The whims of officials dictate the behavior of the entrepreneurs. Sometimes officials are able to extract money from entrepreneurs, and sometimes entrepreneurs are successful at evading taxes or, if not, simply quit their businesses. As a consequence, the central government is deprived of revenue for infrastructure and regional development, thereby eroding the wealth of the nation.

To ward off official corruption and tax evasion, the government is pushing the system toward a new paradigm governed by laws. Table 6.1 on government income from the private sector shows that with every passing year, the government's income from the private sector is increasing, thereby indicating progress toward a more effective system.

In fact, in 1992 the government collected 20.3 billion yuan ($3.5 billion) in taxes from the private sector, which was 7.8 percent of the nation's total. It was forecasted that by 1997 the private sector might pay taxes up to 50 billion yuan ($8.62 billion).[97]

On January 7, 1986, the State Council promulgated Interim Regulations of the People's Republic of China on Income Tax Concerning Urban and Rural Individual-Operated Industrial and Commercial Businesses,[98] to

Table 6.1
State Income from the Private Sector (100 million yuan)

Year	Private Business	Individual Business
1976	—	3.94
1977	—	4.63
1978	—	5.07
1979	—	5.30
1980	—	6.36
1981	—	8.84
1982	—	35.23
1983	—	35.75
1984	—	40.99
1985	—	79.59
1986	—	52.00
1987	—	68.00
1988	—	92.00
1989	—	132.00

Source: Kraus, 44.

replace the previous tax laws governing the income tax of the individually-run economy. The taxable income consisted of the excess of gross income for the given year over deductible costs—expenses, wages, losses, and before-tax expenses allowed by the law (Article 2). The income tax for individual firms was based on a ten-level progressive tax (Article 3; see Table 6.2), and a 10 to 40 percent surtax was levied on individuals with an income over 50,000 yuan (Article 4).

The individual business tax law of January 7, 1986 showed some signs of the government's desire to improve the economic environment for entrepreneurs. First, the tax law was a legal endorsement of private entrepreneurship, thus a move away from the life-uncertainty factor toward the new paradigm. Second, some groups were given incentives for tax reductions and exemptions to venture into the private market economy. The people's governments for provinces, autonomous regions, or municipalities directly under the central government were allowed to grant tax reductions and exemptions to the following taxpayers who had

Table 6.2
Income for Individual Firms

Level	Annual Income (yuan)	Tax Rate (%)	Amount Withheld
1	Not over 1,000	7	0
2	1,000–2,000	15	80
3	2,000–4,000	25	280
4	4,000–6,000	30	480
5	6,000–8,000	35	780
6	8,000–12,000	40	1,180
7	12,000–18,000	45	1,780
8	18,000–24,000	50	2,680
9	24,000–30,000	55	3,880
10	30,000–	60	5,380

Source: Xinhua News Agency, 24 January 1986.

experienced difficulties in paying taxes: (1) the childless elderly, handicapped, and family members of martyrs involved in individual business; and (2) those who provided badly needed services by using high labor intensity and yielded lower incomes than the given standard (Article 5). Article 5 proves that the government was not only trying to create job opportunities for the unemployed and those dependent on government welfare, but was also pushing for the service sector to develop at the lowest level, which meant more individual entrepreneurs and more constituents for the reformers.

With the success of the *getihu*, the economy followed a natural course, which was a move away from the life-uncertainty factor. This gave rise to private businesses hiring more than eight employees. The private businesses were taxed like the *getihu*, and in cases where 60 to 70 percent of the employees were unemployed youths, income taxes for two or three years were waived.[99] On June 28, 1988, the Interim Regulations of the People's Republic of China on the Income Tax of Private Enterprises were issued. Total yearly income, minus expenses and costs, was taxed under the new law at the rate of 35 percent. However, tax reductions or exemptions were offered to those private businesses that used waste water, waste gas, and residues as the main raw materials, or had problems paying taxes because of natural disasters or another extraordinary crisis. Private businesses were allowed to carry over their business losses for three years. To encourage private businesses to reinvest, the tax regulations stated that 50 percent of after-tax profits should be used to expand production. Any amount used for expanding production was exemp from the adjustment tax on individual income, whereas any amount of after-tax profit used for personal consumption was taxed at the rate of 40 percent.[100]

To further demonstrate the reformers' desire to move toward the new paradigm, Provisional Regulations of the People's Republic of China on Enterprise Income Tax were adopted at the 12th general meeting of the State Council on November 26, 1993, and went into effect on January 1, 1994. According to this tax law, all enterprises are required to pay an enterprise income tax, except foreign investment enterprises and foreign enterprises. Thus, state-owned, collective, private, joint venture, joint stock, and other enterprises are required to pay taxes at the rate of 33 percent, but enterprises functioning in autonomous regions "requiring special incentives and encouragement" will be offered tax reductions or exemptions. Taxpayers will pay taxes to the local tax authorities. With the adoption of the new enterprise income tax laws, previous tax regulations governing state-owned, collective, and private enterprises were nullified. This signaled a major move toward the new paradigm, where all enterprises will be taxed equally.[101]

The reformers in the CCP have also laid the groundwork needed to strengthen the central authority by adopting a new tax system where the central government will control 60 percent of the state revenue. Forty percent will be used by the central government and 20 percent will be allocated to local governments through transfer grants.[102] If the new tax reform is successful in the future, China will face less turmoil and conflict between the central and provincial authorities, and between regions. This will give the system an opportunity to move toward the new paradigm, where economic development will occur through entrepreneurial activities and entrepreneurial consumers will also play a major role.

ENTREPRENEURIAL CONSUMERS—AN EVOLVING GROUP

Just as entrepreneurs need the freedom to make full use of resources for maximum benefit, consumers need the freedom of choice to reject and the right to criticize and hold accountable the producers for the goods they produce. If this freedom is not available for consumers, even with the freedom given to entrepreneurs, an economy will face distortion. If entrepreneurs face no challenges from the consumers to produce better quality goods, consumers will lose faith and confidence in the goods on the market, thereby reducing consumption.

However, in an economy where consumers enjoy the above-mentioned freedom, the innovative drive of entrepreneurs is complemented. In a free market, entrepreneurial consumers always look for opportunities to buy goods at a lower price, thus pushing the market toward equilibrium by purchasing surplus goods, and exiting the market as soon as consumers face a market equilibrium. In this process of buying goods from the market, a consumer is protected by law to demand equal value for money spent. If faced with shoddy products, a consumer has the right to demand money back and if that right is not respected by the sellers, the sellers face the consequences of the law and a loss of credibility in the market.

In this process of pushing the market toward equilibrium and holding sellers accountable for the quality of goods sold in the market, entrepreneurial consumers contribute to bringing the best out of entrepreneurs and lawmakers alike. Entrepreneurs in a new paradigm, faced with an equilibrium governed by usual uncertainty, are forced to look for new markets to meet unsatisfied demand and also create new demands, thus making an economy dynamic with a fresh circulation of funds. On the other hand, the lawmakers face the wrath of entrepreneurial consumers if they fail to protect their rights in the market.

Although in present-day China entrepreneurial consumers are not able to hold national decisionmakers accountable, this does not mean that they are not able to hold the producers and sellers of goods accountable for the quality of the goods produced and sold in the market. Consumers are asserting their rights and demanding quality goods in return for their money. At the same time, with the diminishing effect of the life-uncertainty factor in the economy, both consumers and entrepreneurs are able to handle factors that come along with a market economy, such as inflation and personal savings, rationally, unlike in the past, when the concept of a market economy in a communist system was first introduced.

Previously, consumers in the Maoist era were accused of criticizing the government if they merely complained about the quality of goods in the state-owned stores, but present-day consumers are a different breed. With the introduction of the market economy, and the movement of the Chinese system toward the new paradigm, Chinese consumers are faced with new challenges; they must take responsibility for deciding what and how much to buy from the market. In a market economy guided by established laws, consumers, like entrepreneurs, will try to maximize their satisfaction with the resources at their disposal. If consumers fail to get maximum satisfaction from the goods and services purchased from the market, they will try to protect themselves by forming organized groups and pushing for strict consumer rights laws. It is quite natural for a government in a market economy to address the rights of consumers.

Chinese consumers are becoming assertive in their efforts to protect their rights. No doubt, consumers today are enjoying greater satisfaction because of new technology and efficiencies introduced by entrepreneurs. However, consumers are not taking things for granted. They are demanding better quality goods, and with the easing of restrictions in China, they have the opportunity to compare domestic goods with imported goods. In many cases, Chinese consumers are rejecting shoddy products made by state-owned enterprises (and private entrepreneurs), thus challenging the Chinese entrepreneurs to upgrade their products in order to compete with imported goods.

Due to the increasing role of consumers, the Chinese mass media have marked the importance of consumers by having a nationally telecast phone-a-thon to address consumers' complaints. Approximately eighteen operators received 600 calls in approximately two hours.[103] It was reported in August 1992 that complaints from consumers in the second quarter of 1992 exceeded the figure for both the first quarter and for the same period in 1991. About 89,817 complaints were filed by consumers by August 1992, an increase of 25.6 percent over the first quarter, and 17 percent over the second quarter of 1991. The China Consumers Association (CCA) was able to settle more than 97 percent of the complaints, and 30.15 million yuan ($5.58 million) was recovered by the CCA and its 2,000-odd branches as compensation on behalf of consumers.[104]

One may argue over the validity of the above report about consumers' rights in the Chinese government press. However, one should not take the report lightly. The fact that a group's problem was addressed in the government media is an important step toward the new paradigm. It means that the interests of consumers are being treated by the government as an integral part of the economic development process. The government, and China observers, know very well that in the past entrepreneurial activities were hindered by the CCP and the entrepreneurial role of consumers was neglected or suppressed, resulting in stagnation of the Chinese economy.

The government introduced the consumer rights law, which went into effect on January 1, 1994. A woman named Liu Xin took shelter under the consumer rights law and received 1,000 yuan ($115) as compensation because a heel on the shoes she bought for her wedding broke in front of her guests. These kinds of complaints by consumers are not new in China. From 1985 until March 1994, more than 1.5 million complaints were received by the CCA (which had about 2,550 county-level associations and about 18,000 grassroots committees), and over 666 million yuan ($76.5 million) was paid as compensation to consumers. It is not only consumers who are fighting back against shoddy products; state-owned mass media are also joining in to protect the interests of consumers, thus furthering the Chinese economic development process.[105]

In January 1994, Zheng Wenjuan wrote an editorial calling on Chinese consumers to become quality watchdogs. He said that consumers should not rely solely on inspection teams to solve their problems. Consumers should try to protect their rights by using the existing laws on consumer's rights. He went on to say, "It's my belief that only when all consumers become quality watchdogs and all producers realize the importance of making solid goods, can efforts be truly fruitful."[106]

Reformers in the government are pushing the Chinese system toward the new paradigm. The government is trying to protect the interests of both buyers and sellers through enforcement of laws. A day might eventually come when the threat of life uncertainty will vanish from the Chinese system, to be replaced by economic uncertainty, which will govern the behavior of entrepreneurs, consumers, and the government. Then all three parties will be willing to take chances with policies and products and enjoy the fruits of success, or exit the process to begin again.

These kinds of developments, where not only government leaders but also other agencies with the approval of the reform-minded leaders, come forward to protect consumer interests and help consumers gain confidence in the Chinese system, diminish the life-uncertainty factor. In 1988, both consumers and entrepreneurs, when threatened by unreliable government policies and overt threats of coercion, went into a buying panic. By contrast, in 1993, even in the face of inflation, the same consumers and entrepreneurs did not go on spending sprees but accepted inflation as one of the factors of a market economy. With a reduced life-uncertainty factor, consumers and entrepreneurs ventured into other projects, such as second jobs, to protect themselves from inflation. Interestingly, bank savings for both urban and rural Chinese increased by 107.7 billion yuan ($18.6 billion) in the third quarter of 1993, compared to the second quarter of 1993, an increase of over 66.6 billion yuan ($11.5 billion) from the same period in 1992. In a survey of 1,650 families in Beijing, Tianjin, and Shanghai, most agreed that inflation was a serious problem but insisted they were not going to panic. Twenty-nine percent viewed inflation as a "normal phenomenon common to all market economies," and 69 percent said that savings deposits were "safe and reliable," compared to buying valuable goods or investing in stocks and bonds. However 49 percent were still haunted by the memories of 1988, and one-fourth of the group said that panic buying was "very likely" to happen again.[107]

Consumers and entrepreneurs are gaining confidence in the government's ability to keep its promise to let the reform process continue. This means a reduction in the life-uncertainty factor, moving away from the past, the erosion of old cultural values, and the recognition that entrepreneurial talents are a valuable asset to China. If the government allows entrepreneurs and consumers to enjoy the minimum freedom required to let the system move toward the new paradigm, the day will come when the government will also be freed from the institutions of coercion, become entrepreneurial in nature, and gain the confidence of the masses through effective policy-making and implementation. But for now, entrepreneurs and consumers are benefiting from the limited freedom available to push the Chinese system slowly toward the new paradigm. Today, China's markets are more colorful than before, with varieties of goods produced by entrepreneurs to provide maximum satisfaction to the consumers. This limited freedom may have a snowball effect in the long run, and without any violent disruption, the reforms will be an improvement for China, and the world as a whole.

Chapter 7

Conclusion

History and the recent politics of the 1980s, all prejudiced by culture, have had a great impact on the entrepreneurial class of China, making them sensitive to uncertain government policy and cultural attitudes conveyed by the Chinese society. Contemporary entrepreneurs in China suffer from a lack of confidence regarding government policy and often feel insecure about their future. This has given rise to the life-uncertainty factor, whereby entrepreneurs feel that they might become victims of government policy and face the wrath of the masses through mass campaigns. Entrepreneurs fear they might lose their businesses and properties, and possibly be thrown in jail. Their family members might be harassed, disgraced, or even worse, killed, for trying to revive the Chinese economy after the ruin left behind by the Maoist era. This feeling of insecurity hinders the entrepreneurs' abilities to maximize their contributions toward China's economic development.

Historical legacy and traditional culture have been both a blessing and a curse for the entrepreneurial class. Because of historical dependency on authority and the traditional entrepreneurial culture, China's entrepreneurs were able to make a comeback after the chaos of Maoist rule. When Deng's government, in spite of the hardliners' opposition led by Chen Yun, allowed private entrepreneurship to flourish in the late 1970s, traditional entrepreneurial spirit sprang up in almost every corner of China and contributed toward the economic development of China.

However, traditional authoritarianism and culture have made entrepreneurs very sensitive and fragile. Their dependency on the whim of those in power and cultural disdain for entrepreneurial activities have made the position of entrepreneurs in society conspicuous and uncertain.

Nevertheless, with the approval of the reformers in the Deng camp and the reduction of the life-uncertainty factor, entrepreneurs in China have been able to thrive. Entrepreneurs are being protected by the macropolicy of the government, but at the microlevel entrepreneurs are still being harassed by bureaucrats including the notorious tax collectors. In some cases, entrepreneurs are still looked down on by certain segments of society.

The consumers in China are slowly realizing the importance of entrepreneurial activities and how entrepreneurs are bringing convenience to their lives by providing goods and services. These activities create jobs, savings, investments, and facilitate the circulation of funds. In short, entrepreneurial activities increase the wealth of the nation. Many consumers now view entrepreneurs in a positive way, thus alleviating the poor social status of entrepreneurs in many cases. Due to these changing attitudes, entrepreneurs are feeling good about themselves. This is a big step, because if a positive self-image governs an individual's occupation, it will produce creativity and innovation.

This slow change of cultural values toward entrepreneurs is convincing others in the society to view the entrepreneurial occupation in a positive and profitable way. Today, academics, scholars, and others are going into business or learning about new professions through vocational training in order to venture into entrepreneurial activities for profit.

With the vanishing of the Maoist past and the revival of the traditional entrepreneurial culture, the Chinese are learning to be Chinese again. This means, among other things, past Confucian attitudes about women are returning. Women are losing ground in the job market, social status, and human relationships—all of which had improved during the CCP rule. Women during the Dengist economic era are reverting to sex objects to please traditional Chinese men. This is, no doubt, a waste of human resources and a drain on China's economic development.

With the progress of entrepreneurship, economic development of China, and the diminishing power of the hardliners, the Chinese system, as a whole, is slowly moving toward a new paradigm governed by usual uncertainty. This may, in the long run, be a blessing for Chinese women, and for the rest of society. But for now, the government, entrepreneurs, and consumers are developing a matrimonial contract and learning to respect each others' rights in the marketplace. Government policies are becoming more concrete with the introduction of new labor laws, monopoly laws, a new private banking system, ownership laws, improved rights of consumers, and tax laws. The government is moving away from microcontrol of the economy and letting market forces govern the behavior and activities of entrepreneurs and consumers. Consumers are no longer dependent on the government or their *danwei* for their livelihood. This, no doubt, helps to bring the best out of Schumpetarian entrepreneurs to be creative and innovative.

With the new economic freedom in the marketplace, entrepreneurs and consumers are asserting their rights. Entrepreneurs are using the power of their newfound wealth to fill in the gaps left by the government. They are contributing as philanthropists to the local economy. Their acts improve the lives of the citizens and create new projects, such as the building of roads, highways, bridges, clinics, schools, and airports. This translates into more jobs, increased purchasing power, improved circulation of funds, and so on. These activities also help entrepreneurs to win the support of local people, contribute toward minimizing traditional scorn for entrepreneurs, and help reduce the life-uncertainty factor. In the long run, these activities may contribute toward forming loyal followers of the entrepreneurs.

The consumers, to protect their interests in the marketplace, are bonding together as a group and as individuals to assert their rights; the government is also encouraging consumer action in the marketplace. Consumers are helping the economy by asserting their rights by demanding hight quality products and creating or destroying equilibrium. This forces entrepreneurs to face the challenge of a new evolving group of consumers by being innovative and competitive.

The longer this process of a triangular relationship between the government, entrepreneurs, and consumers continues without any major disruption by the hardliners or supporters of Maoist philosophy, the better the Chinese as a whole will be able to adjust to this evolving system. China may slowly move away from some of its traditional authoritarian and cultural past and adopt a new culture to meet the needs of the current electronic age. The Chinese will be able to overcome the fear of the life-uncertainty factor and the government will be able to discard the shackles of its authoritarian past and embrace the new system through new institutions, policy-making, and implementation.

Entrepreneurs will be able to overcome the fear of life uncertainty, take the leading role in the economic development of China, and help close the door to the past. With entrepreneurs' positive contributions toward economic development, the society will also learn to move away from the traditional values of the past and accept entrepreneurship as an honorable occupation, thus giving impetus for China to grow economically and politically.

Appendix A

Though questions differed from person to person, circumstances permitting, I tried to ask each person the following questions:

1. Tell me something about yourself.
2. How long have you been a businessman?
3. Why did you become a businessman?
4. Please describe a real entrepreneur in China.
5. What is a *getihu*? Describe the qualities of a *getihu*.
6. What is the difference between a *getihu* and a private enterprise?
7. How many employees do you have?
8. How much was your initial investment?
9. How much investment do you have now?
10. What are your hours of operation?
11. What government policies affect your company?
12. How do government policies help you?
13. What motivates you to work hard?
14. Tell me about the history of individual entrepreneurship.
15. What is the future of *getihu*?
16. Can you expand your business?
17. Do you want to expand your business?
18. How easy is it for you to borrow money from the bank?
19. How long will it take you to open a business?
20. Tell me about the social and cultural aspects of being a *getihu*?
21. If you met Jiang Zemin, what would you tell him?
22. What changes would you bring if you were the mayor of Tianjin?

23. What do you think of the current tax policy?
24. How much do you pay in taxes?
25. What makes you continue in the face of failure?
26. What do you need to do to open a new business?
27. What advice would you give to a potential entrepreneur?
28. What do you think of corruption in China?
29. What do you think of the officials who check on you or visit you?
30. Some entrepreneurs stop expanding their business once they can meet their financial needs. What do you think of this phenomenon?

Appendix B

REGISTRATION PROCEDURES FOR PRIVATE ENTERPRISES

1. Who can apply:

   Those who are living in the district and have a formal residency permit, or those who have a stable place of business and a long-term residency permit.

   Unemployed young people, idle people, individual business people, people who resigned from state-owned enterprises, retired people, scientists and technocrats employed without pay, party leaders who resigned more than two years ago, and so on.

   a. Unemployed young people must show an unemployment certificate provided by the community labor service unit.

   b. Idle people must show community certificate.

   c. Individual business people must show license.

   d. Resigned and retired people must show the certificate given by their work units (*danwei*).

2. Fields:

   Industry, building, transportation, business, food, services, repairing, scientific advisory, recreation, planting, breeding, and so on.

   a. Private industry with noise and pollution problems must be approved by the District Environment Protection Bureau.

   b. Private enterprise in construction must be approved by the District Building Committee.

   c. Transportation:
   - Freight transportation must apply for a certificate through the highway transportation management unit.

- Passenger transportation must apply for a certificate through the passenger transportation management unit.

d. Food businesses must get permission from the public health bureau.

e. Printing, reprinting, and private hotels (motels) must be approved by the public security ministry.

f. Repairs:
- Electric appliance business must get permission from the district science committee.
- Car mechanics must get permission from the motor vehicle repairing management bureau.

g. Scientific advisory units must get permission from the district science committee.

h. Recreation units must get permission from the police station and community committee.

3. Credentials:

a. Applicant's written application, name of enterprise, address, amount and source of funds, equipments, field, category, investment, employees.

b. Applicant's identification card. Joint ventures and limited companies must show partners' identification cards and their resumes.

c. Usage certificate of place, such as rent contract, land deed, and so on.

d. Contract, employee's roles, and so on. The contract must include qualifications, number of employees required, work time, pay, working condition, welfare, insurance, contract period, praise, and punishment, and so on.

e. Joint ventures must show partners' written agreement. It must include the investment form, amount, profit distribution, debt burden, ending, and so on.

Notes

CHAPTER ONE

1. *Guangming Ribao*, 15 January 1990, 3.

2. Interview with an optician in Tianjin. Interview occurred sometime between April–July 1991. (All future citations to interviews occurred in Tianjin during this same time period.)

3. From interview with officials of Tianjin's Business Administration Bureau.

4. Ludig Von Mises, *Socialism—An Economic and Sociological Analysis* (London: Jonathan Cape Ltd., 1936), 443.

5. *Peking Review*, no. 52, 29 December 1978, 6–16.

6. Adam Smith, *An Inquiry into the Nature and Causes of the Wealth of Nations*, ed. Edwin Cannan (New York: Random House, 1937), 48, 47–54.

7. Leon Walras, *Elements of Pure Economics or the Theory of Social Wealth* (George Allen and Unwin Ltd., 1954), 222–227, 423.

8. Alfred Marshall, *Principles of Economics*, 7th ed. (London: Macmillan and Co., Ltd., 1916), 291–293, 661–665, 745–749.

9. Frank Knight, *Risk, Uncertainty and Profit* (Houghton Mifflin Company, 1921), 231–233, 267, 268, 278–279.

10. Joseph A. Schumpeter, *The Theory of Economic Development* (1911; reprint, Cambridge, MA: Harvard University Press, 1959), 65–69, 71–72, 74–76, 78–85. See also *Business Cycles*, vol. 1 (New York: McGraw-Hill Book Company, Inc., 1939), 102–105; and *Capitalism, Socialism and Democracy*, 3rd ed. (New York: Harper and Brothers, 1942), 132–133.

11. Gustav F. Papanek, *Pakistan's Development: Social Goals and Private Incentives* (Cambridge, MA: Harvard University Press, 1967), 27–30, 32–36, 40–58.

12. Yusif A. Sayigh, *Entrepreneurs of Lebanon—The Role of the Business Leader in a Developing Economy* (Cambridge, MA: Harvard University Press, 1962), 18–29, 52–53. Sayigh carried out a survey of 207 Lebanese entrepreneurs whose actions and decision-making positions qualified them to be the subject of his research.

13. John J. Carroll, *The Filipino Manufacturing Entrepreneur—Agent and Product of Change* (Ithaca, NY: Cornell University Press, 1965), 18–20, 39–40, 136, 213.

14. Wayne E. Nafziger, *Class, Caste, and Entrepreneurship—A Study of Indian Industrialists* (Honolulu: East-West Center, University Press of Hawaii, 1978), 25–26.

15. Anita M. Weiss, *Culture, Class and Development in Pakistan—The Emergence of an Industrial Bourgeoisie in Punjab* (Boulder, CO: Westview Press, 1990), 9.

16. Andrew A. Beveridge and Anthony R. Oberschall, *African Businessmen and Development in Zambia* (Princeton, NJ: Princeton University Press, 1979), 276–277.

17. Maurice Dobb, *Capitalist Enterprise and Social Progress*, 2nd impression (George Routledge and Sons, Ltd., 1926), 3.

18. Kalman Rupp, *Entrepreneurs in Red—Structure and Organizational Innovation in the Centrally Planned Economy* (Albany: State University of New York Press, 1983), 10, 19, 38–39.

19. Anthony Jones and William Moskoff, *KO-OPS—The Rebirth of Entrepreneurship in the Soviet Union* (Indianapolis: Indiana University Press, 1991), 27–34.

20. Myers S. Ramon, "The Agrarian System," in *The Cambridge History of China,* vol. 13, *Republican China 1912–1949,* part 2, ed. John K. Fairbank and Albert Fenerwerker (Cambridge, England: Cambridge University Press, 1986), 234.

21. Mao Zedong, *Selected Works of Mao Tse-Tung,* vol. 4, 1st ed. (Peking: Foreign Languages Press, 1961), 183 and 421.

22. John Gardner, "The Wu-fan Campaign in Shanghai: A Study in the Consolidation of Urban Control" in *Chinese Communist Politics in Action,* ed. A. Doak Barnett (Seattle: University of Washington Press, 1969), 479. See also Harry Harding, *Organizing China—The Problem of Bureaucracy 1949–1976* (Stanford: Stanford University Press, 1981), 48.

23. Chu-Yuan Cheng, *China's Economic Development—Growth and Structural Change* (Boulder, CO: Westview Press, 1982), 137.

24. June Grasso, Jay Corrin, and Michael Kort, *Modernization and Revolution in China* (Armonk, NY: M. E. Sharpe Inc., 1991), 154.

25. Grasso, Corrin, and Kort, 154.

26. Chu-Yuan Cheng, 144–145.

27. From interview with the part-time manager of a clothing store.

28. From interview with the owner of a food factory.

29. From interview with the part-time manager of a clothing store. The interviewee's last statement, "It enjoys preferential treatment from the government," was made to protect herself from being regarded as criticizing the government.

30. Luca Romano, "A Country Changes Course," *Time,* 6 January 1986, 46–50.

31. Hong Qi, "Factory Bosses Feel the Pressure as Atmosphere of Paranoia Reigns," *China Daily,* 9 July 1992.

32. Zhong Huai, "How to Handle Reformer's Errors?" *Renmin Ribao,* 29 September 1985.

33. From interview with the owner of a fruit business.

34. From interview with the an individual barber.

35. From interview with the owner of a computer and consulting firm.

36. Robert C. Hsu, *Economic Theories in China, 1978–1988* (Cambridge, England: Cambridge University Press, 1991), 67; see also 64–65.

37. From interview with the owner of a computer and consulting firm.

38. Willy Kraus, *Private Business in China—Revival Between Ideology and Pragmatism,* trans. Erich Holtz (Honolulu: University of Hawaii Press, 1991), 65.

39. From interview with a car dealer.

40. From interview with a car parts dealer.

41. From interview with the officials of Tianjin's Business Administration Bureau.

42. Lincoln Kaye, "Robots and Puppets—Manchu Princess Remembers the Past," *Far Eastern Economic Review*, 5 November 1992, 14.

CHAPTER TWO

1. Yen-ping Hao, "Commercial Capitalism Along the China Coast During the Late Ch'ing Period," in *Modern Chinese Economic History*, ed. Chi-ming Hou and Tzong-Shian Yu (Taipei: The Institute of Economics, Academia Sinica, 1979), 303–304, 310.

2. Marie-Claire Bergère, *The Golden Age of the Chinese Bourgeoisie 1911–1937*, trans. Janet Lloyd (Cambridge, England: Cambridge University Press, 1989), 28.

3. Marie-Claire Bergère, "The Chinese Bourgeoisie, 1911–37," in *The Cambridge History of China*, vol. 12, *Republican China 1912–1949*, part 1, ed. John K. Fairbank (Cambridge, England: Cambridge University Press, 1983), 744.

4. *Peking and Tientsin Times*, 19 April 1923. Reproduced from Lucian W. Pye, *Warlord Politics—Conflict and Coalition in the Modernization of Republican China* (New York: Praeger, 1971), 161.

5. James E. Sheridan, *China in Disintegration—The Republican Era in Chinese History, 1912–1949* (New York: Free Press, 1975), 51.

6. T. C. Woo, *The Kuomingtang and the Future of the Chinese Revolution* (London: George Allen and Unwin Ltd., 1928), 244–245.

7. James E. Sheridan, 102, 103.

8. Kang Chao, "The Growth of a Modern Cotton Textile Industry and the Competition with Handicrafts," in *China's Modern Economy in Historical Perspective*, ed. Dwight H. Perkins (Stanford: Stanford University Press, 1975), 170, 171.

9. Joseph Fewsmith, *Party, State, and Local Elites in Republican China—Merchant Organizations and Politics in Shanghai, 1890–1930* (Honolulu: University of Hawaii Press, 1985), 47–48.

10. Albert C. Muhse, "Trade Organization and Trade Control in China," *American Economic Review*, vol. 6, no. 2 (June 1916): 309–23. Reproduced from Myers S. Ramon, "The Agrarian System," in *The Cambridge History of China*, vol. 13, *Republican China 1912–1949*, part 2, ed. John K. Fairbank and Albert Fenerwerker (Cambridge, England: Cambridge University Press, 1986), 233–234.

11. Higashi Norimasa, *Chubu Shina Keizai Chosa (Research on the Economy of Central China)*, vol. 1 (Tokyo: Fuzambo, 1915), 361. Reproduced from Ramon, 234.

12. Gail Hershatter, *The Workers of Tianjin, 1900–1949* (Stanford: Stanford University Press, 1986), 30–35.

13. Bèrgere, *The Golden Age*, 229–236.

14. Martin C. Wilbur, "Nationalist China, 1928–1950: An Interpretation," in *China—Seventy Years After the 1911 Hsin-Hai Revolution*, ed. Hungdah Chiu with Shao-Chuan Leng (Charlottesville: University Press of Virginia, 1984), 13–14.

15. Bergère, *The Golden Age*, 275.

16. Parks M. Coble, Jr., *The Shanghai Capitalists and the Nationalist Government, 1927–1937* (Cambridge, MA: Harvard University Press, 1980), 22–41. For Green Gang discussion see also Fewsmith, 115; and Bergère, *The Golden Age*, 280.

17. Bèrgere, *The Golden Age*, 284.

18. H. D. Fong, *Cotton Industry and Trade in China*, 4.2 vols., vol. 1 (Tianjin: Nankai Institute of Economics Industry Series, 1932), 319. Reproduced from Kenneth Lieberthal, *Revolution and Tradition in Tientsin, 1949–1952* (Stanford: Stanford University Press, 1980), 83; and see Hershatter, 36.

19. Qian Zhaoxiong, "Shangye Ziben Caozongxia de Wuxi can sang" (Wuxi Sericulture under the Control of Commercial Capital), *Zhongguo nongcun*, vol. 1, no. 4 (January 1935): 73–74. Reproduced from Lynda S. Bell, "From Comprador to County Magnate: Bourgeois Practice in the Wuxi County Silk Industry," in *Chinese Local Elites and Patterns of Dominance*, ed. Joseph W. Esherick and Mary Backus Rankin (Berkeley: University of California Press, 1990), 132–133.

20. Lloyd E. Eastman, *Seeds of Destruction—Nationalist China in War and Revolution 1937–1949* (Stanford: Stanford University Press, 1984), 122; see also 109–123.

21. *Outline for Cooperative Development*, Department of National Economy (Wayapao, Shensi: November 1935): 4. Reproduced from Edgar Snow, *Red Star Over China*, 1st revised and enlarged ed. (New York: Grove Press, Inc., 1968), 227–228.

22. Edgar Snow, 227–228, 246–248.

23. Thomas R. Jernigan, *China's Business Methods and Policy* (Hong Kong: Kelly & Walsh, Ltd., 1904), 317–318.

24. Helen Foster Snow, *Inside Red China* (1939; reprint, New York: Da Capo Press, 1977), 221–223.

25. Mao Zedong, *Selected Works of Mao Tse-Tung*, vol. 4, 1st ed. (Peking: Foreign Languages Press, 1961), 167–169.

26. Liu Suinian and Wu Qungan, eds., *China's Socialist Economy—An Outline History (1949–1984)* (Beijing: Beijing Review, n.d.), 21–22.

27. Jin Jian, "Upholding Socialist Public Ownership," *Beijing Review*, 29 January–11 February 1990, 15–20.

28. Gong Shiqi, "Economic Features of Primary Stage of Socialism," *Beijing Review*, 15–28 February 1988, 18–21.

29. Thomas B. Gold, "Urban Private Business in China," *Studies In Comparative Communism*, vol. 22, no. 2/3 (summer/autumn 1989): 187–201.

30. Willy Kraus, *Private Business in China—Revival Between Ideology and Pragmatism*, trans. Erich Holtz (Honolulu: University of Hawaii Press, 1991), 58.

31. From interview with the owner of a computer and consulting firm.

32. Mao Zedong, 183, 421.

33. John Gardner, "The Wu-fan Campaign in Shanghai: A Study in the Consolidation of Urban Control," in *Chinese Communist Politics in Action*, ed. A. Doak Barnett (Seattle: University of Washington Press, 1969), 479.

34. Harry Harding, *Organizing China—The Problem of Bureaucracy 1949–1976* (Stanford: Stanford University Press, 1981), 48.

35. The phrase was used by Bo Yibo to justify the *San-fan* campaign. *Renmin Ribao (People's Daily)*, 10 January 1952. Reproduced from John Gardner, 493.

36. John Gardner, 493.

37. When this book was published, Ching was vice-mayor of Shanghai, a deputy to the National People's Congress, and vice-chairman of the Shanghai People's Political Consultative Conference. See Ching Chung-Hwa, "San Fan–Wu Fan—The

Big Cleanup (September–October 1952)," in *China in Transition—Selected Articles 1952–1956* (Peking: China Reconstructs, 1957), 148.

38. Before escaping to Hong Kong in 1957, Chow served for eight years in high-ranking positions in the CCP. He was also one of the vice-chairmen of the Thrift Supervisory Committee at the headquarters of the China Democratic League and also a victim of the Three-Anti campaign. See Chow Ching-Wen, *Ten Years of Storm—The True Story of the Communist Regime in China*, trans. and ed. Lai Ming (New York: Holt, Rinehart and Winston, 1960), 126.

39. Chow Ching-Wen, 127.

40. Ching Chung-Hwa, 146.

41. A. Doak Barnett, *Communist China: The Early Years 1949–55* (New York: Frederick A. Praeger, 1964) 138.

42. Chow Ching-Wen, 131.

43. Barnett, 140.

44. Chow Ching-Wen, 132.

45. Barnett, 147.

46. Chow Ching-Wen, 133.

47. Gardner, 484–489.

48. Gardner, 520–522. "Become meritorious small teams" were those businessmen who willingly confessed their "sins" and in turn received reduced punishment.

49. Gardner, 525.

50. Chow Ching-Wen, 158–159.

51. Li Fu-chun was vice-premier of the state council and chairperson of the state planning commission of the People's Republic of China. The report was delivered on July 5 and 6, 1955, at the second session of the First National People's Congress. See Li Fu-chun, *Report on the First Five-Year Plan for Development of the National Economy of the People's Republic of China in 1953–1957* (Peking: Foreign Languages Press, 1955), 74.

52. Chao Kuo-chun, *Economic Planning and Organization in Mainland China—A Documentary Study (1949–1957)*, vol. 1 (Cambridge, MA: Harvard University Press, 1959), 72. Article 2 of the provisional regulations on public-private jointly operated industrial enterprises (2 September 1954), explained that:

> A Public-private jointly-operated industrial enterprise is an industrial enterprise with investments made by the state or by other public-private jointly-operated enterprises, and jointly operated by the capitalists and by cadres assigned by the state.
>
> Public-private joint operation of capitalists industrial enterprises should be based on the needs of the state, the practicability of transforming the enterprises, and the willingness of the capitalists.
>
> Public-private joint operation of enterprises should be subject to approval by the People's Government.

53. Li Fu-chun, 75.

54. *The Constitution of the People's Republic of China* (Beijing: Foreign Languages Press, 1954), 76.

55. Barnett, 190; see also p. 151 for discussion about malaria patient.

56. Chu-yuan Cheng, *China's Economic Development—Growth and Structural Change* (Boulder, CO: Westview Press, 1982), 148.

57. From interview with the owner of a fruit business.

58. From interview with an individual barber.

59. Barnett, 194; Chu-yuan Cheng, 145–146.

60. Li Fu-chun, 81.

61. Barnett, 194.

62. *China News Analysis*, no. 88 (17 June 1955): 1.

63. Chi Chao-Ting, "Shanghai Steps into the Future," *China in Transition—Selected Articles 1952–1956* (Peking, 1957), 153.

64. Barnett, 194.

65. Chi Chao-Ting, 152–153.

66. Chi Chao-Ting, 157

67. Chu-yuan Cheng, 149–150.

68. *China News Analysis*, no. 88 (3 June 1955): 4, 6.

69. *Ta Kung Daily*, 7 December 1954. Reproduced from *China News Analysis*, no. 86 (3 June 1955): 6.

70. *China News Analysis*, no. 86 (3 June 1955): 7; see also 6.

71. Chi Chao-Ting, 154.

72. *China News Analysis*, no. 86 (3 June 1955): 5.

73. Chao Kuo-chun, 74.

74. He Jianzhang, "On the Dual Character of Individual Economy and Private Economy," *Guangming Ribao*, 15 January 1990, 3.

75. Sun Ping, "Individual Economy Under Socialism," *Beijing Review*, 13 August 1984, 25–28.

76. Sun Ping, 26.

77. He Jianzhang and Zhang Wenmin, "The System of Ownership: A Tendency Toward Multiplicity," in *China's Economic Reforms*, ed. Lin Wei and Arnold Chao (Philadelphia: University of Pennsylvania Press, 1982), 193–194. See also Chu-yuan Cheng, 151; see also *China Daily*, 13 July 1992, 4.

78. Yao Cao, "Prospects for Individual Economy," *Ta Kung Pao* (31 October–6 November, 1985).

79. *Peking Review*, no. 29, 19 July 1968, 25.

80. See Gong Shiqi, "Economic Features of Primary Stage of Socialism," *Beijing Review*, 15–28 February 1988, 18–21; see also Sun Ping, 25–28; and He Jianzhang, 3; and "Newly Emerging Economic Forms," *Beijing Review*, 25 May 1981, 15–18.

81. Thomas B. Gold, "Urban Private Business and Social Change," in *Chinese Society on the Eve of Tiananmen—The Impact of Reform*, ed. Deborah Davis and Ezra F. Vogel (Boston, MA: The Council on East Asian Studies, Harvard University, 1990).

82. *Peking Review*, no. 11, 17 March 1978, 5–14.

83. John A. Reeder, "Entrepreneurship in The People's Republic of China," *Columbia Journal of World Business* (fall 1984): 43–51.

84. *Peking Review*, no. 52, 29 December 1978, 6–16.

85. *Beijing Review*, no. 19, 10 May 1982, 27–47.

86. Karin Plokker, "The Development of Individual and Cooperative Labour Activity in the Soviet Union," *Soviet Studies*, vol. 42, no. 3 (July 1990): 403–428.

87. From interview with the owner of a computer and consulting firm. See also Robert C. Hsu, *Economic Theories in China 1978–1988* (Cambridge, England: Cambridge University Press, 1991), 64.

88. Charles Parmiter, "The Red Aristocrats," *Reader's Digest*, October 1990, 151–156.

89. Claudie Broyelle, Jacques Broyelle, and Evelyne Tschirhart, *China: A Second Look*, trans. Sarah Matthews (New Jersey: Harvester Press, 1980), 71–73.

90. *Beijing Review*, no. 30, 19 September 1983, 7.

91. Yue Haitao, "Leasing Invigorates Small Businesses, *Beijing Review*, no. 27, 6 July 1987, 24–27.

92. Zhao Ziyang, "Report on the Work of the Government," (delivered at the Second Session of the Sixth National People's Congress on May 15, 1984), *Beijing Review*, no. 24, 11 June 1984.

93. *Beijing Review*, no. 42, 15 October 1984.

94. *Beijing Review*, no. 44, 29 October 1984, 1–16.

95. Yao Cao, *Ta Kung Pao* (31 October–6 November 1985).

96. Dong Jin, "Be Alert to the Rebound Coming After the Sluggish Market," *Jingji Ribao* (28 February 1990): 2.

97. Gong Shiqi, "Economic Features of Primary Stage of Socialism," *Beijing Review*, 15–28 February 1988, 18–21. See also Table 2.5.

98. He Jianzhang, "Newly Emerging Economic Forms," *Beijing Review*, no. 21, 25 May 1981, 15–18.

99. Zhang Zeyu, "The Role of Private Enterprises," *Beijing Review*, no. 39, 28 September 1987, 4–5.

100. *Beijing Review*, vol. 30, no. 45, 9–15 November 1987, 1–27.

101. *Beijing Review*, 18–24 July 1988, 6.

102. From interview with the owner of a fruit business.

103. *Jingji Guanli*, no. 12 (1989): 12.

104. *Liaowang*, overseas edition, Hong Kong, no. 8, 19 February 1990, 6.

105. *China Daily*, 6 January 1993, 4.

106. *The Standard*, 23 January 1992; see also *South China Morning Post*, 18 December 1992.

107. Xinhua, cited in *China Daily*, 12 November 1993, 4.

108. *South China Morning Post*, 27 April 1992.

109. Sheryl WuDunn, "China Shakes Up Central Committee, Replacing Some Hard-Liners," *New York Times*, 19 October 1992, A5.

110. *China Daily*, 9 December 1992, 4; see also *China Daily*, 4 January 1993.

111. *China Daily*, document supplement, 21 October 1992, 1–4.

112. *China Daily*, 9 December 1992, 2.

113. Ma Zhiping, "Private Sector Set to Boom in 1993," *China Daily*, 30 January 1993, 3.

114. It was reported on October 19, 1992 in *China Daily* that in China there were "150,000 plus" private enterprises. But in a later issue of *China Daily*, it was mentioned that by the end of 1992 there were 139,000 private enterprises employing 2.3 million employees, a rise of 28 and 26 percent, respectively compared to previous years. See *China Daily*, 19 October 1992, 3; and Xie Liangjun, "CPPCC Gives Voice to Private Sector of the Economy," *China Daily*, 31 March 1993, 4.

115. Xie Liangjun, 4.

116. Zhang Weiqun, "Pawning Back in Fashion in the Capital," *China Daily*, business weekly section, 15 March 1993, 2.

CHAPTER THREE

1. Susan Young, "Policy, Practice and the Private Sector in China," *The Australian Journal of Chinese Affairs*, no. 21 (January 1989): 57–80. Young reported from her interview.

2. "Soaking the Rich," *The Economist*, 6 June 1992, 32.

3. *China Daily*, 20 July 1992, 6.

4. Cai Hong, "Families Divided by Wrenching Issues," *China Daily*, 30 July 1992, 4.

5. *China Daily*, 4 September 1992, 4.

6. Thomas Metzger, "The State and Commerce in Imperial China," *Asian and African Studies*, vol. 6 (1970) 23–46.

7. Fei Qiang, "Entrepreneurs, Stand Straight—Third Discussion on Economic Phenomenon at Present," *Jingji Cankao*, 26 June 1990.

8. Sheryl WuDunn, "China is Sowing Discontent with Taxes' on the Peasants," *New York Times*, 19 May 1993, 1. *China Daily* also talked about this factor. A farmer in Guizhou province was punched by an official when the farmer refused to pay excessive levies. See *China Daily*, 14 September 1992, 4. See also Carl Goldstein, Lincoln Kaye, and Anthony Blass, "Get Off Our Backs," *Far Eastern Economic Review* (15 July 1993): 68–70. The article states in one place that "one old woman drowned herself in a pond after authorities took her bicycle in lieu of unpaid taxes."

9. Ole Bruun, *Business and Bureaucracy in a Chinese City—An Ethnography of Private Business Households in Contemporary China* (Berkeley: Institute of East Asian Studies, University of California, 1993), 121–125.

10. Susan Mann, *Local Merchants and the Chinese Bureaucracy, 1750–1950* (Stanford: Stanford University Press, 1987), 14.

11. Lin Jinhua, "A Brewing Affair for 4,000 Years," *China Daily*, 6 January 1993, 5.

12. Nicholas D. Kristof, "China Plans Big Layoffs of Coal Mine Workers," *New York Times*, Business Day, 29 December 1992, C-1.

13. "Protect the Entrepreneurs," *Guangming Ribao*, 31 August 1988, 1.

14. Nicholas D. Kristof, "Factories in a Changed China Suffer Strikes and Sabotage," *New York Times*, 11 June 1992, A-1.

15. The last statement was given in response to my inquiry about a twenty-four-hour working system. By Chang's expression it seemed to me that his answer was given to please the government officials present.

16. Confucius, *The Analects (Lun Yu)*, book XVI: 9, trans. D. C. Lau (New York: Penguin Books Ltd., 1979), 140.

17. See James E. Sheridan, *China in Disintegration—The Republican Era in Chinese History 1912–1949* (New York: Free Press, 1975), 16. See also Frederic Wakeman, Jr., *The Fall of Imperial China* (New York: Free Press, 1975), 39.

18. John K. Fairbank, and Edwin O. Reischauer, *China—Tradition & Transformation* (Boston: Houghton Mifflin Company, 1978), 34.

19. Yan Bian, "How Parental Concern Can End in Tragedy," *China Daily*, 14 January 1993, 4.

20. Ming Cai, "School Was the Dream of This Man and Girl," *China Daily* 2 February 1993, 6.

21. Gustav F. Papanek, *Pakistan's Development: Social Goals & Private Incentives* (Cambridge, MA: Harvard University Press, 1967), 49, 51–52.

22. June Grasso, Jay Corrin, and Michael Kort, *Modernization & Revolution in China* (Armonk, NY: M. E. Sharpe, 1991), 13.

23. From interview with the Tianjin's Business Administration Bureau, May 1991.

24. Han Baocheng, "Report from Tianjin: Small Shops Coming Back," *Beijing Review*, 11 July 1983, 19–21.

25. Young, 57–80.

26. Anthony Jones and William Moskoff, *KO-OPS—The Rebirth of Entrepreneurship in the Soviet Union* (Indianapolis: Indiana University Press, 1991), 83–84.

27. Nigel Swain, *Hungary—The Rise and Fall of Feasible Socialism* (London: Verso, 1992), 174.

28. From interview with an individual barber.

29. Carl H. Landè, "The Dyadic Basis of Clientelism," in *Friends, Followers, and Factions—A Reader in Political Clientelism*, ed. Steffen W. Schmidt, Laura Guasti, Carl H. Landè, and James C. Scott (Berkeley: University of California Press, 1977), xv.

30. *China Daily*, business weekly section, 13 July 1992, 2.

31. *China Daily*, 9 March 1990, 1.

32. Hai Bian, "Giving Gifts: A Poor Practice?" *China Daily*, 17 February 1993, 6. See also A. P. Co Wei and A. Evison, *Concise English-Chinese, Chinese-English Dictionary* (Oxford University Press and The Commercial Press, 1986), 424.

33. Nicholas D. Kristof, "Factories in a Changed China Suffer Strikes and Sabotage," *New York Times*, 11 June 1992, A-1.

34. *Beijing Review*, 11 March 1985, 6.

35. Mariusz Mark Dobek, *The Political Logic of Privatization—Lessons from Great Britain and Poland* (Westport, CT: Praeger, 1993), 93–105. See also George J. Church, "Counter Reformation," *Time*, 28 September 1992.

36. From interview with a former loom factory owner.

37. Frank Gibney, Jr., Kari Huss, and Jane Whitmore, "The Great Stonewall," *Newsweek*, 7 June 1993, 26–27.

CHAPTER FOUR

1. Ben J. Wallace, "Technological Impact and Culture Change among the Pagan Gaddang," in *Culture Change in the Philippines*, ed. Mario D. Zamora, Vinson H. Sutlive, and Nathan Altshuler (Williamburg, VA: Studies in Third World Societies, Department of Anthropology, College of William and Mary, 1976), 22.

2. Albert A. Segynola, "The Cultural Factor in the Development of Rural Small Scale Industries: A Case Study from Bendel State of Nigeria," in *Culture and Development in Africa,* ed. Stephen H. Arnold and Andre Netecki (Trenton, NJ: Africa World Press, 1990), 256.

3. Clyde Kluckhohn, *Culture And Behavior*, ed. Richard Kluckhohn (New York: Free Press of Glencoe, 1962), 73.

4. Richard J. Smith, cited in "The Future of Chinese Culture," *Futures*, vol. 21, no. 5 (October 1989): 431–446.

5. Lucian Pye, "Political Culture," in *International Encyclopedia of the Social Sciences*, vol. 12, ed. David L. Sills (New York: Macmillian and Free Press, 1968), 218.

6. Gabriel A. Almond, and Sidney Verba, *The Civic Culture—Political Attitudes and Democracy in Five Nations* (Newbury Park, CA: Sage Publications, 1989), 12–15.

7. Karl W. Deutsch, "Social Mobilization and Political Development," *The American Political Science Review,* vol. 4, no. 3 (September 1961): 493–514.

8. See "Reform Bringing About Profound Social Changes," *China Daily*, 27 May 1993, 4. The article says, "Nearly 100 million rural labourers have entered township

enterprises and 700,000 farmers have poured into cities to make a better living. In cities many people have quit their jobs to hunt for higher paying ones." See also "Why China's People Are Getting Out of Control," *The Economist*, 12 June 1993, 41–42; and Carl Goldstein, "Two Faces of Reform," *Far Eastern Economic Review* (8 April 1993): 15–16.

9. See Xi Mi, " 'Self-Supported' Students Pay Way Through Colleges," *China Daily*, 12 July 1993, 4.

10. See Cai Yan, "Money Fever Becomes Epidemic in China," *China Daily*, 15 July 1993, 4. The article says "that the Chinese are abandoning their traditions and becoming money-worshippers."

11. See Ling Ling, "Beauty Pageants No Longer so Demure," *China Daily*, 6 July 1993, 4.

12. See "Reform Bringing about Profound Social Changes," *China Daily*, 27 May 1993, 4. The article says, "The social evolution is also reflected by the increasingly diversified forms of ownership . . . which have broken up the monopoly of public ownership."

13. Cai Yan, 4. Cai Yan said that along with the rise of the Chinese desire to make a profit, "the idea of equal shares for all has been shattered."

14. From interview with the owner of an ice cream and soft drinks business.

15. Karl Marx and Frederick Engels, *The German Ideology*, part 1, ed. C. J. Arthur (London: Lawrence & Wishart, 1970), 54–55, 94–95.

16. Mao Zedong, *Selected Works of Mao Tse-Tung*, vol. 4, 1st ed. (Peking: Foreign Languages Press, 1961), 428.

17. See Chu-yuan Cheng, *China's Economic Development—Growth and Structural Change* (Boulder, CO: Westview Press, 1982), 32–36. Cheng elaborated in detail on the concepts of "Communist Man" and "class struggle."

18. Liu Shaoqi, "How To Be a Good Communist," *Selected Works of Liu Shaoqi*, vol. 1 (Beijing: Foreign Languages Press, 1984), 136.

19. Hong Yung Lee, "The Implications of Reform for Ideology, State and Society in China," *Journal of International Affairs*, vol. 39, no. 2 (Winter 1986): 77–89.

20. Lei Feng was considered a model communist. His diary was used as the central text during campaigns of the socialist education movement to emulate heroes in the early 1960s. Lei was from a peasant family. He was born on December 18, 1940 in Wangcheng county, Hunan Province and he was orphaned at the age of seven. Lei was chosen as a model worker in a party office, a factory, and a farm. He joined the PLA in 1960. Lei was killed while on duty, in August 1962 (some scholars think he was a fabrication). Lei's diary was read by thousands who were urged to study Mao Zedong's writings and become a model communist like Lei. See Chen Qiuping, "Lei Feng: For Three Decades the Face of Altruism," *Beijing Review*, 29 March–4 April 1993, 16–18.

21. See Liu Chih-chien, "A Great Soldier with a Noble Character," *China Youth Daily*, vol. 5, February 1963; "Fight and Live as Lei Feng Has Done," *China Youth Daily*, 5 February 1963. Reproduced from Richard H. Solomon, *Mao's Revolution and the Chinese Political Culture* (Berkeley: University of California Press, 1971), 444.

22. Karl Marx and Frederick Engels, *Manifesto of the Communist Party* (Peking: Foreign Languages Press, 1965), 57.

23. Zhiling Lin, "How China Will Modernize," *The American Enterprise*, vol. 2 (July/August 1991): 15–18.

24. Lucian W. Pye, *Asian Power and Politics—The Cultural Dimensions of Authority* (Cambridge, MA: Harvard University Press, 1985) 205. Pye also viewed communist China as a blend of Confucianism and Leninism. He wrote that the Chinese did not give up the principles of their Confucianism before adopting communism. See Lucian W. Pye, *The Mandarin and the Cadre: China's Political Cultures* (Ann Arbor: Center for Chinese Studies, University of Michigan, 1988), 31. See also Jack Chen, *Inside the Cultural Revolution* (New York: Macmillan, 1975), 376. Chen said that the attacks on Confucianism during the Cultural Revolution had the power to destroy the old sage's influence in the Chinese society.

25. Khun-Eng Kuah, "Confucian Ideology and Social Engineering in Singapore," *Journal of Contemporary Asia*, vol. 20, no. 3 (1990): 371–383.

26. Agnes Syu, "Field Study of Privatization in the Republic of China on Taiwan: Interactive Dynamics During the Initial Stages of the Privatization Process in Two State-Owned Enterprises" (Ph.D. diss., University of Kansas, 1992), 77–78.

27. Confucius, *The Analects (Lun Yu)*, book XIII: 20, trans. Arthur Waley (Macmillan, 1939), 176. See also *The Analects*, book II: 7, 8; book VIII: 14; book XIII: 18; book XIV: 23, 27, 28; and book XVII: 21 for a discussion about filial piety and obedience to the ruler.

28. Zao Chen, "The Path of Knowledge Leads to Qufu, Zouxian," *China Daily*, 26 February 1994, 5.

29. Ross Terrill, "China's Youth Wait for Tomorrow," *National Geographic*, vol. 180, no. 1 (July 1991): 110–136.

30. Herbert H. Gowen, and Joseph Washington Hall, *An Outline History of China* (New York: D. Appleton, 1927), 73.

31. Charles O. Hucker, *China's Imperial Past—An Introduction to Chinese History and Culture* (Stanford: Stanford University Press, 1975), 97, 127–131, 140–142.

32. See Gowen and Hall, 140–143; James T. C. Liu, *Reform in Sung China—Wang An-Shih (1021–1086) and His New Policies* (Cambridge, MA: Harvard University Press, 1959), 4–7, 54–58; and Hucker, 274–275.

33. Raymond Dawson, *Imperial China* (London: Hutchinson, 1972), 149.

34. Dun J. Li, *The Ageless Chinese—History* (New York: Charles Scribner's Sons, 1978), 57–58, 209. See also Wolfram Eberhard, *A History of China* (Berkeley: University of California Press, 1969), 173.

35. H. R. Williamson, *Wang An Shih*, vol. 1 (Westport, CT: Hyperion Press, 1973), 201; see also 177–203 for a detailed discussion on *baojia*.

36. See John W. Dardess, *Confucianism and Autocracy—Professional Elites in the Founding of the Ming Dynasty* (Berkely: University of California Press, 1983), 197–201.

37. Hucker, 310–311.

38. Edgar Snow, *Red Star Over China*, 1st revised and enlarged ed. (New York: Grove Press, 1968), 220.

39. Franz Schurmann, *Ideology and Organization in Communist China*, 2nd ed. (Berkeley: University of California Press, 1970), 416.

40. Samuel P. Huntington, *Political Order in Changing Societies* (New Haven, CT: Yale University Press, 1968), 89.

41. Jean-Jacques Rousseau, *On the Social Contract*, book II, trans. Judith R. Masters, ed. Roger D. Masters (New York: St. Martin's Press, 1978), 62.

42. Derek J. Waller, *The Government and Politics of the People's Republic of China* (New York: New York University Press, 1981) 105–106; see also 92–93, 103–105.

43. Ross Terrill, *China in Our Time* (New York: Simon & Schuster, 1992), 66.

44. *Condè Nast TRAVELLER*, October 1993, 106–111.

45. Kathy Wilhelm, "Mixed Emotions on Mao," *Lawrence Journal World* (19 December 1993): 15A.

46. Li Kai and Ching Shen, "The Road for Five Hundred Million Peasants," *People's Daily*, 28 November 1955, cited in *Socialist Upsurge in China's Countryside* (Peking: Foreign Languages Press, 1957), 115.

47. Jonathan D. Spence, *The Gate of Heavenly Peace—The Chinese and their Revolution, 1895–1980* (Middlesex, England: Penguin Books, 1982), 382–383.

48. Yunxiang Yan, "The Impact of Rural Reform on Economic and Social Stratification in Chinese Village," *The Australian Journal of Chinese Affairs*, no. 27 (January 1992): 1–23.

49. Gail E. Henderson and Myron S. Cohen, *The Chinese Hospital—A Socialist Work Unit* (New Haven, CT: Yale University Press, 1984), 140.

50. Hu Min (alias). Interviewed when he was visiting the United States in 1993–1994.

51. Gordon Thomas, *Chaos Under Heaven—The Shocking Story of China's Search for Democracy* (New York: Carol Publishing Group, 1991), 30–31.

52. "Why China's People Are Getting Out of Control," *The Economist*, 12 June 1993, 41–42.

53. Nicholas D. Kristof, "4 Years After Tiananmen, the Hard Line is Cracking," *New York Times*, 1 June 1993, 1.

54. Thomas A. Metzger, "The State and Commerce in Imperial China," *Asian and African Studies*, vol. 6 (1970): 23–46.

55. Martin Albrow, *Bureaucracy* (New York: Praeger, 1970), 31–32.

56. William Hinton, *The Great Reversal—The Privatization of China, 1978–1989* (New York: Monthly Review Press, 1990), 168.

57. From interview with the owner of a cement bag machine factory.

58. Marco Polo, *The Travels of Marco Polo*, revised from Marden's translation and edited with introduction by Manuel Komroff (London: Jonathan Cape, 1928), 174–175, 238–244.

59. John K. Fairbank and Edwin O. Reischauer, *China-Tradition & Transformation* (Boston: Houghton Mifflin Company, 1978), 204.

60. Ho Ping-ti, *Studies on the Population of China, 1368–1953* (Cambridge, MA: Harvard University Press, 1959), 199.

61. Jean Baptiste Du Halde, *A Description of the Empire of China and Chinese Tartary*, vol. 1 (London, 1738), 333–334. Cited in Ho Ping-ti, 199.

62. Karin Polkker, "The Development of Individual and Cooperative Labour Activity in the Soviet Union," *Soviet Studies*, vol. 42, no. 3 (July 1990): 403–428.

63. Roy D. Laird, *The Soviet Paradigm* (New York: Free Press, 1970), 14–19, 116–126. See also Viktor Petrovich Danilov, "The Commune in the Life of the Soviet Countryside Between Collectivisation," in *Land Commune and Peasant Community in Russia*, ed. Roger Bartlett (New York: St. Martin's Press, 1990), 299; see also Karel Hulicka and Irene M. Hulicka, *Soviet Institutions—The Individual and Society* (Boston: Christopher Publishing House, 1967), 437–466.

64. Arcadius Kahan, *The Plow the Hammer and the Knout—An Economic History of Eighteenth-Century Russia* (Chicago: University of Chicago Press, 1985), 88–136.

65. William L. Blackwell, *The Beginnings of Russian Industrialization 1800–1860* (Princeton, NJ: Princeton University Press, 1968), 197–198.

66. Cyril E. Black, "Russian and Soviet Entrepreneurship in Comparative Context," in *Entrepreneurship in Imperial Russia and the Soviet Union*, ed. Gregory Guroff and Fred V. Carstensen (Princeton, NJ: Princeton University Press, 1983), 16. For detailed information on Russian and regional entrepreneurs in the nineteenth and early twentieth century, see Alfred J. Rieber, *Merchants and Entrepreneurs in Imperial Russia* (Chapel Hill: University of North Carolina Press, 1982).

67. Nicholas D. Kristof, *New York Times,* June 1, 1993, 1.

68. Ross Terrill, "China's Youth Wait for Tomorrow," *National Geographic,* vol. 180, no. 1 (July 1991): 110–136.

69. *Beijing Ribao,* 18 August, 1980, cited in Zhou Jinghau, "Discussion About Individual Economy," *Beijing Review,* no. 45, 10 November 1980, 20–24.

70. From interview with the owner of an electronic store.

71. Jin Qi, "Productivity and Ideology," *Beijing Review,* 14–20 December 1987, 4–5.

72. Xi Mi, "Non-Governmental High-Tech Firms Blooming," *China Daily,* 8 July 1992, 4.

73. Zhou Jinghua, 23.

74. Polkker, 411.

75. Anthony Jones and William Moskoff, *KO-OPS—The Rebirth of Entrepreneurship in the Soviet Union* (Indianapolis: Indiana University Press, 1991), 130.

76. *Jingji Ribao,* 18 November 1987, 1, cited in Susan Young, "Wealth But Not Security: Attitudes Towards Private Business in China in the 1980s," *The Australian Journal of Chinese Affairs,* no. 25 (January 1991): 115–137.

77. From interview with a former loom factory owner.

78. From interview with the owner of an electric appliance business.

79. Nicholas D. Kristof, "China Applauds Officials who Plunge into Profit," *New York Times,* 6 April 1993, A6.

80. See Ole Brunn, *Business and Bureaucracy in a Chinese City—An Ethnography of Private Business Households in Contemporary China* (Berkeley: Institute of East Asian Studies, University of California, 1993), 144–146.

81. From interview with the owner of an ice cream and soft drinks business.

82. From interview with the owner of a computer and consulting firm.

83. From interview with the owner of an electronics store.

84. Adi Ignatius, "Party Animals: In Capitalist Moscow, Young Business Grads Reap Money and Envy," *Wall Street Journal,* 2 August 1993, 1.

85. *China Daily,* 6 October 1992, 4.

86. Frank Gibney, Jr., "No Time to Waste on Theory," *Newsweek,* 18 January 1993, 43.

87. From interview with the owner of an electronics store.

88. From interview with an individual barber.

89. From interview with the owner of a bicycle repair stand.

90. *China Daily,* 16 February 1993, 1.

91. Li Wen, "Doors Opening for Traders," *China Daily,* 20 July 1992, 6.

92. Urban Development Group, 1987 Survey, *Wenhui bao,* 4 September 1988, Chinese Academy of Social Sciences, Institute of Social Research.

93. *Renmin Ribao,* 12 April 1988, 2, cited in Susan Young, "Policy, Practice and the Private Sector in China," *The Australian Journal of Chinese Affairs,* no. 21 (January 1989): 57–80.

94. From interview with the owner of a general store.

95. Tan Hongkai, "Urban Dwellers Try to Keep Pace with Reforms," *China Daily*, 21 January 1993, 4. A similar result was observed in a previous survey. See Li Wensha, "Survey Lifts Lid on the Current Social Climate," *China Daily*, 6 October 1992, 6.

96. Qian Lijun, "What a Deflating Experience," *China Daily*, 21 September 1992, 6.

97. Ignatius, 1.

98. Bill Keller, "A Brand New Soviet Man, Self-Made," *New York Times*, 29 December 1990, 4. See also Jones and Moskoff, 105.

99. Cai Yan, 4.

100. Hong Lanxing, "Wealthy Farmer Helps the Disabled," *Beijing Review*, 25–31 May 1992, 26–28.

101. Nicholas D. Kristof, *New York Times*, 1 June 1993, 1.

102. "Teachers Finding It Hard To Be 'Props' of Society," *China Daily*, 2 August 1993, 5.

103. Li Xing, "Artists Find New Creative Persona as Entrepreneurs," *China Daily*, 20 February 1993, 4.

104. Cai Beihua, "Lun geti jingji" ("On Individual Economy"), *Shehui Kexue*, (*Social Science*), no. 6 (1980): 16, cited in Linda Hershkovitz, "The Fruits of Ambivalence: China's Urban Individual Economy," *Pacific Affairs*, vol. 58, no. 3 (fall 1985): 427–450.

105. Qian Lijun, "Students Get Off Their High Horses and Work," *China Daily*, 15 September 1992, 6.

106. A picture of a college student in Harbin, capital of Heilongjiang Province, cleaning a car. *China Daily*, 2 August 1993, 3.

107. *China Daily*, 12 September 1992, 3.

108. *China Daily*, 12 September 1992, 3.

109. *Peking Review*, no. 1, 3 January 1969, 14.

110. Christopher J. Smith, *China—People and Places in the Land of One Billion* (Boulder, CO: Westview Press, 1991), 57.

111. Qian Lijun, *China Daily*, 15 September 1992, 6.

112. According to professor Hu Min of Nankai University, many intellectuals sell their expertise to enable them to buy equipment for research. However, in their hearts they dislike it, but due to the economic reality they do not have much choice. Many professors hope for the day when they will not have to sell their talents in the marketplace to support their intellectual pursuits.

113. Lin Shiwei, "University Adapting Courses to Market Place," *China Daily*, 3 March 1993, 5.

114. Kou Zhengling, "Part-Time Jobs: A New Beijing Trend," *Beijing Review*, 8–14 March 1993, 27–30.

115. *China Daily*, 17 July 1993, 4.

116. From interview with the owner of a food factory.

117. From interview with the owner of a photography business.

118. Xi Mi, "Individuals Gain Importance in Drive toward Economic Reforms," *China Daily*, 28 August 1992, 4.

119. Satoshi Imai, "Case Studies of Joint Ventures in China," *China Newsletter*, no. 76 (Sept.–October 1988): 8–13.

120. Lin Shiwei, "Non-degree Schools Booming in Beijing," *China Daily*, 17 August 1993, 5.

121. Arthur Waley, *Chinese Poems* (London: Allen and Unwin, 1946), 84.

122. Reverend J. A. Davis, *Chinese Slave-Girl: A Story of Woman's Life in China* (Chicago: Missionary Campaign Library, 1880), 10–11.

123. Robert Leroy McNabb, *The Women of the Middle Kingdom* (New York: Young People's Missionary Movement, 1907), 17.

124. Delia Davin, *Woman-Work—Women and the Party in Revolutionary China* (Oxford, England: Clarendon Press, 1976), 114.

125. *Peking Review*, no. 11, 16 March 1973, 5–6.

126. *The Economist*, 13 March 1993, 4. Also see cite above for discussion.

127. Jack Anderson and Dale Van Atta, "Infanticide Continues in Rural China," *Washington Post*, 24 October 1991, B23.

128. Lena H. Sun, "Abduction, Sale of Women Reemerges from China's Past," *Washington Post*, 21 June 1992, A1.

129. Shirin Rai, "Watering Another Man's Garden—Gender, Employment and Educational Reforms in China," in *Women in the Face of Change—The Soviet Union, Eastern Europe and China*, ed. Shirin Rai, Hilary Pilkington, and Annie Phizacklea (New York: Routledge, 1992), 30–36.

130. Lena H. Sun, "A Great Leap Back—Chinese Women Losing Jobs, Status as Ancient Ways Subvert Socialist Ideal," *Washington Post*, 16 February 1993, 1.

131. Sheryl WuDunn, "Women Face Increasing Bias as Chinese Focus on Profits," *New York Times*, 28 July 1992, A1. See also *China Daily*, 28 May 1992. This articles says television ads "stereotyped roles of women as temptress, wife and mother."

132. "Chinese Pin-up Girls: Armed and Dangerous," *Lawrence Journal World—Extra*, 29 September 1993, 10. See also *China Daily*, 5 July and 6 July, 1993. The article reported that beauty pageants and supermodel contests, which were taboo during the prereform era, are now in fashion. A beauty pageant is a challenge to the established ethic, which forbids respectable women from showing their beauty openly, particularly their bodies.

133. Margery Wolf, *Revolution Postponed—Women in Contemporary China* (Stanford: Stanford University Press, 1985), 60–64.

134. Xiao Ma, "Women's Work and Marriage in Today's China," *US-China Review*, vol. 17, no. 2 (spring 1993): 11–13.

135. Ignatius, 1.

136. James Gallagher, "Job Discrimination, Cutbacks Strap Educated Russians," *Chicago Tribune*, 1 August 1993, 6/1.

137. Blaine Harden, "Study see Setbacks for Polish Women," *Washington Post*, 24 March 1992, A24.

138. Simons Marlise, "East Europeans Duped into West's Sex Trade," *New York Times*, 9 June 1993, A1.

139. V. I. Lenin, *The Emancipation of Women* (New York: International Publishers, 1984), 73–74.

CHAPTER FIVE

1. "A Serious Lesson," *The Socialist Upsurge in China's Countryside*, vol. 1, cited in *The Thoughts of Chairman Mao Tse-Tung* (London: Anthony Gibbs Library, 1967), 87.

2. Margaret G. Hermann, "When Personality Will Affect Foreign Policy: Some Proposition," in *In Search of Global Patterns*, ed. James N. Rosenau (New York: Free Press, 1976), 327. Although Hermann's discussion of decision-making power referred to foreign policy, the concept can easily be broadened.

3. For the above discussion, see Wolfgang Bartke, *Who's Who in the People's Republic of China*, vol. 1, 3rd ed. (New York: K. G. Saur, 1991), 92–93; see also William R. Doerner, "The Comeback Comrade," *Time*, 6 January 1986, 42–45.

4. Witold Rodzinski, *The People's Republic of China—A Concise Political History* (New York: Free Press, 1988), 213.

5. George J. Church, "China," *Time*, 6 January 1986, 24–41.

6. David Shambaugh, "Deng Xiaoping: The Politician," *The China Quarterly*, vol. 135 (September 1993): 457–490.

7. Vàclav Klaus, "Interplay of Political and Economic Reform Measures in the Transformation of Postcommunist Countries" (speech before The Heritage Foundation on October 15, 1993).

8. James M. Buchanan, "What Should Economists Do?" *The Southern Economic Journal*, vol. 30, no. 3 (January 1964) 213–222.

9. Gray L. Wamsley and Mayer N. Zald, *The Political Economy of Public Organizations* (Lexington, MA: Lexington Books, 1973), 17.

10. Luo Bing, "Inside Information About the Election of Members of the Secretariat of the CCP Central Committee and Other Matters," *Cheng Ming*, no. 40 (1 April 1980).

11. "Chen Yun Criticized Mao Zedong," *Ming Pao*, 15 January 1979; see also *AFP* (HK), 10 January 1979.

12. See *Ming Pao*, 7 January 1979; and Luo Bing, "The Fall of the 'Whatever Faction,' " *Cheng Ming*, no. 16 (February 1979); and see also Qi Xin, "The CCP Has Completed its Sharp Turn—The Frontstage and the Backstage of the Third Plenary Session," *Chishi Nientai*, February 1979.

13. "Correctly Understand and Seriously Implement the Party's Policy Toward the National Bourgeoisie," *Renmin Ribao*, 15 February 1979; see *Kunming Yunnan Provincial Service*, 2 March 1979; see "To Implement the Rural Economic Policies, it is Imperative to Relentlessly Criticize Ultraleftism," *Yunnan Ribao*, 2 March 1979; and see also Xinhua, 7 March 1979.

14. Harold C. Hinton, *The People's Republic of China, 1979–1984—A Documentary Survey*, vol. 1 (Wilmington, DE: Scholarly Resources Inc., 1986), 3–15. See also *Cheng Ming*, 1 March 1980.

15. Deng Xiaoping, "Why China Has Opened Its Doors," *Bangkok Post*, 10 February 1980, cited in Hinton, vol. 2, 451–453.

16. "Expert and the Mass Line," *Renmin Ribao*, 7 March 1980; and see also "The Red Must Be Experts," *Renmin Ribao*, 3 April 1980.

17. "It Is Necessary To Get Rich and Also Achieve Modernization," *Heilongjiang Ribao*, 31 March 1980.

18. *AFP* (HK), 19 March 1980. Qu Qiubai led the CCP from 1927 to 1928 until he was dismissed. He was later executed by Nationalist Chinese on June 18, 1935. Mao was not powerful enough at that time to dismiss Qu, but afterward Mao denounced Qu many times as the representative of "the first leftist opportunist deviation."

19. See "Beijing Removes Rightist Labels from 2,100 Wrongly Designated People," *Beijing Ribao*, 26 January 1979; and *Changsha Hunan Provincial Service*, 12 February 1979; and see also "It is Imperative to Firmly Step Up the Work of

Reversing Incorrect Verdicts on Wrongfully Designated Rightists," *Yunnan Ribao*, 15 February 1979, reported by *Kunming Yunnan Provincial Service*, 15 February 1979.

20. See "Xinhua to Release Facts about Liu Shaoqi's Case," Xinhua, 12 March 1980. Xinhua also reported that the *People's Daily* and all other Beijing newspapers on 12 March 1980 devoted their front page and another half page to an article by Liu Shaoqi written in 1940 titled, "Be a Good Communist and Build a Good Party."

21. *AFP* (HK), 16 March 1980.

22. "Chen Yonggui Loses Power," *Ming Pao*, 12 January 1979.

23. "Lay Down This Stick, 'Opposing Dazhai,' " *Guangming Ribao*, 3 March 1979; and "We Cannot Regard Dazhai's Practical Experience as a Law," *Beijing Domestic Service*, 6 March 1979, reported from *Guangming Ribao*; and see also "Break Through the 'Leftist' Yoke and Implement the Spirit of 3rd Plenary Session of the 11th Central Committee—Comrade Liu Shugang Talks on How Xiyang County Has Initially Rectified the Leftist Errors of the Movement to Learn from Dazhai," *Shanxi Ribao* 6 May 1981.

24. Xinhua, 18 March 1979; and see also Xinhua, 20 March 1979. In their report scientific methods to boost production were encouraged and "taking grain as the key link" was discouraged.

25. "Political Bureau's Meeting Unanimously Approves Hua Guofeng's Resignation from Party Chairmanship," *Ming Pao*, 26 June 1981.

26. "Are There Contradictions Between Party and Army," *Cheng Ming Jih Pao*, 6 July 1981.

27. For example see, Su Da, "We Must Continue to Restore Order Out of Chaos and Wipe Out the Left Influence," *Guangming Ribao*, 9 April 1981; and see, "Uphold and Safeguard the Four Basic Principles," *Jeifangjun Bao*, 17 April 1981. See other Chinese newspapers from May 1981 to June 1981.

28. Fang Yeh-fang, "The Troubles of Deng Xiaoping," *Cheng Ming* (HK), no. 44, June 1, 1981.

29. In the late 1970s and early 1980s, Chen Yun was called a "pragmatist" in Deng's faction; Yao Yilin a "liberal-minded" economic expert; and Deng, Hu Yao-bang, and Chen Yun were considered "identical" in their thinking. See respectively, *AFP* (HK), 10 January 1979; Shih I-Ping, "Deng Xiaoping's Three Strategic Moves," *Tung Hsiang*, 16 April 1981; and *Cheng Ming*, no. 45, 1 July 1981.

30. Lo Ping, "Deng Xiaoping Criticizes Chen Yun at Meeting," *Cheng Ming*, 1 October 1986.

31. Lei Yu was in charge of government affairs in Hainan. Hainan officials were involved in reselling motor vehicles and other imported goods for profit. On this pretext, hardliners led by Chen attacked the special economic zones. To prevent the hardliners movement from gaining any momentum, Deng sacked Lei Yu. See *Cheng Ming*, no. 95, 1 September 1985, and no. 96, 1 October 1985.

32. *Hongqi*, no. 13, 1 July 1985.

33. "Let Privately Run Industry Flourish," *Renmin Ribao*, 22 September 1982.

34. Xinhua, 31 March 1981. For detailed information about the struggle between Deng Xiaoping and the Maoists in the PLA see Paul Humes Folta, *From Swords to Plowshares?—Defense Industry Reform in the PRC* (Boulder, CO: Westview Press, 1991), 23–36.

35. "Zhang Aiping Calls on All Departments of Military Science and Technology and Defense Industry to Help Boost China's National Economy," *Jingi Ribao*, 8 August 1983.

36. "An Important Reform in the Leadership System of Party and State," *Renmin Ribao*, 28 October 1980.

37. See "CPC Central Committee Holds Plenary Session," *Beijing Review*, no. 42, 17 October 1983, 4; see also *Hsin Wan Pao*, 29 October 1983.

38. Deng Liqun, "The Duties of Intellectuals and the Tasks of the Party's Propaganda Departments in the New Period," *Red Flag*, no. 20, 16 October 1983.

39. See "It is Imperative to Make the Administrative Machinery Operate Harmoniously and Rhythmically," *Guangming Ribao*, 17 October 1983. And see also Xinhua 24 October 1983.

40. Lo Ping, "A Fierce Struggle in Zhongnanhai," *Cheng Ming*, no. 76, 1 February 1984.

41. *Guangxi Regional Service*, 27 October 1983.

42. Lo Ping, "Retreat of the Antipollution Tide in Perspective," *Cheng Ming*, no. 75, 1 January 1984.

43. "Let the People's Life Be Full of Variety," *Guangming Ribao*, 17 December 1983; and see also "Adopt a Correct Attitude Toward Peasants Who Are the First to Become Rich," *Ban Yue Tan*, no. 24, 25 December 1983.

44. "Foster Several Viewpoints," *Tianjin City Service*, 9 February 1984.

45. Xinhua, 9 October 1984.

46. "Beginning with the Worries Caused by 'Triple Happiness.' " Xinhua, 10 October 1984.

47. Jin Qi, "The Way to Vitalize Enterprises," *Beijing Review*, no. 45, 5 November 1984, 4–5.

48. *Beijing Domestic Service*, 1 November 1984. From *Jiefangjun Bao* report.

49. *Beijing Domestic Service*, 5 November 1984. From *Jiefangjun Bao* report.

50. *Cheng Ming*, no. 94, 1 August 1985.

51. "Senior Chinese Leadership Has Become Younger," *Zhongguo Xinwen She*, 4 September 1985.

52. Xinhua, 16 September 1985.

53. "Persons Who Persistently Carry Out Reform Are Heroes of Today," *Dazhong Ribao*, 23 September 1985.

54. Xinhua, 18 September 1985; and *Ta Kung Pao*, 31 October–6 November 1985.

55. Li Kelin, "Dazhai Today," *Renmin Ribao*, 5 October 1985.

56. See *Renmin Ribao*, overseas edition, 18 December 1985; and see also "Hu Yaobang's Speech at Party School Criticizes Some People for Regarding Current Situation as Taking a Capitalist Road," *Ming Pao*, 6 October 1985.

57. *Cheng Ming*, no. 95, 1 September 1985.

58. *Beijing Review*, no. 44, 29 October 1984, v.

59. See "The Growth of Consumption Funds Should Be Appropriate," *Renmin Ribao*, 30 August 1985; see "Hidden Growth of Consumption Funds Threatens Reform and Development," *Ming Pao*, 13 January 1986; see also Peter M. Lichtenstein, *China at the Brink—The Political Economy of Reform and Retrenchment in the Post–Mao Era* (New York: Praeger, 1991), 79.

60. *Ming Pao*, 6 October 1985.

61. Ho Feng, "The 'United Front' of Deng Liqun and Wang Zhen," *Cheng Ming*, no. 116, 3 June 1987.

62. See Kuang Pi-hua, "Questions Concerning Who Will Replace Zhao Ziyang to Take the Premiership, and the Mystery of Hu Yaobang's Resignation: The CPC Makes Stipulations on Restricting the Scope of the Drive to Oppose 'Bourgeois

Liberalization,' " *Kuang Chiao Ching*, no. 173, 16 February 1987; and see David Wong, *Hongkong Standard*, 6 February 1987.

63. Xinhua, 14 January 1987; and see also " 'In a Word, We Will Continue Our Work as Planned,' Deng Xiaoping's Important Conversations at Meeting with Foreign Visitors on Three Occasions," *Shijie Jingji Daobao*, 23 February 1987.

64. *Hefei, Anhui Provincial Service*, 11 January 1987. See other newspapers, such as *Renmin Ribao, Guangming Ribao, Jiefangjun Bao*, from the end of December 1986 to April 1987.

65. "No Political Campaign to Be Launched," *Beijing Review*, nos. 5/6, 9 February 1987, 6; and see also *Kuang Chiao Ching*, no. 173, 16 February 1987.

66. Ma Encheng, "Let a Large Number of Peasant Entrepreneurs Spring Up," *Renmin Ribao*, 10 February 1987; see "Rural Reform is to Develop In-Depth," *Ban Yue Tan*, 10 January 1987; see "The Position and Quality of Entrepreneurs," *Gongren Ribao*, 27 February 1987; see "A Probe into the Operation of Small State-Run Enterprises on a Leasing Basis," *Renmin Ribao*, 6 February 1987; and see also *Tianjin City Service*, 13 March 1987. Tianjin's Mayor Li Ruihuan also came forward to advocate enterprise reform and practicing of economy.

67. No one voted against Hu Yaobang as a member of the presidium and on top of this Hu received warm applause from the 2,000 delegates when he ascended the podium to take his seat. For the above discussion see *South China Morning Post*, 26 March 1987; and see also *Cheng Ming*, no. 115, 1 May 1987.

68. " '*Hongqi*' Commentator's Article Points Out that Opposing Bourgeois Liberalization is Different From 'Bringing Order Out of Chaos,' " *Hsin Wan Pao*, 4 April 1987.

69. Rao Xinjian, "Opposing Bourgeois Liberalization Promotes Reform and Opening Up to the Outside World," *Jeifangjun Bao*, 14 April 1987.

70. Liu Jui-shao, "Zhao Ziyang Corrects Erroneous Tendencies," *Wen Wei Po*, 18 May 1987.

71. "Be Alert Against Interference from the 'Left,' " *Wen Wei Po*, 23 May 1987.

72. *Ching Pao*, no. 6, 10 June 1987. This Hong Kong-based reformers' mouthpiece reported that Zhao Ziyang criticized Bo Yibo, Hu Qiaomu, and Deng Liqun by name for their leftist deviations. See also *Cheng Ming*, 1 August 1987. It reported that on May 13, 1987, Zhao delivered a speech at a meeting of cadres responsible for propaganda, stating that opposing bourgeois liberalization should not affect reform and the opening up of China. Since that day an open confrontation started between Zhao Ziyang and Hu Qiaomu, Deng Liqun, Peng Zhen, and Bo Yibo. On July 10, 1987 *Renmin Ribao* published Zhao's May 13, 1987 speech, thus indicating the conflict between Zhao and the hardliners.

73. *South China Morning Post*, 19 June 1987.

74. Willy Wo-Lap Lam, *The Era of Zhao Ziyang* (Hong Kong: A. B. Books and Stationery Ltd., 1989), 224, cited in Peter M. Lichtenstein, *China at the Brink—The Political Economy of Reform and Retrenchment in the Post–Mao Era* (New York: Praeger, 1991), 122.

75. Zhao Ziyang, "Advance Along the Road of Socialism with Chinese Characteristics," report delivered at the 13th National Congress of the CCP on October 25, 1987. *Beijing Review*, 9–15 November 1987.

76. *Ching Pao*, no. 125, 10 December 1987.

77. *Ching Pao*, no. 126, 10 January 1988.

78. "Problems Concerning Competitive Bidding for Enterprise Operation: Let Competitive Bidders Surface from Underground," Xinhua, 8 August 1988; see "Wuhan: Enterprises Compete and Thrive," *Beijing Review*, 18–24 January 1988, 20; and see "Private Businesses Produce Millionaires," *Beijing Review*, 21–27 March 1988, 14.

79. *Beijing Review*, 8–14 February 1988, 9.

80. *China Daily*, 21 February 1990.

81. *Cheng Ming*, no. 116, 3 June 1987.

82. *Cheng Ming*, no. 132, 1 October 1988.

83. Lo Ping, "Zhao Ziyang is Encountering a Big Crisis," *Cheng Ming*, no. 130, 1 August 1988.

84. In *Cheng Ming*, no. 131, 1 September 1988, it was reported that Deng said: "I shall not protect anybody and whoever fails to give a good account of himself should go," and in *South China Morning Post*, 25 November 1988, it was reported that Deng said: "I will not protect anyone. If the situation worsens, the general must get killed."

85. Joe Klein, "Twilight of the Emperor," *Newsweek*, 22 November 1993, 43; and see also Tai Ming Cheung, "Serve the People," *Far Eastern Economic Review*, 14 October 1993, 64–66; and *UPI*, 21 April 1994.

86. Dorinda Elliot, "We Need Law and Order—The Army Wants Stability, But It Will Not Step In," *Newsweek*, 5 April 1993, 26; see *China Daily*, 24 January 1994; see *The Economist*, 29 January 1994, 23–25, 58; and see also *The Economist*, 5 March 1994, 58.

87. Nicholas C. McBride, "Government Closes in a Fraud Indictments in Pentagon Scandal," *Christian Science Monitor*, 23 November 1988, 4; and see Leonard Buder, "File-Destroying Efforts Cited by Arms Fraud Investigators," *New York Times*, 27 October 1988, B13. See also other U.S. newspapers from July to December 1988.

88. From interview with the owner of a food factory.

89. Max Weber, *The Theory of Social and Economic Organization*, trans. A. M. Henderson and Talcott Parsons (New York: Oxford University Press, 1947), 329–337.

90. Liu Binyan, *China's Crisis, China's Hope*, trans. Howard Goldblatt (Cambridge, MA: Harvard University Press, 1990), 59–68. Liu Binyan's look at Bin County in Heilongjiang Province illustrates the intricacy of this family network affair.

91. Nicholas D. Kristof, "Slaying Creates an Uproar in China's 'Model' Village," *New York Times*, 30 March 1993, A7.

92. Xi Mi, "Individuals Gain Importance in Drive Toward Economic Reforms," *China Daily*, 28 August 1992, 4.

93. *Kyodo*, 15 June 1992.

94. Yin Xiao-huang, "China's Gilded Age," *Atlantic Monthly*, April 1994, 42–53.

95. From interview with the owner of a food factory.

96. "Free-loaders Ruin Restaurant," *China Daily*, 17 June 1986, 3.

97. From interview with an individual barber.

98. From interview with the owner of an electric appliances business.

99. Xinhua, 9 March 1990.

100. Wang Xianghong, "Beijing Exposes Company of Thieves," *Beijing Review*, no. 1, 6 January 1986, 8.

101. From interview with the owner of an electronics store.

102. From interview with the a car parts dealer.

103. *China Daily*, 30 August 1993, 4.

104. "Pakistan—Big Fish, Big Catch," *The Economist*, 30 April 1994, 40. See also Edward Gargan, "Corruption's Many Tentacles Are Choking India's Growth," *New York Times*, 10 November 1992, A1.

105. Zafar Altaf, *Entrepreneurship in the Third World—Risk and Uncertainty in Industry in Pakistan* (New York: Croon Helm, 1988), 8.

106. Kalman Rupp, *Entrepreneurs in Red—Structure and Organizational Innovation in the Centrally Planned Economy* (Albany: State University of New York Press, 1983), 90.

CHAPTER SIX

1. From interview with a car parts dealer.

2. From interview with a car parts dealer.

3. *Beijing Review*, 13–19 June 1988, 28. See also Susan Young, "Wealth But Not Security—Attitude Towards Private Business in the 1980s," *Economic Reform and Social Change in China*, ed. Andrew Watson (London: Routledge, 1992), 77–78.

4. Chen Xiao, "Private Business Taps Advantages of State Firms," *China Daily*, 5 May 1993, 4.

5. *Beijing Review*, 27 June–3 July 1988, 7.

6. *Beijing Review*, 26 Sept.–3 October 1988.

7. *Hongkong Standard*, 29 March 1990.

8. *China Daily*, 5 November 1992.

9. Tayseer Baquir Khunaizi, "Economic, Social, and Political Development in Saudi Arabia: A Historical Analysis" (Ph.D. diss., University of Kansas, 1993), 336–344.

10. Youssef M. Ibrahim, "Saudi Arabia to Slash Its Budget as Oil Prices Continue to Plunge," *New York Times*, 3 January 1994, A3.

11. Edward Mason, et al., *The Economic and Social Modernization of the Republic of Korea* (Cambridge, MA: Harvard University Press, 1980), 254.

12. Li Zhuoyan, "Private Firms Now Likely to Engage in Business Overseas," *China Daily*, 21 October 1992, 1.

13. Wang Yong,"Freer Rein Granted to Small Businesses," *China Daily*, 26 February 1993, 2.

14. Wang Tianjun, "Private Business Takes Area by Storm," *China Daily*, 30 July 1993, 2.

15. "Nanjing Fosters Private Business," Xinhua, reported in *China Daily*, 22 February 1993.

16. Cai Yan, "New Labour Rules Take Effect for Private Firms," *China Daily*, 9 August 1993, 4.

17. "Reform of Labour System Seen Beneficial," *China Daily*, 22 January 1994, 4.

18. From interview with the owner of a food factory.

19. Sun Shangwu, "Private Sector Needs State's Help," *China Daily*, 15 March 1994, 4.

20. From interview with the owner of a computer and consulting firm.

21. From interview with an individual barber.

22. Xiao Zheng, "Private Businesses Starved for Capital," *China Daily*, business weekly, 28 February 1994, 4.

23. *China Daily*, 20 and 21 January 1994.

24. *The Economist*, 30 November 1991, 35.

25. "China-Return to Go," *The Economist*, 4 July 1992.

26. *The Economist*, 20 November 1993, 36.

27. William J. Baumol, "Toward Operational Models of Entrepreneurship," in *Entrepreneurship*, ed. Joshua Ronen (Lexington, MA: Lexington Books, D. C. Heath, 1982), 30.

28. Dai Yannian, "Speed Up Reform, Open the Doors Wider," *Beijing Review*, 9–15 March 1992, 4–5.

29. *The Economist*, 25 July 1992, 34.

30. Ren Kan, "Sweeping Power to Big State Firm," *China Daily*, 5 August 1992, 2.

31. *China Daily*, 5 August 1992.

32. Ma Zhiping, "Leasing of State Shops to Citizens Paying Off," *China Daily*, 23 July 1993, 3.

33. *China Daily*, 7 September 1993, 4.

34. *China Daily*, 3 December 1993, 13 and 14 January 1994.

35. *China Daily*, 4 September 1992, 4.

36. From interview with the owner of a computer and consulting firm.

37. *China Daily*, 8 March 1994, 6.

38. From interview with the owner of an ice cream and soft drinks business.

39. *China Daily*, 28 June 1993.

40. From interview with the part time manager of a clothing store.

41. "Li Yining Points Out that Unemployment Affects Social Stability," *Wen Wei Po*, 26 March 1990, 2.

42. *China Daily*, 8 October 1992.

43. Li Hong, "City Jobless Rate Is Still a Low 2.3%," *China Daily*, 25 August 1993.

44. Le Ngoe Hung, and Dennis A. Rondinelli, "Small Business Development and Economic Transformation in Vietnam," *Journal of Asian Business*, vol. 9, no. 4 (fall 1993): 2.

45. "Myopic Traders Urged to Think about Insurance," *China Daily*, 15 September 1992.

46. *China Daily*, 5 December 1992.

47. "Real Estate Business Grows Rapidly in China," *China Market*, no. 11, 1992, 11–12.

48. Cao Min, "Entrepreneurs Invest in the Public," *China Daily*, business weekly, 21 February 1994.

49. Thomas Joseph Weiss, *The Service Sector in the United States—1839 Through 1899* (New York: Arno Press, 1975), 2.

50. "Service Industry Needs Market System to Thrive," *China Daily*, 10 May 1993.

51. "Day Offers Extra Hour of Leisure in Tianjin," *China Daily*, 14 November 1994, 3.

52. From interview with a former owner of a loom factory.

53. From interview with the owner of an ice cream and soft drinks business.

54. Sun Ping, "Individual Economy Under Socialism," *Beijing Review*, 3 August 1984, 25–28.

55. From interview with the owner of an electronics store.

56. Peter Morris, "The Social Barriers to African Entrepreneurship," *Journal of Development Studies* (October 1968): 29–38.

57. *China Daily*, 25 August 1992.

58. From interview with the owner of an electronics store.

59. Da Lin, "Harvest Time," *China Daily*, 22 September 1992.

60. Chen Ya, "Village Women's Labour Brings Life to a Valley," *China Daily*, 11 November 1993.

61. *Jingji Guangli*, no. 12, 1989.

62. From interview with the owner of an ice cream and soft drinks business.

63. Ma Zhiping, "Private Sector Set to Boom in 1993," *China Daily*, 30 January 1993.

64. Cai Hong, "Private Businesses Play a Subsidiary Role," *China Daily*, 12 March 1994.

65. Gao Shangquan, "Market-Oriented Reforms Can Work in Nation's System," *China Daily*, 10 September 1992.

66. Ma Zhiping, "Business in Free Markets Rises 50%," *China Daily*, 22 February 1994.

67. *China Daily*, 2 February 1994.

68. "More Small State Enterprises Leased to Individuals," *China Daily*, 7 September 1993.

69. Li Hong, "Put in Private Hands, State Shops Prosper," *China Daily*, 1 July 1993.

70. Carl Goldstein, "China Under License—Deng Blesses Guandong's Economic Reforms," *Far Eastern Economic Review*, 23 April 1992.

71. *The Economist*, 10 October 1992.

72. Wang Yonghong, "'Vegetable Baskets' Are Fuller These Days," *China Daily*, 23 July 1993.

73. *China Daily*, 30 March 1994.

74. *China Daily*, 20 January 1994.

75. Anita M. Weiss, *Culture, Class and Development in Pakistan—The Emergence of an Industrial Bourgeoisie in Punjab* (Boulder, CO: Westview Press, 1990), 148.

76. Kalman Rupp, *Entrepreneurs in Red—Structure and Organizational Innovation in the Centrally Planned Economy* (Albany: State University of New York Press, 1983), 98.

77. Arnold Mindell, *The Leader as Martial Artist—An Introduction to Deep Democracy* (New York: HarperCollins Publishers, 1992), 100.

78. *Jingji Guangli*, no. 12, 1989.

79. For the above discussion see Xie Liangjun, "CPPCC Gives Voice to Private Sector of the Economy," *China Daily*, 31 March 1993.

80. *China Daily*, 31 March 1993.

81. From interview with the owner of a photography business.

82. Cao Min, "Entrepreneurs Invest in the Public," *China Daily*, business weekly, 21 February 1994.

83. Cai Hong, *China Daily*, 12 March 1994.

84. Nicholas D. Kristof, "Chinese Communist's Secret Aim: Capitalism," *New York Times*, 19 October 1992.

85. Cai Hong, 1994. See also Susan Young, "Policy, Practice and the Private Sector in China," *The Australian Journal of Chinese Affairs*, no. 21 (January 1989): 65.

86. Emily MacFarquhar and Susan V. Lawrence, "Following Deng's Lead," *U.S. News & World Report*, 15 March 1993.

87. Ross Terrill, "China's Youth Wait for Tomorrow," *National Geographic*, vol. 180, no. 1 (July 1991): 110–136.

88. For the above discussion, see Willy Kraus, *Private Business in China—Revival Between Ideology and Pragmatism*, trans. Erich Holtz (Honolulu: University of Hawaii

Press, 1991), 161; and see also Li Jinyan, *Taxation in the People's Republic of China* (New York: Praeger, 1991), 85.

89. Robert Delfs, "Fiscal Feudalism," *Far Eastern Economic Review*, 6 April 1989.

90. Willy Kraus, *Private Business in China—Revival Between Ideology and Pragmatism*, trans. Erich Holtz (Honolulu: University of Hawaii Press, 1991), 160–161.

91. "New Rules for Private Firm," *Beijing Review*, 18–24 July 1988, 7.

92. *The Economist*, 8 April 1989.

93. From interview with the owner of a general store.

94. From interview with an individual barber.

95. From interview with the owner of an electronics store.

96. *China Daily*, 20 October 1993.

97. Xie Liangjun, "CPPCC Gives Voice to Private Sector of the Economy," *China Daily*, 31 March 1993.

98. Xinhua, 24 January 1986.

99. Kraus, 162.

100. See *Beijing Review*, 6–12 March 1989, ix–xvi.

101. *China Daily*, business weekly, 14 February 1994.

102. *China Daily*, 25 November 1993.

103. Lincoln Kaye, "Beware the Buyer—China's Consumers Demand Value for Money," *Far Eastern Economic Review*, 23 April 1992, 55.

104. Ma Zhiping, "Consumer Criticism on the Rise," *China Daily*, 31 August 1992.

105. Xiao Fei, "Consumers Armed with Rights," *China Daily*, 9 March 1994.

106. Zheng Wenjuan, "Chinese Consumers Must Start Becoming Quality Watchdogs," *China Daily*, 6 January 1994.

107. Tan Hongkai, "Inflation Has Not Sparked Panic in Cities, Says Survey," *China Daily*, 28 October 1993.

Selected Bibliography

Albrow, Martin. *Bureaucracy*. New York: Praeger Publishers, 1970.

Almond, Gabriel A., and Sidney Vebra. *The Civic Culture—Political Attitudes and Democracy in Five Nations*. Newbury Park, CA: Sage Publications, 1989.

Altaf, Zafar. *Entrepreneurship in the Third World—Risk and Uncertainty in Industry in Pakistan*. New York: Croon Helm, 1988.

Anderson, Jack, and Dale Van Atta. "Infanticide Continues in Rural China." *Washington Post*, 24 October 1991, B23.

Barnett, A. Doak. *Communist China: The Early Years 1949–55*. New York: Frederick A. Praeger, 1964.

Bartke, Wolfgang. *Who's Who in the People's Republic of China*. Vol. 1, 3rd edition. New York: K. G. Saur, 1991.

Baumol, William J. "Toward Operational Models of Entrepreneurship." In *Entrepreneurship*, edited by Joshua Ronen. Lexington, MA: Lexington Books, 1982.

Bell, Lynda, S. "From Comprador to County Magnate: Bourgeois Practice in the Wuxi County Silk Industry." In *Chinese Local Elites and Patterns of Dominance*, edited by Joseph W. Esherick and Mary Backus Rankin. Berkeley: University of California Press, 1990.

Bergère, Marie-Claire. *The Golden Age of the Chinese Bourgeoisie 1911–1937*. Translated by Janet Lloyd. Cambridge: Cambridge University Press, 1989.

Beveridge, Andrew A., and Anthony R. Oberschall. *African Businessmen and Development in Zambia*. Princeton, NJ: Princeton University Press, 1979.

Blackwell, William L. *The Beginnings of Russian Industrialization 1800–1860*. Princeton, NJ: Princeton University Press, 1968.

Broyelle, Claudie, Jacques Broyelle, and Evelyne Tschirhart. *China: A Second Look*. Translated by Sarah Matthews. New Jersey: Harvester Press, 1980.

Bruun, Ole. *Business and Bureaucracy in a Chinese City—An Ethnography of Private Business Households in Contemporary China*. Berkeley: Institute of East Asian Studies, University of California, 1993.

Buchanan, James M. "What Should Economists Do?" *The Southern Economic Journal* 30, no. 3 (January 1964): 213–222.

Burns, John P. "China's Governance: Political Reform in a Turbulent Environment." *The China Quarterly* 119 (September 1989): 481–518.

Butterfield, Fox. *China—Alive in the Bitter Sea*. New York: Times Books, 1982.

Cai, Beihua. "Lun geti jingji" ("On Individual Economy"). *Shehui Kexue* (Social Science). No. 6. 1980.

Carroll, John J. *The Filipino Manufacturing Entrepreneur—Agent and Product of Change*. Ithaca, NY: Cornell University Press, 1965.

Central Intelligence Agency. *The Republic of the Former Soviet Union and the Baltic States: An Overview*. January 1992.

Chao Kuo-chun. *Economic Planning and Organization in Mainland China—A Documentary Study (1949–1957)*. Vol. 1. Cambridge, MA: Harvard University Press, 1959.

Chen, Jack. *Inside the Cultural Revolution*. New York: Macmillan, 1975.

Cheng, Chu-yuan. *China's Economic Development—Growth and Structural Change*. Boulder, CO: Westview Press, 1982.

Chi Chao-Ting. "Shanghai Steps into the Future." In *China in Transition—Selected Articles 1952–1956*. Peking: China Reconstructs, 1957.

Ching Chung-Hwa. "San Fan-Wu Fan—The Big Cleanup, (September–October 1952)." In *China In Transition—Selected Articles 1952–1956*. Peking: China Reconstructs, 1957.

Chow Ching-Wen. *Ten Years of Storm—The True Story of the Communist Regime in China*. Translated and edited Lai Ming. New York: Holt, Rinehart and Winston, 1960.

Coble, Parks M. Jr. *The Shanghai Capitalists and the Nationalist Government, 1927–1937*. Cambridge, MA: Harvard University Press, 1980.

Confucius. *The Analects (Lun Yu)*. Book XVI: 9. Translated by D.C. Lau. New York: Penguin Books, 1979.

Confucius. *The Analects (Lun Yu)*. Book XIII: 20. Translated by Arthur Waley. Macmillan, 1939.

The Constitution of the People's Republic of China. Beijing: Foreign Languages Press, 1954.

Dardess, John W. *Confucianism and Autocracy—Professional Elites in the Founding of the Ming Dynasty*. Berkeley: University of California Press, 1983.

Davin, Delia. *Woman-Work—Women and the Party in Revolutionary China*. Oxford, England: Clarendon Press, 1976.

Davis, Rev. J. A. *Chinese Slave-Girl: A Story of Woman's Life in China*. Chicago: Missionary Campaign Library, 1880.

Dawson, Raymond. *Imperial China*. London: Hutchinson & Co., 1972.

Deng Liqun. "The Duties of Intellectuals and the Tasks of the Party's Propaganda Departments in the New Period." *Red Flag*, no. 20 (16 October 1983).

Deng Xiaoping. "Why China Has Opened Its Doors." *Bangkok Post*, 10 February 1980.

Deutsch, Karl W. "Social Mobilization and Political Development." *The American Political Science Review* 4, no. 3 (September 1961): 493–514.

Dobb, Maurice. *Capitalist Enterprise and Social Progress*. 2nd impression. George Routledge and Sons, 1926.

Dobek, Mariusz Mark. *The Political Logic of Privatization—Lessons from Great Britain and Poland*. Westport, CT: Praeger, 1993.

Du Halde, Jean Baptiste. *A Description of the Empire of China and Chinese Tartary*. Vol. 1. London, 1738.

Eastman, Lloyd E. *Seeds of Destruction—Nationalist China in War and Revolution 1937–1949*. Stanford, CA: Stanford University Press, 1984.

Eberhard, Wolfram. *A History of China*. Berkeley: University of California Press, 1969.

Fairbank, John K., and Edwin O. Reischauer. *China—Tradition & Transformation*. Boston: Houghton Mifflin Company, 1978.

Feuerwerker, Albert. *State and Society in Eighteenth-Century China: The Ch'ing Empire in Its Glory*. Ann Arbor: Center for Chinese Studies, University of Michigan, 1976.

Fewsmith, Joseph. *Party, State, and Local Elites in Republican China—Merchant Organizations and Politics in Shanghai, 1890–1930*. Honolulu: University of Hawaii Press, 1985.

Folta, Paul Humes. *From Swords to Plowshares?—Defense Industry Reform in the PRC*. Boulder, CO: Westview Press, 1991.

Fong, H. D. *Cotton Industry and Trade in China*. 4.2 vols. Tianjin: Nankai Institute of Economics Industry Series, 1932.

Foster, George M. "Peasant Society and the Image of Limited Goods," *American Anthropologist* 67, no. 2 (April 1965): 293–315.

Gardner, John. "The Wu-fan Campaign in Shanghai: A Study in the Consolidation of Urban Control." In *Chinese Communist Politics in Action*, edited by A. Doak Barnett. Seattle: University of Washington Press, 1969.

Gold, Thomas B. "Urban Private Business and Social Change." In *Chinese Society on the Eve of Tiananmen—The Impact of Reform*, edited by Deborah Davis and Ezra F. Vogel. Cambridge, MA: The Council on East Asian Studies, Harvard University, 1990.

Gold, Thomas B. "Guerrilla Interviewing Among the Getihu." In *Unofficial China: Popular Culture and Thought in the People's Republic*, edited by Perry Link, Richard Madsen, and Paul G. Pickowicz. Boulder, CO: Westview Press, 1989.

Gowen, Herbert, H., and Joseph Washington Hall. *An Outline History of China*. New York: D. Appleton and Company, 1927.

Grasso, June, Jay Corrin, and Michael Kort. *Modernization and Revolution in China*. Armonk, NY: M. E. Sharpe, 1991.

Harding, Harry. *Organizing China—The Problem of Bureaucracy 1949–1976*. Stanford, CA: Stanford University Press, 1981.

He Jianzhang, and Zhang Wenmin. "The System of Ownership: A Tendency Toward Multiplicity." In *China's Economic Reforms*, edited by Lin Wei and Arnold Chao. Philadelphia: University of Pennsylvania Press, 1982.

Henderson, Gail E., and Myron S. Cohen. *The Chinese Hospital—A Socialist Work Unit*. New Haven, CT: Yale University Press, 1984.

Hershatter, Gail. *The Workers of Tianjin, 1900–1949*. Stanford, CA: Stanford University Press, 1986.

Hershkovitz, Linda. "The Fruits of Ambivalence: China's Urban Individual Economy." *Pacific Affairs* 58, no. 3 (fall 1985): 427–450.

Higgins, Benjamin. *Economic Development*. Revised edition. New York: W. W. Norton, 1968.

Hinton, Harold C. *The People's Republic of China, 1979–1984—A Documentary Survey.* Vol. 1. Wilmington, DE: Scholarly Resources, 1986.

Hinton, William. *The Great Reversal—The Privatization of China, 1978–1989.* New York: Monthly Review Press, 1990.

Ho, David Yau-fai. "On the Concept of Face." *American Journal of Sociology*, 81, no. 4 (1976): 867–884.

Ho Ping-ti. *Studies on the Population of China, 1368–1953.* Cambridge, MA: Harvard University Press, 1959.

Hong Yung Lee. "The Implications of Reform For Ideology, State and Society in China." *Journal of International Affairs* 39, no. 2 (Winter 1986): 77–89.

Hook, Brian, ed. *The Cambridge Encyclopedia of China.* 2nd edition. Cambridge, England: Cambridge University Press, 1991.

Hsu, Robert C. *Economic Theories in China, 1978–1988.* Cambridge, England: Cambridge University Press, 1991.

Hucker, Charles O. *China's Imperial Past—An Introduction to Chinese History and Culture.* Stanford, CA: Stanford University Press, 1975.

Jernigan, Thomas R. *China's Business Methods and Policy.* Hong Kong: Kelly & Walsh, 1904.

Jones, Anthony, and William Moskoff. *KO-OPS—The Rebirth of Entrepreneurship in the Soviet Union.* Indianapolis: Indiana University Press, 1991.

Kahan, Arcadius. *The Plow the Hammer and the Knout—An Economic History of Eighteenth-Century Russia.* Chicago: University of Chicago Press, 1985.

Khunaizi, Tayseer Baquir. "Economic, Social, and Political Development in Saudi Arabia: A Historical Analysis." Ph.D. diss., University of Kansas, 1993.

Kluckhohn, Clyde. *Culture And Behavior,* edited by Richard Kluckhohn. New York: Free Press of Glencoe, 1962.

Knight, Frank. *Risk, Uncertainty and Profit.* Houghton Mifflin Company, 1921.

Kraus, Willy. *Private Business in China—Revival Between Ideology and Pragmatism.* Translated by Erich Holtz. Honolulu: University of Hawaii Press, 1991.

Laird, Roy D. *The Soviet Paradigm.* New York: Free Press, 1970.

Lam, Willy Wo-Lap. *The Era of Zhao Ziyang.* Hong Kong: A. B. Books and Stationery, 1989.

Landè, Carl H. "The Dyadic Basis of Clientelism." In *Friends, Followers, and Factions—A Reader in Political Clientelism,* edited by Steffen W. Schmidt, Laura Guasti, Carl H. Landè, and James C. Scott. Berkeley: University of California Press, 1977.

Lenin, V. I. *The Emancipation of Women.* New York: International Publishers, 1984.

Li, Dun J. *The Ageless Chinese—History.* New York: Charles Scribner's Sons, 1978.

Li Fu-chun. *Report on the First Five-Year Plan for Development of the National Economy of the People's Republic of China in 1953–1957.* Peking: Foreign Languages Press, 1955.

Lichtenstein, Peter M. *China at the Brink—The Political Economy of Reform and Retrenchment in the Post-Mao Era.* New York: Praeger, 1991.

Lieberthal, Kenneth. *Revolution and Tradition in Tientsin, 1949–1952.* Stanford, CA: Stanford University Press, 1980.

Lin, Zhiling. "How China Will Modernize." *The American Enterprise* 2 (July/August 1991): 15–18.

Liu Binyan. *China's Crisis, China's Hope.* Translated by Howard Goldblatt. Cambridge, MA: Harvard University Press, 1990.

Liu, James T. C. *Reform in Sung China-Wang An-Shih (1021–1086) and His New Policies.* Cambridge, MA: Harvard University Press, 1959.

Liu Shaoqi. "How To Be a Good Communist." *Selected Works of Liu Shaoqi.* Vol. I. Beijing: Foreign Languages Press, 1984.

Liu Suinian, and Wu Qungan, eds. *China's Socialist Economy—An Outline History (1949–1984).* Beijing: Beijing Review.

Mackerras, Colin, and Amanda Yorke. *The Cambridge Handbook of Contemporary China.* Cambridge, England: Cambridge University Press, 1991.

Mann, Susan. *Local Merchants and the Chinese Bureaucracy, 1750–1950.* Stanford, CA: Stanford University Press, 1987.

Mao Zedong. *Selected Works of Mao Tse-Tung.* Vol. 4, 1st ed. Peking: Foreign Languages Press, 1961.

Mao Zedong. *The Thoughts of Chairman Mao Tse-Tung.* London: Anthony Gibbs Library, 1967.

Marshall, Alfred. *Principles of Economics.* 7th ed. London: Macmillan, 1916.

Marx, Karl, and Frederick Engels. *The German Ideology.* Part 1. Edited by C. J. Arthur. London: Lawrence & Wishart, 1970.

Marx, Karl, and Frederick Engels. *Manifesto of the Communist Party.* Peking: Foreign Languages Press, 1965.

Mason, Edward, et. al. *The Economic and Social Modernization of the Republic of Korea.* Cambridge, MA: Harvard University Press, 1980.

McNabb, Robert Leroy. *The Women of the Middle Kingdom.* New York: Young People's Missionary Movement, 1907.

Metzger, Thomas A. "The State and Commerce in Imperial China." *Asian and African Studies* 6 (1970): 23–46.

Mindell, Arnold. *The Leader as Martial Artist—An Introduction to Deep Democracy.* New York: HarperCollins Publishers, 1992.

Morris, Peter. "The Social Barriers to African Entrepreneurship." *Journal of Development Studies* (October 1968): 29–38.

Muhse, Albert C. "Trade Organization and Trade Control in China." *American Economic Review* 6, no. 2 (June 1916): 309–323.

Nafziger, Wayne E. *Class, Caste, and Entrepreneurship—A Study of Indian Industrialists.* Honolulu: East-West Center, University Press of Hawaii, 1978.

Nee, Victor, and Frank W. Young. "Peasant Entrepreneurs in China's 'Second Economy': An Institutional Analysis." *Economic Development and Cultural Change* 39 (January 1991): 293–310.

Ng, Kwok Kit. "The Social and Organisational Implications of Post-Mao Chinese Management Reform." *Journal of Contemporary Asia* 20, no. 4 (1990): 540–556.

O'Leary, Greg. "Redefining Workers' Interests—Reform and the Trade Unions." In *Economic Reform and Social Change in China,* edited by Andrew Watson. London: Routledge, 1992.

Papanek, Gustav F. *Pakistan's Development: Social Goals and Private Incentives.* Cambridge, MA: Harvard University Press, 1967.

Polkker, Karin. "The Development of Individual and Cooperative Labour Activity in the Soviet Union." *Soviet Studies* 42, no. 3 (July 1990): 403–428.

Polo, Marco. *The Travels of Marco Polo.* Revised from Marden's translation and edited with an introduction by Manuel Komroff. London: Jonathan Cape, 1928.

Prybyla, Jan S. *The Political Economy of Communist China.* Scranton, PA: International Textbook Company, 1970.

Pye, Lucian W. *Asian Power and Politics—The Cultural Dimensions of Authority*. Cambridge, MA: Harvard University Press, 1985.

Pye, Lucian W. *The Dynamics of Chinese Politics*. Cambridge, MA: Oelgeschlager, Gunn & Hain, 1981.

Pye, Lucian W. *The Mandarin and the Cadre: China's Political Cultures*. Ann Arbor: Center for Chinese Studies, University of Michigan, 1988.

Pye, Lucian W. "Political Culture." *International Encyclopedia of the Social Sciences*. Vol. 12. Edited by David L. Sills. New York: Macmillian and Free Press, 1968.

Pye, Lucian W. *Warlord Politics—Conflict and Coalition in the Modernization of Republican China*. New York: Praeger, 1971.

Rai, Shirin. "Watering Another Man's Garden—Gender, Employment and Educational Reforms in China." In *Women in the Face of Change—The Soviet Union, Eastern Europe and China*, edited by Shirin Rai, Hilary Pilkington, and Annie Phizacklea. New York: Routledge, 1992.

Reeder, John A. "Entrepreneurship in The People's Republic of China." *Columbia Journal of World Business* (fall 1984): 43–51.

Rieber, Alfred J. *Merchants and Entrepreneurs in Imperial Russia*. Chapel Hill: University of North Carolina Press, 1982.

Rodzinski, Witold. *The People's Republic of China—A Concise Political History*. New York: Free Press, 1988.

Rong, Jingben. "Reform and Society." *World Marxist Review* 32, no. 1 (January 1989): 14–16.

Rousseau, Jean-Jacques. *On the Social Contract*, edited by Roger D. Masters and translated by Judith R. Masters. New York: St. Martin's Press, 1978.

Rupp, Kalman. *Entrepreneurs in Red—Structure and Organizational Innovation in the Centrally Planned Economy*. Albany: State University of New York Press, 1983.

Sayigh, Yusif A. *Entrepreneurs of Lebanon—The Role of the Business Leader in a Developing Economy*. Cambridge, MA: Harvard University Press, 1962.

Schumpeter, Joseph A. *Business Cycles*. Vol. 1. New York: McGraw-Hill, 1939.

Schumpeter, Joseph A. *Capitalism, Socialism and Democracy*. 3rd ed. New York: Harper and Brothers, 1942.

Schumpeter, Joseph A. *The Theory of Economic Development*. Cambridge, MA: Harvard University Press, 1959.

Schurmann, Franz. *Ideology and Organization in Communist China*. 2nd ed. Berkeley: University of California Press, 1970.

Segynola, Albert A. "The Cultural Factor in the Development of Rural Small Scale Industries: A Case Study from Bendel State of Nigeria." In *Culture and Development in Africa*, edited by Stephen H. Arnold and Andre Netecki. Trenton, NJ: Africa World Press, 1990.

Sheridan, James E. *China in Disintegration—The Republican Era in Chinese History 1912–1949*. New York: Free Press 1975.

Smith, Adam. *An Inquiry into the Nature and Causes of the Wealth of Nations*, edited by Edwin Cannan. New York: The Modern Library, Random House, 1937.

Smith, Christopher J. *China—People and Places in the Land of One Billion*. Boulder, CO: Westview Press, 1991.

Snow, Edgar. *Red Star Over China*. 1st revised and enlarged edition. New York: Grove Press, 1968.

Solomon, Richard H. *Mao's Revolution and the Chinese Political Culture*. Berkeley: University of California Press, 1971.

Spence, Jonathan D. *The Gate of Heavenly Peace—The Chinese and their Revolution, 1895–1980*. Middlesex, England: Penguin Books, 1982.

Swain, Nigel. *Hungary—The Rise and Fall of Feasible Socialism*. London: Verso, 1992.

Syu, Agnes. "Field Study of Privatization in the Republic of China on Taiwan: Interactive Dynamics During the Initial Stages of the Privatization Process in Two State-Owned Enterprises." Ph.D. diss., University of Kansas, 1992.

Thomas, Gordon. *Chaos Under Heaven—The Shocking Story of China's Search for Democracy*. New York: Carol Publishing Group, 1991.

Von Mises, Ludwig. *Socialism—An Economic and Sociological Analysis*. London: Jonathan Cape, 1936.

Wakeman, Frederic Jr. *The Fall of Imperial China*. New York: Free Press, 1975.

Wallace, Ben J. "Technological Impact and Culture Change Among the Pagan Gaddang." In *Culture Change in the Philippines*, edited by Mario D. Zamora, Vinson H. Sutlive, and Nathan Altshuler. Williamsburg, VA: Studies in Third World Societies, Department of Anthropology, College of William and Mary, 1976.

Waller, Derek J. *The Government and Politics of the People's Republic of China*. New York: New York University Press, 1981.

Walras, Leon. *Elements of Pure Economics or The Theory of Social Wealth*. London: George Allen and Unwin, 1954.

Wamsley, Gray L., and Mayer N. Zald, *The Political Economy of Public Organizations*. Lexington, MA: Lexington Books, 1973.

Wang, N. T. "Entrepreneurship in China." *Hungarian Scientific Council for World Economy*. No. 66. Budapest: 1990.

Weber, Max. *The Theory of Social and Economic Organization*. Translated by A. M. Henderson and Talcott Parsons. New York: Oxford University Press, 1947.

Weiss, Thomas Joseph. *The Service Sector in the United States—1839 Through 1899*. New York: Arno Press, 1975.

Weiss, Anita M. *Culture, Class and Development in Pakistan—The Emergence of an Industrial Bourgeoisie in Punjab*. Boulder, CO: Westview Press, 1990.

Williamson, H. R. *Wang An Shih*. Vol. 1. Westport, CT: Hyperion Press, 1973.

Wolf, Margery. *Revolution Postponed—Women in Contemporary China*. Stanford, CA: Stanford University Press, 1985.

Woo, T. C. *The Kuomingtang and the Future of the Chinese Revolution*. London: George Allen and Unwin Ltd. Ruskin House, 1928.

Yeh Chou. "Shanghai Steps into the Future." In *China In Transition—Selected Articles 1952–1956*. Peking: China Reconstructs, 1957.

Yen-ping Hao. "Commercial Capitalism Along the China Coast During the Late Ch'ing Period." In *Modern Chinese Economic History*, edited by Chi-ming Hou and Tzong-Shian Yu. Taipei: The Institute of Economics, Academia Sinica, 1979.

Young, Susan. "Policy, Practice and the Private Sector in China." *The Australian Journal of Chinese Affairs*, no. 21 (January 1989): 57–80.

Young, Susan. "Wealth but Not Security—Attitude towards Private Business in the 1980s." In *Economic Reform and Social Change in China*, edited by Andrew Watson. London: Routledge, 1992.

Yunxiang Yan. "The Impact of Rural Reform on Economic and Social Stratification in Chinese Village." *The Australian Journal of Chinese Affairs*, no. 27 (January 1992): 1–23.

Zhao Ziyang. "Advance Along the Road of Socialism with Chinese Characteristics."
       Report delivered at the 13th National Congress of the CCP on October 25,
       1987. *Beijing Review* (9–15 November 1987).
Zhao Ziyang. "Report on the Work of the Government." Report delivered at the
       Second Session of the Sixth National People's Congress on May 15, 1984).
       Beijing Review, no. 24 (11 June 1984).

Index

RASHID MALIK, who received his doctorate from the University of Kansas, is an independent researcher.